T0367692

Inequality and Global
Supra-surplus
Capitalism

Inequality and Global
Supra-surplus
Capitalism

E Ray Canterbery
Florida State University, USA

World Scientific

NEW JERSEY · LONDON · SINGAPORE · BEIJING · SHANGHAI · HONG KONG · TAIPEI · CHENNAI · TOKYO

Published by

World Scientific Publishing Co. Pte. Ltd.

5 Toh Tuck Link, Singapore 596224

USA office: 27 Warren Street, Suite 401-402, Hackensack, NJ 07601

UK office: 57 Shelton Street, Covent Garden, London WC2H 9HE

Library of Congress Cataloging-in-Publication Data

Names: Canterbery, E. Ray, author.

Title: Inequality and global supra-surplus capitalism / E Ray Canterbery
   (Florida State University, USA).

Description: 1 Edition. | World Scientific : New Jersey, [2018] |
   Includes bibliographical references and index.

Identifiers: LCCN 2017045430 | ISBN 9789813200821

Subjects: LCSH: Equality. | Income distribution. | Wealth. | Economic policy. | Business cycles.

Classification: LCC HM821 .C36 2018 | DDC 305--dc23

LC record available at https://lccn.loc.gov/2017045430

British Library Cataloguing-in-Publication Data

A catalogue record for this book is available from the British Library.

For any available supplementary material, please visit
http://www.worldscientific.com/worldscibooks/10.1142/10302#t=suppl

Desk Editor: Shreya Gopi

Typeset by Stallion Press
Email: enquiries@stallionpress.com

Printed in Singapore

In fond memory of John Kenneth Galbraith

CONTENTS

ABOUT THE AUTHOR

A former Professor of Economics at Florida State University (Tallahassee), **E.Ray Canterbery** is one of the most respected economists of his generation. In 2003, John Kenneth Galbraith, who knew both Michal Kalecki and John Maynard Keynes, called Canterbery, "the best". He conducted research as a Truman Scholar in 2004, which led to his recent book, *Harry S Truman: The Economics of a Populist President* (2014). Canterbery is the author of many acclaimed
books (and articles), including *The Global Great Recession*, the tour de force *Wall Street Capitalism*, biographies of *Alan Greenspan* and of *F Scott Fitzgerald* (co-authored with Thomas Birch), the classic, *The Making of Economics*, and the best-selling *A Brief History of Economics*, many of which are available in several languages. After the Truman book was safely in press, he returned to his global concerns with the engaging *The Rise and Fall of Global Austerity* (2015), which is ahead of today's newspaper headlines. He is also the author of two novels, the most recent being *Scott: A Novel of F. Scott Fitzgerald*.

Canterbery served as President of the Eastern Economics Association in 1986–1987 and of the International Trade and Finance Association in 1997–1998. In January 1996, Prentice-Hall, Inc. selected Canterbery for their Hall of Fame Economist Baseball Cards for "significant contributions to the economics discipline," including the development of one of the first complete mathematical theories of foreign exchange, a new theory of the labor market and of personal incomes (vita theory), which later was integrated into international trade theory.

The international Biography Centre in Cambridge, England includes Canterbery among 500 persons worldwide in its *Living Legends* (2004), among 2000 scholars worldwide in its *Outstanding Scholars in the 21st Century* (2002), among *One Thousand Great Intellectuals* (2002), among *2000 Outstanding People* (2003) worldwide, and among *One Thousand Great Americans* (2002). The American Biographical Institute includes Canterbery in its *Great Minds of the 21st Century* (2002) and *American Biography* (2003). He is also listed in selected issues of Marquis *Who's Who in the World* and *Who's Who in America*, as well as many other biographical sources.

Part I

INTRODUCTION

Chapter 1

THE PARAMOUNT POSITION OF PRODUCTION

In his elegant and persuasive magnum opus, John Kenneth Galbraith (JKG) devoted a chapter with the above title. We repeat it here, with a summary of Galbraith's chapter in *The Affluent Society*. This position of production is not simply a matter of belief, though that is important, but rather of reality. First, we spread caution to the winds about production, then we take a look at the national income accounts and the place of production there. We end on the quite unconventional note that income is more important than production, followed closely by employment. As promised, the first words of caution emanate from JKG. Why, we must ask, does production have such a prominent position in the USA and other economies?

Increases in production have long been celebrated. Higher production is a measure of achievement. When it comes to production as a test of performance, there is no difference between Republicans and Democrats, right and left, white and middle-class blacks, Catholics and Protestants. It is common ground for the Chair of Americans for Democratic Action, the President of the U.S. Chamber of Commerce, and the President of the National Association of Manufacturers. Even the head of the AFL–CIO can concede on this one, though full employment cannot be taken off the table.

A small voice regularly tells us that production is not everything. Perhaps it is the voice of an angel for we hear constant reminders that there is a spiritual side to life. Those who remind us of this will receive a respectful if not attentive hearing. Still, to be sensible and practical is to believe in the prestige that production accords us. To say that CEOs understand production is to pay them the highest of complements. For one to be useful, they must be productive. Anything that interferes with the supply of more and better things is resisted with religious-like enthusiasm. In fiction, Ayn Rand's Hank Rearden is a vindication of the creativity of the industrialist, the author of material production.[1]

The importance of production transcends USA boundaries, but is not confined therein. In what Galbraith calls the conventional wisdom, the level of GNP is the most frequent justification of American civilization. It is often said in this regard that the American standard of living is "the marvel of the world." While to a considerable extent, it is, we will nonetheless raise questions regarding the sanctity of GNP. Still, the perspective of the world is often the one given by a picture of relative GNP such as that of Figure 1.1, which shows the relative positions of seven economies in 2015. From the perspective of the International Monetary Fund (IMF), the Economic Union (EU) is like a United States of Europe. The rank order has the USA first, followed respectively by the European Union, China, Japan, India, Brazil, and Canada. The rank order for most of the "countries" of the world is provided in Appendix A for 2016 (IMF), 2016 (World Bank), and 2015 (United Nations). Ignoring the EU as a "country," China and Japan are followed by Germany, the UK, France, India, Italy, and then Brazil.

In the supra-surplus economies, goods are comparatively abundant. The abundance of sun and rain, though they are no less important, are taken for granted. Still, worldwide there is much malnutrition, but more die in the supra-surplus countries from too much food and drink than of too little. As Galbraith suggests: "For many women and some men, clothing has ceased to be related to protection from exposure and has become, like plumage, almost exclusively erotic."[2] Those who doubt this do not go

---

[1] See Ayn Rand, *Atlas Shrugged* (New York: Random House, 1957), p. 480 as well as many other pages.
[2] John Kenneth Galbraith, *The Affluent Society* (Boston/New York: Houghton Mifflin Company, 1998) [1958], p. 101.

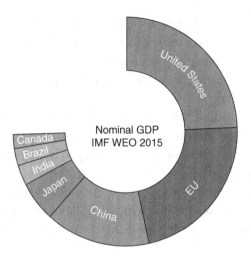

Figure 1.1 A Pie Chart Displaying the World's Seven Largest Economies by Nominal GDP — The United States, the European Union, China, Japan, India, Brazil, and Canada.

to the movies or nightclubs. And, yet, production remains central to our thoughts. It continues to measure the quality and progress of civilization. So large does production bulk in our thought that we can only suppose a vacuum must remain if it should be relegated to a smaller role. As we soon shall see, there are other things. But first we will examine more closely our present preoccupation with production.

Ways to Expand Production

There is more than one way to expand production. In principle, according to Galbraith, there are five distinct ways worth listing formally.[3]

(1) The available productive resources, namely labor and capital (including raw materials), can be more fully employed. Even capital can be idle, though traditionally this condition has been applied to labor.

---

[3] John Kenneth Galbraith, *The Affluent Society, ibid.*, p. 102. Although the list is pretty much what Galbraith had in mind, I have amended it.

(2) Given available production techniques, these resources can be more efficiently utilized. There are different ways of combining capital with labor, but there should be one especially advantageous way.
(3) The labor force can be increased, through new entrants, immigration, or population increases.
(4) The supply of capital, which in some theories can serve as a substitute for labor, can be increased. We should stress that in the economist's long run, capital and labor are more likely to be substitutable. We will return to this issue.
(5) Technological innovation can occur. As a consequence, more output can be obtained from the given supply of labor and capital. Moreover, the new capital will likely be enhanced by the new technology.

It is difficult to know which is more important or effective. Perhaps an equal emphasis should be placed on each. That having been said, economists generally have focused on the top two because they best fit the orthodox paradigm. Changes are closely interrelated and studies of the comparative effect of these five measures do not produce unambiguous results. An early study, still cited as important, was for the period between 1859–1873 and 1944–1953. It shows that net national output increased at an average annual rate of 3.5 percent, of which about half (1.7 percent) can be attributed to the increase in capital and labor supply. The remainder probably was due to technological improvement in capital and parallel improvement in the people who devise the better capital equipment and operate it. In more recent times, a growing share of the increase in output is attributable to such technological advances and a declining share to mere increases in the *quantities* of capital and labor.[4]

No one questions the importance of technological advance for increasing production (and also generating new products) from available resources. Little, however, is done to improve the volume of this investment, except when mandated by some military emergency. We tend to

---

[4] See, as examples, Moses Abramovitz, *Resources and Output Trends in the United States Since 1870*, and John W. Kendrick, *Productivity Trends: Capital and Labor*, Occasional papers 52 and 53 of the National Bureau of Economic Research, New York, 1956. The NBER then and since has been a major source of such studies.

accept whatever investment in technology is being made and applaud the outcome.

Economic growth depends on the growth rates of productivity and the labor force. Paul M. Romer (born November 7, 1955), currently Chief Economist and Senior Vice President of the World Bank, is responsible for intensive research on productivity and its causes. Yet, he is of several minds regarding the relationship of inputs and technology to final output. For example, he has taken the contrary positions that economic growth is endogenous *and* exogenous. The role of technology is often the source of these two positions. Technology is endogenous when it is embodied in existing capital and exogenous when it is viewed as a residual (after capital and labor quantities are accounted for). In one paper he concludes that an increase in the size of the market or in the trading area in which a country operates increases the incentives for research and thereby increases the share of investment and the rate of growth of output, with no fall in the rate of return on capital.[5] A higher level of income seems to be associated with a higher rate of savings and investment. Interestingly, higher exogenous savings have little relationship with higher technological change and productivity growth. This finding does considerable damage to the long-held belief that thriftiness is next to Godliness.

In another paper, Romer focuses on economic growth as endogenous.[6] As he notes, endogenous growth distinguishes itself from neoclassical growth theory by emphasizing that economic growth is an endogenous outcome of an economic system, not the result of forces that impinge from outside. In this paper he rejects some of his earlier research findings. In particular, he rejects the idea that the *quantity* of physical capital is an important determinant of productivity. His earlier emphasis on production functions using capital and labor inputs was mistaken. Instead, he now likes an early paper (1987) he did on research and knowledge as being in the right direction. He refers to five facts that can be used to explain economic growth. (1) There are many firms in a market economy. While

---

[5] Paul M. Romer, *Capital, Labor, and Productivity*, Working Paper No. R1496, National Bureau of Economic Research, New York, January 1991.

[6] Paul M. Romer, "The Origins of endogenous Growth," *Journal of Economic Perspectives*, 8(1), 1994.

monopolies exist, output is not concentrated in a single, economy-wide monopolist. (2) Discoveries differ from other inputs in the sense that many people can use them at the same time. Such discoveries include the idea behind the transistor, the principles behind internal combustion, the organizational structure of a modern corporation, and the concepts of double entry bookkeeping. These all have the property that it is techno-logically possible for everybody and every firm to make use of them at the same time. (3) It is possible to replicate physical activities.

The aggregate production function can be estimated. If the function is represented in the form $Y = AF(K, H, L)$, then doubling all three of K, H, and L should allow a doubling of output (Y). A represents technology and is non-rival (see Fact 2) because the existing pieces of information can be used in all instances of productive activity at the same time. H represents human capital and L is physical labor. Note that land is not an input, which would be very embarrassing for the output of farming and fisheries. (4) Technological advance comes from things that people do. Discovery will seem to be an exogenous event in the sense that forces outside our control seem to determine whether it succeeds. The *aggregate* rate of dis-covery is endogenous. When more people start prospecting for gold or experimenting with bacteria, more valuable discoveries will be found. (5) Many individuals and firms have market power and earn monopoly rents on discoveries. Though information from discoveries is non-rival (Fact 2), economically important discoveries usually do not meet the other criterion for a public good; they typically are partially excludable, or excludable for at least some period of time. Because people and firms have some control over the information produced by most discoveries, it cannot be treated as a pure public good. If a firm can control access to a discovery, it can charge a price that is higher than zero. It thus earns monopoly profits because information has no opportunity costs.

We must not forget the orthodoxy, which remains firmly neoclassical. A combo of American economists in the mid-1950s wrote a new, neoclas-sical orchestration with themes that are still played today. The new virtu-oso was Robert Solow.[7] Solow in the front row and Paul Samuelson in the

---

[7]Robert M. Solow's seminal articles are "A Contribution to the Theory of Economic Growth," *Quarterly Journal of Economics*, 70, 1956, 65–94 and "Technical Change and Aggregate Production Function," *Review of Economics and Statistics 39*, 1957.

second forsook any chorus about production taking place at fixed proportions of capital and labor. In a return to neoclassical growth rendition, the interest rate and wage rates are flexible and capital and labor easily substitutable, one for the other, depending on whether a low interest rate favors capital investment or a low wage rate favors bringing labor off the bench. These substitutions are sufficiently fine that the economy never really diverges from its stable path. Thus, the knife-edge threat to capitalistic stability is dulled by a new arrangement.

The nerves of the capitalist were soothed. The economy could be compared to a long-distance jogger who never changes pace and yet runs forever. Neoclassical growth theory still dominated Macro-dynamics in the late 1970s and remains textbook bound to this day. The theory, like the economy, had the endurance of the long-distance runner.

Robert Solow's Nobel Prize in Economics came in 1987 and it was for his contributions to the theory of economic growth. His was a popular choice, for Solow is one of the most likeable persons on the planet. His main contribution to growth theory was to introduce the theme of technological flexibility. There was a variety of compositions for total production prior to factories and equipment being put into place. Thereafter, such production techniques became fixed, as indeed they are. The degree of intensity with which capital is utilized in production can vary over time and is a source of great flexibility for capitalist (or socialist) economies. It turns out that the permanent growth of output per unit of labor input (productivity) is independent of the saving and the investment rate. Rather, productivity growth depends solely on technological progress in a broad sense. Technological progress, little studied by economists, is the key that unlocks productivity growth.

The Solow Economic Growth Model

Solow served on the staff of the President's Council of Economic Advisers and the neoclassical growth model provided a framework within which macroeconomic policies could be used to sustain full employment. Solow's ideas were written into the *1962 Economic Report of the President* for John F. Kennedy. Admittedly, however, steady growth depended upon tranquil conditions, the conditions prevailing during the late 1950s and early 1960s. As Solow has written, "the hard part of disequilibrium growth is that we do not have — and it may be impossible to have a really good theory of asset valuation under turbulent conditions."[8] He made that observation near the end of 1987, shortly after the stock market crash of October. We will address turbulent conditions later.

The basic Solow growth model can be simply expressed. During 1870–1999, national output in the USA increased at an annual rate of 3.5 percent. At the same time, per capita output increased at an annual rate of 1.8 percent. What factors, it is fair to ask contributed to these growth rates — population growth, capital expansion, improvements in education, natural resources growth? The simplest way to begin to answer this question is to write an aggregate production function for the economy that relates the level of output to the level of basic factor inputs, so

$$Y = A(t)F(K, N),$$

where $A(t)$ represents technological change which is presumed to depend only on time, K is the capital stock, and N is the size of the labor force. Since $A(t)$ is multiplicative, more output will be produced for the same amount of factor inputs (K and N). This means that technological change does not alter the relative marginal productivities of the factor inputs. Not surprisingly, such technological change is called neutral technological change. Neutral technological change favors neither machines nor labor. As he studied shifts in the aggregate production function over time, Robert Solow found evidence that technological change in the USA had indeed been neutral.[9] Unlike Romer, Solow ignores human capital, unless it is embodied in the quantities of labor.

From this production function we can show how output grows over time by using the rate of change in the variables.[10] That is,

$$dY/Y = dA/A + w_k(dK/K) + w_n(dN/N),$$

---

[8] Robert M. Solow, "Growth Theory and After," Nobel lecture, December 8, 1987, in Karl-Goran Maler, editor, *Nobel Lecture, Economic sciences, 1981–1990* (Singapore/New Jersey/London: World Scientific, 1992), p. 203.

[9] Robert M. Solow, "Technical Change and the Aggregate Production Function," *op. cit.*, pp. 312–320.

[10] The calculus operator d is used to denote "change" in a variable.

an equation that says that the rate of change in output(dY/Y) depends on the rate of technological change (dA/A), the rate of change in capital stock, and the rate of change in the number of workers employed (dN/N). Note that weights (w_k, w_n) are attached to the factor inputs that are their shares in national output and reflect the importance of each in the production process. This growth equation says that the rate of growth in production depends on the rate of growth in technology and of factor supplies over time. It is an equation for economic growth.

There is much more to the Solow model than this, particularly if we express the variables in per capita terms. For example, there is something called the comparative statics of the steady state. A dramatic conclusion from the Solow model is that absent productivity growth, an economy reaches a steady state in the long run. A steady state is where an economy's output per worker, consumption per worker, and capital stock per worker are constant. In turn, if output, consumption and capital stock per worker are constant, then total output (Y), consumption (C) and capital (K) are all growing at the rate of growth in the labor force. Steady-state investment (I) is the sum of net investment and depreciation, so

$$I = nK + dK = (n + d)K,$$

where n is the rate of net investment and d equals the rate of depreciation.

This is about all we need to know about the Solow model for now.[11] However, we will consider a few more of its conclusions. An increase in the savings rate lowers current consumption in order to provide higher future consumption. The savings rate (s) depends on the capital–labor ratio. There is a trade-off between the present and the future. A government policy change might cause the savings shift. For example, a higher value added tax (VAT) on consumption might raise the savings rate. Alternatively, a cultural drift toward greater thrift might shift the savings rate upward.

---

[11] The complete model, including graphics, can be found in a readable format in E. Ray Canterbery, *The Making of Economics, Volume 2 The Modern Superstructure,* 4th edition (Singapore/New Jersey/London: World Scientific, 2009), pp. 89–106. In the complete model, new savings per worker is $sf(k)$, where k is the capital–labor ratio.

What of the effects of population growth? An excessive population growth rate is a problem for many developing countries; reducing the rate often is a major policy goal. The Solow model can be used to illustrate the relationship between population growth and the levels of economic development. An increase in the population growth rate raises investment per worker. Since workers are entering the labor force at a faster clip, these new workers must be equipped with capital, so the amount of investment per worker must rise. However, per capita output and income are lower. Output increases are not sufficient to offset the growth of population and its effect on per capita output and income. Thus the Solow model suggests that increased population growth will lower living standards in developing countries. It may seem like a Malthusian conclusion but absent the checks and balances of Thomas Malthus.

In reality in many industrialized or industrializing countries, productivity is not constant. In the Solow model an improvement in productivity results in an upward shift in the per-worker production function. Now each worker can produce more at each capital–labor ratio. With savings still proportional to output, savings per worker rise. The productivity boast has elevated the capital–labor ratio and thus increases output and income as well as per capita consumption. The standard of living improves.

The Solow model reveals some stylized facts about the standard of living. We will have more to say about this later. (1) An increase in the saving rate will cause output, consumption, and capital per worker to rise. A higher level of saving facilitates more investment and a larger capital stock. (2) An increase in the rate of population growth will cause output, consumption, and capital per worker to fall. With faster population growth, more output must be utilized to equip workers with capital, leaving less output available for consumption or to increase capital per worker. (3) An increase in productivity will cause output, consumption, and capital per worker to rise. The higher productivity advances output; by raising income, it also raises savings and the capital stock.

Economic Growth Accounting

Before departing from the idea of economic growth, we should consider the idea of "growth accounting," which emanated from Solow's brilliant theory of the growth process. Economist Edward Denison used this device to study economic growth in the United States. *Real* output grew at an annual rate of 2.9 percent in the U.S. during 1929–1982. This era included the Roaring Twenties, followed by the great decline of the Great Depression of the thirties. Denison estimated that 32 percent, or about a third of this growth, was due to increases in the amounts of labor.

The other sources of growth are those things that raise labor productivity. Denison estimated that 14 percent of the growth was due to increased education of the labor force. In turn, capital formation accounted for slightly less than a fifth of U.S. growth. Technological change (Solow's focus) accounted for 28 percent of this growth. Denison included new technological knowledge (e.g., ways to employ robots in the production process) as well as new ways to organize businesses (managerial strategies) as technological advances. Since at a given technology, greater amounts of inputs seemed to cause more than a proportional increase in output, Denison estimated that 9 percent of U.S. growth came from economies of scale. Finally, other elements such as the effects of weather on farm output and work stoppages had a net negative effect equal to 2 percent of economic growth. Though Denison had a slightly longer list of sources of growth than did Solow, his results did not conflict with Solow's initial estimates. Technology remains the capitalist engine for growth, with human capital investment following about midway in the growth train.

There remains much to be explained. American economic growth between 1970 and 2016 was not at the steady pace of the long-distance runner. There have been deep recessions, money panics, the great stagnation of the 1970s, the hyper-speculation in securities during the 1980s and 1990s, the financial collapse of 2008–09, the Global Great Recession, and the recent slow recovery. Still, Solow's model can explain the steady growth of the 1950s and 1960s. Perhaps we need different models for different eras.

Nations have more than one measure of economic well-being, economic growth being an important one. Economic growth is normally measured as the rate of growth in real (price adjusted) gross domestic production (GDP). This is only one measure of income and output in the national income account. While some attempts were made to estimate national incomes as long ago as the 17th century, the systematic keeping of national accounts only began in the 1930s, in the United States and some European countries. The impetus for this major statistical effort was the Great Depression and the rise of Keynesian economics, which made it necessary for the government to obtain accurate information so that its interventions into the economy could proceed as well-informed as possible.

To count a good or service, it is necessary to place a value on it. The value that the national income account uses is the market value of a good or service — the price it fetches when bought or sold. This does not prevent accountants from measuring the "real" value of the products by deflating their values by a price index. The actual usefulness of a product (its use-value) is not measured. However, since economists have a price fetish, they are loath to separate the price-value of a product from its use-value. A Marxist will often complain that the neoclassical economist knows the price of everything but the value of nothing. For the sake of argument, let us say that we need a common denominator for value and price serves that purpose. So, we are dealing with market values.

Measuring Gross Output and Income

Three strategies have been used to obtain the market values of all the goods and services produced within some defined boundary. They are the product (or output) method, the expenditure method, and the income method. The product method examines industry-by-industry so that total output of the economy is the sum of the outputs of every industry. However, since an output of one industry may be used by another industry and become part of the output of that second industry, to avoid counting the item twice we use not the value output by each industry, but the value added; that is, the difference between the value of what it puts out and what it takes in. The total value produced by the economy is the sum of the values added by every industry. A value-added tax (VAT) is a tax placed on the value of production at each stage of value added.

The expenditure method is based on the idea that all products are bought by somebody or some organization. Therefore, we sum up the total amount of money people and organizations spend in buying things. This amount must equal the value of everything produced. Usually expenditures by private individuals, by businesses, and by governments are calculated separately and then summed to give the total expenditure. Finally, a correction must be made to account for imports and exports outside the national boundary. A distinction must be made between what is produced in the U.S. and what, for example, is produced in China.

The income method sums the incomes of all producers within the defined boundary. Since what they are paid is just the market value of their product, their total income must be the total value of the product. This sounds circular because it is. Wages, proprietor's incomes, and corporate profits are the major subdivisions of income.

The above can be distilled into simple formulas. First is the output approach.

$$GDP = Q - \text{intermediate goods, or}$$

$$GDP \text{ (at factor cost)} = GDP \text{ at market price} - D$$
$$+ NFIA - \text{Net Indirect Taxes,}$$

where Q equals output, D equals depreciation (capital consumption allowances) and NFIA equals net factor income from abroad. Those who see production as paramount focus on GDP. The income method formula is

$$NDP \text{ at factor cost} = \text{Wages and Salaries} + \text{Net Interest}$$
$$+ \text{Rental \& Royalty Income} + \text{Profits}$$
$$\text{of Incorporated and Unincorporated}$$
$$\text{Enterprises.}$$

The expenditure method is the following sum:

$$GDP = C + G + I + (X - M),$$

where C equals household consumption expenditures or personal consumption expenditures, I equals gross private domestic investment, G equals government consumption and gross investment expenditures, X equals gross exports of goods and services, and M equals gross imports of goods and services. $(X-M)$ is often written as NX. All items are expressed in market prices.

We should note that all three accounting methods should in theory give the same final figure. However, in practice minor differences are obtained for several reasons, including changes in inventory levels and errors in the statistics. There is a fundamental reason for differences in output and income to which we will return.

Further breakdowns of the data are useful for various purposes. Net national product is

$$NNP = GNP - D: NDP = GDP - D,$$

where the difference between *GNP* and *GDP* is receipts of factor income from abroad minus payments of factor income to the rest of the world. Receipts minus payments are near zero much of the time. However, in politics, even small differences lead to great debates between Congress and the President. National income (*NI*) is

$$NI = NNP - \text{Indirect Business Taxes.}$$

NI is also equal to the sum of wages, salaries, supplements to wages and salaries, rent, net interest, profits and proprietors' income. Sales taxes are the largest part of indirect business taxes. We are almost, but not quite, finished with the national income accounts.

Personal income (PI) equals NI minus transfer payments. Transfer payments which are added to NI are: social security and pension payments, welfare and unemployment payments. Transfer payments deducted from NI are: social security contributions, undistributed corporate profits, and corporate income taxes. Generally, the transfer payments remaining in PI are those items that households can freely spend.

Disposable income (DI) equals PI less PI taxes. In turn, DI is distributed between personal consumption expenditure and savings. DI generally is what an employee receives from the employer in the form of a paycheck. Savings are measured as a residual after consumption expenditures have been subtracted from DI. It is important to make a note of the following: savings as measured by the Federal Reserve System differ from the savings in the NI accounts. If you are rich, you will notice the difference right away.

Ideas About Surplus Value

Since this book is about supra-surpluses, as well as simply surpluses, at some point you will want a measure of such surpluses. The NI accounts will give some clues, but more is afoot here than meets the accountant's eye. Notions of "surplus produce" have been used in economic thought and commerce for a long time (notably by the Physiocrats). In *Das Kapital, Theories of Surplus Value* and the *Grundrisse*, Karl Marx gave the concept a central place in his interpretation of economic history. Today the concept is mainly used in Marxian economics. That's too bad because it has a useful place in economics to which we hope to elevate it. After all, Marx began to work out his idea of surplus product in his 1844 notes on moderate James Mill's *Elements of Political Economy*.

Save for the fact that profits go to "capitalists" and wages to the working class, the NI accounts say little about the distribution of their benefits. In great part this is due to their focus on aggregate production. We nonetheless know that the scientific and engineering resources by which modern technology is advanced are most unevenly distributed between industries. Where firms are few and comparatively large — oil, metallurgy, automobiles, chemicals, rubber, heavy engineering — investment in technological advance is considerable. The research and development work on which this advance depends is well financed and comprehensive. Little David has little chance against such giants.

There nonetheless are many industries where the firms are Malthusian in number and small in stature. They include home construction, clothing manufacture, natural-fiber textile industry, the service industries such as cleaners and restaurants. These are the least developed industries and often dominate the developing nations. The investment in innovation is negligible, save for finance, as we will come to note in more detail. Except for agriculture, there is little to no publicly financed research and development. As JKG notes, "We attach great importance to the fact that some industries advance. We attach almost no importance to the fact that others do not." Americans love winners, even if they be giants.

In everyday discourse, nothing is more frequently taken as an index of economic growth than the volume of capital formation. Countries hoping to industrialize set at the Altar to capital. This is a by-product of abstaining from consumption in order to have funds for such investment. The capitalist that forgoes luxury goods spending — perhaps sacrificing a Rolls Royce or a private plane — has greater profits for investment. As with technological advance, we generally content ourselves with whatever investment is taking place. This, despite routine preachments on the Godly virtues of thrift. As to the truth, thrift is largely beside the point, for more savings do not guarantee more investment in capital goods. Capitalists do not frequent church for such sermons.

Increasing the capital stock is a safe route to economic growth whereas increasing the number of workers is dangerous. There was a time — the era of princes and feudal lords — when imported craftsmen increased their productive wealth. The practice has gone the way of Robin Hood. The size and skill composition of the labor force can be a limitation on the growth rate. Around the world rest many recruits for the American labor force, but they are viewed with suspicion even though we are a "nation of immigrants." Equally resisted are calls for a higher birth rate. In the Solow growth model, a rising population does increase total production, but decreases per capita consumption. Thus, we need not look to population growth as the golden path of the future.

Once production is lost, we do not grieve for it. We cannot worry about something which is no longer there. Rather, what is bemoaned are the lost jobs and income. Perhaps there is a lesson in this. Production may have a purpose beyond itself. After all, we take seriously the loss of production that results from the deliberate holding of labor or capital out of production. Moreover, we deplore the malingering workman. We also are deeply aroused by the featherbedding union. In theory the monopoly leads to less than optimum labor and capital employment and thus diminishes production. For this reason, economists often have protested the presence of monopolies and urged breaking them up. Anti-trust laws were aimed at monopoly abuses. Still, economists and the public have run hot and cold on the subject.

Private-social Imbalance

The 19th century scholar was not concerned with invention and innovation as a means to greater production. This is a modern phenomenon and related to the growth of the giant corporate enterprise. In the past, inventions were mostly by accident except as they might be encouraged by the patent office. Oddly enough, our present concern is with increased efficiency in the allocation of resources as the means to greater production. This is likely due to the economist's fondness for perfect competition which requires many small firms. As noted, the small firm does not do research and is loath to enlarge its capital stock. It is far better to tinker with the way labor and capital is mixed in an optimum manner. Efficiency and thrift are the rallying points, something nonetheless much more appropriate for the 19th century.

Still, we have managed to greatly increase production during wartime. Under the stress of war conditions, the conventional wisdom is abandoned. We use all the relevant dimensions of production. We make serious efforts to expand the labor force, including inviting women to man assembly lines for tanks and jeeps. Where investment is inadequate, more is made. There is no involuntary idleness. War has brought an astonishing increase in production as the machines are run to their limits. Even the enforcement of anti-trust laws has been lifted because of the emphasis on output. It is a pity that we cannot concentrate our energies in the interest of peace.

Galbraith suggests that there is still another respect in which our concern for production is traditional and irrational. We view the production of some of the most frivolous goods with pride and regard the production of some the most significant and civilizing services with regret. In part, this is the consequence of our worshiping the Holy Grail of GNP, which treats all goods and services as equal. The increased supply of educational services has a standing not different in kind from an increased output of television sets. Worse, government allocation of resources beyond warfare is downright subversive.

This paradox leads to some contradictions. While we welcome the expansion of cell phone services as improving the general well-being, the curtailment of postal services on occasion is a necessary economy measure. Increases in private wealth is wonderful but outlays for police to protect that private property is a waste. We watch television commercials of the latest vacuum cleaner with rapt attention but view the cleaning of city streets as an unfortunate expense. As a result, our houses are usually clean and our streets filthy. Such distinctions are not made in our GNP and therefore are easily ignored. As Galbraith puts it, "alcohol, comic books and mouthwash all bask under the superior reputation of the market. Schools, judges, patrolmen and municipal swimming pools lie under the reputation of bad kings."[12]

Public goods come under suspicion for still another reason. Normally, such goods are paid for by taxation. They are consumed more by the ordinary citizen than by the rich. Even if the rich and poor pay equal tax rates the net advantage of the public good accrues to the poor and the middle class. In their defense the rich build mansions which can be admired and provide vicarious satisfaction to the poor. Moreover, the rich can afford artwork out of reach of the lower classes and can display such artwork in museum's where they can be protected. Obviously, we are not content to deal with production for its own sake, but we must wrestle with the issue of how equally it is distributed. This is a matter which will be taken up in a later chapter.

Global Comparisons of GDP and Prosperity

GDP is by its nature a gross figure, but it is a popular one. Appendix 1.A shows the rank order of countries by nominal GDP. In the first column, the United States ranks first, followed closely by the European Union (EU). China, Japan, Germany, the United Kingdom, and France follow in that order. Surprisingly, India ranks number 7 despite its widespread poverty. The developing nations of Brazil, South Korea, Mexico, Indonesia, and Turkey go from 9th to 17th. Figures are given for 2016 for the IMF, 2015 for World Bank, and 2014 for the United Nations. The rankings for the seven richest countries are identical for the IMF, the World Bank, and the UN. Toward the bottom are poor nations such as Dominica, Swaziland, Liberia, Lesotho, Belize, Liberia, and Lesotho. The IMF primarily focuses on finance and the public debt. The World Bank ranking for 2016, in the second column, has a few more countries, perhaps because the focus of the World Bank is on economic development. The cluster at or near the bottom include Dominica, Micronesia, Palau, the Marshall Islands, Kiribati and Tuvalu as the poorest. At the top the rich countries follow the

---

[12] Galbraith, *The Affluent Society, op. cit.,* p. 111.

same order as in the IMF ranking. Again, the third column was compiled in 2015 by the United Nations (UN). The list of countries is longer for the UN because it recognizes every country in the world, regardless of GNP size, and the poorest countries are also the smallest.

The Legatum Prosperity Index for 2015 (https://www.li.com/activities/publications/2015-legatum-prosperity-index) has a different rank order. This ranking takes into account the economy, entrepreneurship & opportunity, governance, education, health, safety & security, personal freedom, and social capital. The U.S. is no longer number 1; rather, it ranks 11th in prosperity. Though she gets high rankings for health, she is 33rd for safety & security. The U.S. ranks 9th in education, despite its highly-touted public school system. In terms of prosperity, Norway, Switzerland, Denmark, New Zealand, Sweden, and Canada are at the top, respectively. They greatly outrank the U.S. in social capital. This is not surprising since most are socialist nations or social democracies. Iceland, Luxembourg, Germany, United Kingdom, Austria, and Singapore follow the U.S. closely. Little Singapore's economy ranks No. 1 as a major contributor to her prosperity. Countries such as Belgiium, Japan, France, Hong Kong, Taiwan, Malta, Spain, Czech Republic, Portugal, and South Korea are in the top one-third despite their relative low GDPs. At or near the bottom are the usual suspects, such as Republic of Congo, Ethiopia, Nigeria, Pakistan, Angola, Yemen, Syria, and Afghanistan. African and Middle East countries are among the least prosperous, excepting notably United Arab Emirates (30th), Kuwait (36th), Israel (38th), and Saudi Arabia (42nd).

Still, prosperity depends on more than simply the level of GDP. Geography is often destiny. For example, South Korea (28th) would rank much higher in prosperity if she did not share a border with North Korea. Israel would rank much lower absent US aid in technology and in military equipment.

In 2016 the Legatum Prosperity Index was updated (Appendix 1.B), with some changes in country rankings. New Zealand went from 4th to 1, based on improvements in its economy, going from 14th to 1st, related in part to improvements in entrepreneurship, going from 17th to 2nd. In an apparent contradiction, New Zealand slipped in education, but notably remained 1st in "social capital." Finland moved up from 9th to 3rd, while

Iceland went from 12th to 14th, which was not exactly earth-shaking. Again, the economy was important in Finland's move, as its economy rating went from 33rd to 12th, and again with improvements in entrepreneurship. Other changes in Finland were modest. Singapore's economy dropped from 1st to 8th; however, this high ranking flies in the face of a GDP ranking between 36th to 39th in the world (depending on the source). When the rank-ordering in Appendices A.1 and B.1 are compared by country, GDP clearly does not dominate the prosperity index. Prosperity depends not only on economic conditions, but also on entrepreneurship and opportunity, governance, education, health, safety and security, personal freedom, and social capital.

Chapter 2

THE SUPRA-SURPLUS SOCIETY

Some years ago John Kenneth Galbraith (JKG) wrote of the affluent society. A major theme of Galbraith was that the production of goods and services is a measure of civilized progress. The Gross Domestic Product (GDP) remains the accepted measure of not only economic but of larger social achievement. The counterpart to GDP is Gross National Income (GNI). National Income is somewhat smaller than GNI: it excludes the consumption of fixed capital and a statistical discrepancy. In the latter, business executives, athletes such as Bubba Watson and movie/TV stars such as Taylor Swift are handsomely rewarded. Of course, in the case of business executives, especially those in the financial sector, they essentially set their own pay, even though the boards of directors (also business executives, for the larger part) oversee this wonderful process. When challenged about being overpaid, the executives blithely answer: "the income is not the important thing; rather, it is the jobs we are creating." This establishes the business executive as a person of compassion. The movie star and star athlete do not get off so lightly; they must prove their compassion through public service. And so Brad Pitt, Harrison Ford, George Clooney, Angelina Jolie, and even Tiger Woods (with his Foundation for youngsters) have their favorite public charities. Billionaire industrialist Charles Koch has a foundation that, in one way or another, aims to please conservatives.

We need to distinguish **income** from **wealth**. Income is what people earn from work, but also from dividends, interest, and any rents or royalties paid to them on properties they own. Need we say, for the rich most of their income does not come from what we normally think of working. In 2008, for example, though not a very good year, only 19 percent of those 13,480 individuals making over $10 million had any income from wages and salaries. **Wealth** is the value of everything a person or family owns, minus any debts. In studying the wealth distribution, economists define wealth in terms of marketable assets, such as real estate, stocks, and bonds, leaving aside consumer durables like cars and household items because these are not as readily converted into cash and are more valuable to their owners for *use* purposes than they are for resale. Besides, in the marketplace, these items depreciate rapidly in great part because they are part of surplus production. Once we have the value of all marketable assets, then all debts, such as home mortgages and credit card debts, are subtracted, which yields a person's **net worth**. To the economist, net worth and wealth are identical. Financial wealth is treated a bit differently. **Financial wealth** is defined as net worth *minus* net equity in owner-occupied housing. It is important to note that financial wealth is more liquid than marketable wealth, since it is difficult to convert one's home into cash in the short run, the exception being during the height of real estate bubbles.

Much Ado about Production

Returning to Galbraith, he suggests that the productive process incorporates the means by which wants are created, and these are further sustained by fashion, social aspiration, and simple imitation. That is, what your neighbor does or has, you should do and have. The most evident source of consumer demand is the advertising and salesmanship of those providing the product. First the good is made, then so too is the market for it. We hardly need to suggest that this contradicts the concept of consumer sovereignty, not to mention scarcity, that is the bread and butter of orthodox economics. Galbraith suggests that such concepts serve the interests of those in the top of the income and wealth distributions.

1958–1998: The Shift of Concern from Inflation to Deflation

Galbraith's *The Affluent Society* appeared in four editions, the first in 1958 and the 40th anniversary issue in 1998.[1] Throughout the early editions was a stern warning about a choice between inflation and unemployment. It was then viewed as the primary threat afflicting the public's well-being. This was the case at home and abroad, though such a choice barely existed in the developing world. In Latin America, for example, inflation was rampant and so too was unemployment. The principle cause of inflation in the developed countries was the interaction of prices and wages. In the developed world management and unions negotiated higher wages partly because of past price increases. From the higher prices came demands for higher wages to keep real wages from falling. This led to a wage–price spiral. Tight monetary and fiscal policies were effective only insofar as they reduced national income and employment. The remedy — reducing real GNI to slow wage growth — was worse than the disease. Only occasionally and with little enthusiasm was an incomes policy deployed. An incomes policy uses a carrot or stick approach in which incomes (wages or profits) are directly or indirectly tempered.

As JKG noted in 1998, the dismal prospect of an upward wage–price spiral is now less of a threat. In the industrialized nations production has shifted away from traditional manufacturing where unions were once strong. The services, the professions and the arts, the entertainment and communications industries have become increasingly important areas of employment. Not only that, but the main players have changed. Doctors and nurses have become more important even as Tiger Woods is being apparently replaced by Jordan Spieth, Jason Day, Rory McKIlroy, Adam Scott, Bubba Watson, and Rickie Fowler. That so many are needed to replace the once number one — Tiger Woods — speaks volumes about *his* stature. Michael Jordan, Tiger's friend, was a billionaire in 2016. In Hollywood, an ageless Harrison Ford was still in the 2016 *Star Wars* film. Anyway, as early as 1998 there was little inflation at high levels of

---

[1] See John Kenneth Galbraith, *The Affluent Society* (New York: Houghton Mifflin Company, 1958, 1969, 1976, 1998).

employment. As Galbraith was writing in the final edition, the United States had had low unemployment and little inflation, a circumstance worthy of celebration. While this led Ken Galbraith to delete some paragraphs, the present circumstance is not only a cause of alarm but reason for many new paragraphs in the present book.

Since about 2008 and the collapse of the American, European and Japanese financial markets, the main problem has been deflation or at least the flirtation with it. We have been living with zero or near-zero short-term interest rates since December 16, 2008. The Federal Reserve Open Market Committee (FOMC) reset the shortest of rates, the federal funds rate in March 2015, to a range of 1.00 percent to 1.25 percent, a range prevailing just prior to zero or near zero rates. Despite fears of inflation on Wall Street, historically low interest rates, prevailing for a very long time, have not ignited price levels. If, during this time, a plot of the targeted federal funds rate is a flat-liner; a person with an EKG of this nature would be dead. While the USA economy was not moribund, it nonetheless was growing at the below-average rate of 2 percent per year, again as measured by the rate of change in real GNP. More recently, the growth rate has been a mere 1 percent per annum. This slow growth has been — at least temporarily — overtaken by the so-called "Trump Rally." While it would be premature to question the use of GNP growth as a measure well-being, the stock markets live and die by these numbers.

Social Imbalance

In 1958, JKG wrote of the maldistribution of money and effort between the public and private living standards, as well as the important question of the environment. His case is still strong. We have expensive cars such as the Porsche 211 and poor schools, clean houses and filthy streets, weak public services combined with anxiety for what the government spends (local, state, and federal). The federal government does spend willingly on national defense, a euphemism for war, and for corporate welfare. Otherwise, there is still persistent and powerful pressure for restraint on public outlays. While we are ever more affluent in our private consumption where incomes are adequate, the inadequacy of our schools, libraries, public recreation facilities, even law enforcement, are matters of daily discussions. In *The Affluent Society*, Galbraith is writing mostly about the United States of America.

In 1998, JKG admits that views on the environment have changed, where attitudes are mildly better. Today at least half of the general public agree about global warming. When he finished the original manuscript, he concluded that one piece of prose on the subject was too rich. The dubious passage nonetheless was retained and remains in the 40th anniversary edition. It bears quoting in full, as follows:

> The family which takes its mauve and cerise, air-conditioned, power-steered and power-braked automobile out for a tour passes through cities that are badly paved, made hideous by litter, blighted buildings, billboards and posts for wires that should long since have been put underground. They pass on into a countryside that has been rendered largely invisible by commercial art. (The goods which the latter advertise have an absolute priority in our value system. Such aesthetic considerations as a view of the countryside accordingly come second. On such matters we are consistent.) They picnic on exquisitely packaged food from a portable icebox by a polluted stream and go on to spend the night at a park which is a menace to public health and morals. Just before dozing off on an air mattress, beneath a nylon tent, amid the stench of decaying refuse, they may reflect vaguely on the curious unevenness of their blessings. Is this, indeed, the American genius?[2]

Besides the many references to the conventional wisdom, which has become part of the world's lexicon, the above paragraph was the most widely quoted. As we will come to note, driverless cars now would have to be mentioned.

There is much more to production than is revealed by the aggregates of GNP. The output of steel, oil, and machine tools is related to the production of automobiles. The production of automobiles is related to glass and plastic, as well as aluminum. Investment in railways must take into account the products to be shipped. These relationships have led to the construction of input–output tables which show how changes in the production in one industry will increase or diminish the demands on

---

[2] *Ibid.*, pp. 187–188.

other industries. The founder of input–output was a short, kindly Professor at Harvard, Wassily Leontief (1906–1999), who eventually received the Nobel Prize in economics (1972).[3] (Input–output is sufficiently important that we will return later to provide more detail.) Suffice to say, the changes in production between industries are called *coefficients* by economists. If expansion in one part of the economy is not matched by the requisite expansion in other parts, wherein the need for balance is not respected, then bottlenecks and shortages, speculative hoarding of scarce supplies and sharply increasing costs would be the outcome. The existence of inventories and some flexibility (in the longer run) in the coefficients as a result of substitution, ensures that these difficulties do not arise. For example, if the price of steel (because of shortages) rises, aluminum can be substituted in automobile production. That is, the coefficient between steel and aluminum and automobiles changes. Of course, warfare can create shortages that cannot be easily managed. Still, when surpluses are sufficiently large, war is more or less a sideshow.

Oddly and without reason, Leontief was held under suspicion because he came from Russia and later, the USSR used planning to manage its economy. Input–output was considered by some to be the ideal tool for a planned economy. A free-market economy is more likely to lead to substitution of one product for another and the input–output coefficients are more likely to be stable. This is not the first or last time that ideology plays a role in economics. Common sense trumps ideology. If we consume more automobiles, we need more gasoline. If we need more gasoline, we need more crude oil. If we need more crude oil, we need more derricks. As to services, more automobiles require more insurance as well as more roadways. The increased consumption of tobacco and alcohol per capita places a greater burden on medical services. More vacations require more hotels, resorts, golf clubs, tennis racquets, and fishing tackle. And so forth.

Such relationships are not confined to the private sector. Not only are private services involved but so too are public services. To Kenneth Galbraith, this raises the problem of social balance. That increase in the consumption of automobiles requires an ample supply of streets, highways,

---

[3] See especially Wassily Leontief, *Input–output Economics* (Oxford: Oxford University Press, 1986).

traffic control, and parking spaces. Traffic accidents place an increased demand on medical services. The use of the private automobile has often gotten out of line with the supply of these related public services. The city of Los Angeles, not to mention the major cities of Japan, is a classic study in the consequent problem of social balance. There is also ubiquitous traffic congestion, human massacre of impressive proportions and chronic congestion in the cities, even the small ones. Congestion is not confined to ground transportation. Look to the sky and you see planes delayed or colliding at airports with adverse consequences for passengers when the public provision of air traffic control fails to keep pace with the private demand for the airways.[4] One of the worst cases of public neglect came to light in January and February of 2016. CNN revealed that Flint, Michigan's water pipes were corroded to the point of breakage. Worse, they were made of lead, which meant the drinking water was poisonous. Children were found to have unsafe levels of lead in their bodies. While the Governor of Michigan called it "a failure of government," the deeper cause was social imbalance.

There is an affirmative side to social balance. By failing to expand public production, we are missing opportunities for enjoyment which otherwise we might not have. A community can be well rewarded by building better schools or better parks. In purely economic terms, falling short in the public goods arena is to fail to maximize satisfaction. The contrast is invidious. Satisfying private needs and wants with reckless abundance, while practicing self-denial in the case of public goods is to sacrifice much of the future. Those with sufficient income and wealth can fly off to a private resort whereas public goods are mostly designed for the poor and middle class. Even private schools have been known to supplant public education. The rich can own expensive art works, but only museums can display art to the general public. On the night of November 9, 2015 in Manhattan, Christie's auctioned off Arnedeo Modigliani's "Nu Couche," a painting of a voluptuous nude lady in dramatic color, smiling in a post-coital slumber. Its hammer price was $170.4 million, and for an

---

[4] For many more negative examples of social imbalance in the USA, see Chapter 17 of John Kenneth Galbraith, *The Affluent Society*, *op. cit.*

artist on no one's top 20 list. There is some consolation in the aftermath; 10 other works failed to sell at their high reserve prices.

The Importance of the Income Distributions

We will return to *The Affluent Society* in the next chapter. As the alert reader of the title of the present book may suspect, it is a sequel to JKG's magnum opus. The themes of the two books diverge at several points. My emphasis will be upon inequality and production surpluses, though demand will not be ignored. The corpus of my work comprises a theory of supra-surplus capitalism, both as it exists in the USA and abroad. Hence, my concerns go global. Supra-surplus applies to an economy sufficiently productive so as to produce more than the society wants and needs. This does not mean that wants and needs are met equally. The idea that surpluses even exist is an unpopular notion among conventional economists. Why this is so and why this departure from convention has important implications will require some explanation. In recent history this surplus increasingly has been distributed more to the top than to the bottom or to the middle. This is true both at the margin (income distribution) and for surplus accumulation (wealth distribution). Surpluses imply a high level of development for an economy. Although our main focus will be on industrialized economies, we are reminded that even in ancient Greece surpluses of a different kind existed for the upper class. Slaves and even many free persons lived at the margins of society. Poverty exists even absent industrialization.

In this perspective the income distribution is important in deciding what is produced and what the rewards to particular factors of production will be. In the traditional world of economics wages and profits are factor payments to labor and capital. In the economy we have been describing, this is not so. Income payments are made to persons and, therefore, we are concerned with the *personal* income distribution. A society with surpluses has labor that goes beyond subsistence wages that simply meet basic physiological needs. The poor barely exist at a subsistence level and live amidst affluence. Some labor generates sufficient incomes to indulge in non-spending that is in line with wealth accumulation. When such persons purchase income-producing financial assets they can then share (though indirectly) in total profits of business enterprises. In short, the reliance on a stereotyped income division between workers and capitalists is an inadequate explanation for the income distribution of a supra-surplus society. Although the income and wealth distributions are related, the wealth distribution in in most of the developed world is much more lop-sided than the income distribution.

We turn now to near the tip of the top of the wealth distributions, and even higher as we reach the highest peaks.

The Wealth Distribution: The Forbes 400

Admission to the Forbes 400 richest Americans in October 2015 required a $1.7 billion net worth (wealth), nearly 10 percent higher than the previous year's then record $1.55 billion. This raising of the bar for the richest rich eliminated 31 now former members of this exclusive club. Five others passed away; immortality is one of the few things that the rich cannot buy. There were seven unlucky people who would have cleared the 2014 bar of $1.55 billion but were too poor to make the 2015 list. Compassion mandates that their names should be mentioned — Carol Jenkins Barnett of Publix Super Markets (a mere $1.59 billion), Alexander Spanos of real estate and the San Diego Chargers ($1.69 billion), Jeffrey Lurie of the Philadelphia Eagles ($1.65 Billion), Nicolas Berggruen of investments ($1.65 billion), Alexander Karp of software ($1.6 billion), Jeff Rothschild of Facebook ($1.6 billion), and the poorest of these castoffs, Leslie Alexander of the Houston Rockets ($1.55 billion). The then Presidential hopeful Donald Trump made the cut with an estimated $4.5 billion net worth, though he claimed to be worth $10 billion. He still ranked 121st instead of the aspired for 37th.

Looking up to the very top, we find Bill Gates ($76 billion) still at number 1 and Warren Buffet ($62 billion) at number 2. Gates made his fortune by co-founding Microsoft with Paul Allen (No. 28). He now has just under 3 percent of the company which is about 13 percent of his fortune. The world's richest man is deploying his billions primarily to improve humanity's lot. He has focused on social policy in the USA, giving more than $25 million to the Clinton Foundation. Buffet is a Hillary Clinton supporter and contributed to her campaign for President of the

United States. While he has sided with Clinton, he has made admiring comments about Bernie Sanders, known as a far-left politician. Many of the rich consider Gates and Buffet to be traitors to their own class. Such cannot be said for number 5 Charles Koch ($41 billion), tied with his brother David Koch ($41 billion). Charles compares his crusade for smaller government and economic liberty to the civil rights campaign, and his network of several hundred wealthy conservatives hoped to spend up to $300 million on candidates and another $600 on efforts to reduce regulations and reform the criminal justice system. This is pocket-change out of some $82 billion in wealth, but it is highly significant for conservative politicians. High technology still plays a role in the making of fortunes as big gains by Amazon's Jeff Bezos and Facebook's Mark Zuckerberg vault the 2 tech pioneers into the ranks of the 10 wealthiest Americans for the first time.

The Maldistribution of the Koch Brothers' Fortune

So, does it really matter that about 0.001 percent of the American population have a total net worth equaling some 12 percent of the nation's GNI? Does it really matter that the Koch brothers have a wealth level greater than the GNI of several countries, including Panama with its population 3.9 million? More realistically is a larger economy like Argentina, wherein the Koch brothers fortune is *only* about 15 percent of its GNI. An important book by Jane Mayer has put the spotlight on what she calls "Dark Money."[5] At the heart of the book are the Koch brothers, who inherited an industrial conglomerate, which is the second-largest private company in the USA. The company is diverse, with interests in energy, chemicals, commodities and consumer goods; its owners focus on advancing their narrow conservative agenda. Among other things, the Koch's deny climate change and oppose government regulation, welfare, and taxes. They view the rise of the Democrats and Barack Obama's election in 2008 in apocalyptic terms, while the counterinsurgency they have funded has changed the face of politics in the USA. Rich conservatives, like the Koch's, set up

---

[5] Jane Mayer, *Dark Money: The Hidden History of the Billionaires Behind the Rise of the Radical Right* (New York: Doubleday, 2016).

private foundations, which allow them quietly to divert money to their favorite political causes free of taxes. These foundations, besides those set up by the Koch's, include Richard Mellon Scaife, the John M. Olin Foundation, and Harry Bradley, which are not subject to much disclosure or oversight. They can transfer money secretly into partisan think-tanks like the conservative Cato Institute, the Heritage Foundation, the American Enterprise Institute and the Hoover Institution. These wealthy individuals use "charitable" foundations to influence politics at the expense of ordinary taxpayers.

They go beyond contributions to politicians to attempt to alter public discourse without leaving a trace. The Koch's and other rich conservatives support academic research that is allied to their political ideologies. In short, they want to take the liberal out of liberal arts. To be fair, we should note that Democratic donors, such as the hedge-fund billionaires, George Soros and Tom Steyer, have funneled money into their own political causes. However, these are open individuals who do not use the secretive tactics of the right. Much of the Soros' fortune goes to finance emerging democracies in developing nations. There is no attempt to secretly make the rich richer. The Koch network has become one of the most powerful political forces in the USA. Some 1,200 people work full-time for the Koch network, which is more than three times the number of people who work for the Republican National Committee. According to Harvard scholars Theda Skoepol and Alexander Hertel-Fernandez, the Koch's have established a nationally-federated, full-service, ideologically focused machine that operates on the scale of a national USA political party. They make democracy for sale.[6] In a hasty retreat from presidential politics, the Koch brothers are supporting neither Donald Trump nor Hillary Clinton. However, they have amassed (with help from others) about a trillion dollars to disperse to Republican Senate and House candidates.[7]

While there is inequality at the tip of the top of the income and wealth distributions, we should not neglect the top 1 percent. The top 1 percent

---

[6] See Jane Mayer, "New Koch," *The New Yorker*, January 25, 2016, p. 38.
[7] See Isaac Chotiner, "Are the Koch's Really Sitting This One Out?" *Slate*, May 21, 2016. As to the Koch's backing Hillary Clinton, Jane Mayer in an interview in the same article opined, "I would say the odds are greater that a meteorite will take out the planet Earth."

has been the traditional cut-off point for "the top" in academic studies. With notable exceptions, such as Edward N. Wolfe at New York University and Thomas Piketty of the Paris School of Economics, the wealthy have been studied mostly by sociologists and political scientists. Among the latter, G. William Domhoff is a pioneer. Domhoff is a psychologist and a sociologist. Thus, most economists have chosen to ignore him, economics having claimed to be a "hard science." That's too bad, because he has not ignored economists who have studied the income and wealth distributions. His main thesis is: income and wealth distributions are indicators of power.[8] He was influenced by sociologists E. Digby Baltzell and C. Wright Mills, economist Paul Sweezy and distinguished political scientist Robert A. Dahl (1915–2014). Sweezy (1910–2004) was a Harvard economist and a friend of the conservative Joseph Schumpeter. JKG called Sweezy "the most noted American Marxist scholar of the late 20th Century."[9] Later, we will have more to say about power.

The International Spectra

Is the USA the most unequal in income and wealth distributions? The answer is not simple, and we will return to this issue in more detail later. One measure of income inequality is the Gini coefficient. It is a mathematical ratio that puts all countries on a scale with values that range from zero (everyone in the country has the same income) to 100 (one person in the country has all the income). These extremes of zero and 100, of course, are hypothetical. On this measure, the USA is 95th out of some 134 countries that have been studied — that is, only 39 of the 134 countries have worse income inequality. The USA has a Gini index of 45.0. Sweden is the lowest at 23.0, and South Africa is near the top with 65.0.[10] While the income distribution is not as concentrated as the wealth distribution, it

---

[8] See G. William Domhoff, *Who Rules America?* 6th edition (New York: Prentice Hall, 2009) and on the internet, Who Rules America.net.

[9] John Kenneth Galbraith, *Economics in Perspective* (Boston: Houghton Mifflin, 1987), p. 189.

[10] G. William Domhoff, "Wealth, Income, and power," Who Rules America.net, pp. 15–16.

nonetheless can be a power indicator. Those with higher incomes in democracies can donate more to political parties, make greater payments to lobbyists, and generally realize wishes, or reach goals, even in the face of opposition. The same can be said for wealth, except more so.

As noted, income inequality can also be measured by the share of income going to the Top 1 percent compared with the Bottom 99 percent. One of the most striking differences is between Sweden and the USA. The differences narrowed in the 1950s and 1960s, but after that went their separate ways, with the USA becoming much more unequal.[11] One might suppose that the income distribution becomes more equal after taxes and transfers, but not in the USA, according to the Gini index. Another way to use income as a power indicator is to compare average CEO annual pay to average factory worker pay. In the USA the ratio of CEO pay to factory worker pay rose from 42:1 in 1960 to as high as 531:1 in 2000, at the height of the stock market bubble, when CEOs were cashing in big stock options. It was at 411:1 in 2005 and 344:1 in 2007. The same ratio was about 25:1 in Europe.[12]

We next consider the wealth distribution, again to be looked at in more detail later. The top 10 percent of the world's adults control about 85 percent of global household wealth — defined broadly as all assets (not simply financial assets), minus debts. This compares with about 70 percent for the top 10 percent in the USA. Only Switzerland with 71.3 percent tops the USA. Denmark, France, Sweden, the UK, and Canada follow, in that order.[13] All of these are industrialized nations. Consider the top 1 percent. In 2010 in the USA, the top 1 percent of households (the upper class) owned some 35 percent of all privately held wealth. The next 19 percent (the managerial, professionals, and small business class) had 54 percent, which means that just one-fifth of the people owned a remarkable 89 percent, leaving only 11 percent of

---

[11] Domhoff, *ibid.*, p. 16. This is based on the Top 1 percent with data from F. Alvaredo, T. Atkinson, T. Piketty, & E. Saez, World Top Incomes Database. Retrieved March 14, 2012 from http://g-mond.parisschoolofeconnomics.eu/topincomes/.

[12] Domhoff, *Ibid.*, pp. 17–18. *Bloomsberg/Business Week* keeps close track of CEO pay.

[13] Domhoff, *Ibid.*, pp. 9–10. These figures are for the year 2000. They can be updated with data from the very top, the Forbes 400.

wealth for the bottom 80 percent (wage and salary earners). The inequality only grows when we narrow wealth to financial holdings only. Financial wealth is total net worth minus the value of one home. In the USA the top 1 percent of households had 42 percent, the next 19 percent, 54 percent, and at the bottom 80 percent, 4.7 percent.[14]

When we look at the richest people in the world in 2014, we find more money, more newcomers, more women, more billionaires, faster horses. Records were not simply broken, they were shattered. There were 1,545 billionaires worth some $6.4 trillion, an 18.5 percent advance from 2013. Around 268 of them made their first appearance on the list in 2014, and there are now 172 women billionaires — 42 of them newcomers. You could make the top 20 if you had $31 billion dollars, another new record. The top 50 comprise only 0.000001 percent of the world's population. Half of these are USA citizens, but extreme wealth is spreading around the world. Now at least one member of this elite club can be found on every continent except Antarctica. Any billionaire there would have moved to Florida or Hawaii by now. After 4 years behind Carlos Slim of Mexico (or at least, one of the Mexico's), Bill Gates was back on top, at a whopping $76 billion. The rich got richer in 2014. Mark Zuckerberg of Facebook gained a hefty $15.2 billion, Lui Che Woo gained $11.3 billion in net worth, when his company Galaxy Entertainment hit the jackpot, and Aliko Dangote lagged behind with a mere $8.9 billion gain, wherein shares in Dangote Cement, his largest asset, climbed more than 60 percent over the prior year.[15] At third among the gainers, he nonetheless is a concrete example.

Money goes where money is. Foreign billionaires are parking their money in the USA at an accelerated pace, snapping up landmark properties from commercial towers like New York's General Motors Building to trophy residences in New York, California and Florida. As examples, Michael Ashley, the reclusive British founder of retailer Sports Direct, purchased a gold-leaf-accented estate in Miami for $30 million, while Japan's Masayoshi Son, the Softbank chief, purchased a hilltop estate in a horsey neighborhood in Woodside, CA for $117.5 million. Most everyone

---

[14] Domhoff, *Ibid.*

[15] *Forbes Special Issue*, March 24, 2014.

agrees that Son overpaid, but poetically, he can afford it.[16] These are buys that are almost impossible to comprehend by the average worker in any nation. The typical household income (median) in the USA in 2014 was about $54,000, not enough for a week's rent for one of these estates.[17] Besides, they are not for rent.

At the very bottom are the poor. With a USA population that had grown since 1959, the number in poverty was 45.7 million with an official poverty rate of 14.8 percent in 2014. There has been some progress. The poverty rate was about 23 percent during the nostalgic 1950s, falling dramatically during the 1970s, rising dramatically during the early 1980s, reaching 14.8 percent in 1993, dipping for a while, but rising to a plateau of 14.8 percent following the Great Recession in 2010. It has not been an easy ride for the poor compared to the rich. Thanks to social security and income tax credits, the greatest improvement has been for those aged 65 and older; their poverty rate fell from 35 percent in 1959 to 10 percent in 2014. The young should be wary of limiting social security since, with a longer-living population, the ranks of the aged is growing. Many lament such a great number in poverty in the biggest economy in the world, especially since the USA is a showplace for supra-surplus capitalism.

Although the orthodoxy places priority on the paramount position of production, the reality regarding inequality is to be found in the income and wealth distributions. The focus on surplus production is a diversion.

We next consider in detail what JKG meant by "conventional wisdom."

---

[16] *Ibid.*, p. 38.

[17] The median is such that half of households have higher incomes and half have lower.

Chapter 3

UNCONVENTIONAL WISDOM

Before unconventional wisdom came conventional wisdom, a term that has become part of the global lexicon. Many elements contribute to the acceptability of ideas. We often associate truth with convenience; that is, with what most closely aligns with self-interest and personal well-being or in the least promises to best avoid awkward effort or unwelcome dislocation of life. Most acceptable is what contributes to self-esteem. We like to hear speeches from those which we best understand. No self-respecting Republican will listen intently to a speech by a Democrat, no matter how much sense the speech-maker is making, and vice-versa. The understanding of economic and social behavior is complex and mentally tiring. We are always looking for short-cuts to the understanding of complex subjects or issues. In this regard, vested interests play a big role. Frequently we react with something like religious passion in the defense of what we have so laboriously mastered. In this regard familiarity does not bred contempt. Familiarity in the realm of social ideas is the touchstone of acceptability.

Acceptable ideas have great stability and therefore are highly predictable. John Kenneth Galbraith thought it convenient to have a name for the ideas which are esteemed at any time for their acceptability, and thought it should be a term that emphasizes this predictability. He therefore referred to those ideas henceforth as the Conventional Wisdom. The conventional wisdom is not the property of any particular political group. Hence, we can speak of the conventional wisdom of, for example, the conservative or the liberal. It is also articulated on all levels of sophistication. At the highest levels of social science scholarship, some novelty is not resisted. An old wine is sometimes put in a new bottle. And this, without being unscientific or parochial, minor modifications can be made, with considerable attention drawn to it. It may elicit a large literature and a certain mystic. Its defenders are able to say that the challengers of the conventional wisdom have not mastered its intricacies. Sound scholars cling to that old time conventional wisdom. At the highest level of sophistication, originality remains acceptable only in the abstract. The vigorous advocacy of originality becomes a substitute for originality itself. There is little mystery here: there are many reasons why people like to hear articulated that which they approve. If nothing else, it massages the ego.[1]

In some respects, the articulation of the conventional wisdom is a religious rite, or so it might seem. Faith certainly is required. Reading the conventional wisdom is an act of affirmation like reading aloud the Scriptures or going to church. Participating in the ritual is important. At its highest level in the social sciences, it is known as *normal science*. Scientists belong to a scientific community. This does not mean that they all live together in housing especially set aside for scientists. A scientific community is an invisible college that contains all those who practice or work at a particular scientific specialty — for example, medicine, chemistry, or biology. All of the scientists in a given field have had similar educations, and they all work with the same technical literature. They all know more or less the same things. They can also be identified by the highest academic degrees they hold (in economics, a Ph.D.) and the professional organizations they belong to (the American Economic Association).

In addition, they share a belief in identical rules of exploration and common standards for correctness in their sciences, rather like players of a game who agree to the same rules. This agreement on standards is a prerequisite for normal science, which is the kind of science practiced by

---

[1] This brief introduction to Galbraith's concept of the conventional wisdom is based on John Kenneth Galbraith, *The Affluent Society*, 40th Anniversary Edition (Boston/New York: Houghton Miffllin Company, 1998), especially pp. 6–11. The reader would benefit from the whole of his Chapter 2.

nearly all working scientists at all levels of their profession. *Normal science* is based on the accomplishment of scientists in the past whose work has laid the ground rules for contemporary scientists. As we might expect, normal science is the conventional wisdom of particular scientific field, writ large. The academic who goes up against this conventional wisdom will likely be defrocked.[2]

Closely related to the practice of normal science is what science historian Thomas Kuhn has called a *paradigm*.[3] A paradigm is an outstanding example of scientific achievement that other scientists can use and follow in their own work. For example, the Newtonian world view is a paradigm. It is still used to explain planetary motion and the atom. Newton's explanation of the movements of heavenly bodies was complete and convincing enough to attract many scientific followers, but at the same time it left problems for its followers to solve. A paradigm, then, is the body of knowledge that the members of a particular scientific community share; conversely, a scientific community consists of people who share a paradigm. As Kuhn puts it, "The study of paradigms . . . is what mainly prepares the student for membership in the particular scientific community with which he will later practice."[4]

Despite the title of Kuhn's book, scientific revolutions are rare, happening at best about once a generation, when the former members of a scientific community are safely in their graves. The nature of scientific revolution is most clearly seen in astronomy, where the medieval concept of the universe was ultimately overthrown. The Ptolemaic, Copernican, and Newtonian scientific systems as examples of well-developed and easy to understand paradigms had profound influence on the world view of Western society.[5] Let it be said again: in the academic world, the conventional wisdom in the strictest form is a scientific paradigm.

---

[2] For the definition of normal science and an extended discussion, see E. Ray Canterbery, *The Making of Economics*, 1st edition (Belmont, CA: Wadsworth Publishing Co., 1976), pp. 26–27.

[3] Thomas S. Kuhn, *The Structure of Scientific Revolutions,* 2nd edition (Chicago: University of Chicago Press, 1970).

[4] Kuhn, *op. cit.*, p. 176.

[5] For an extended discussion of these paradigms and their effects on Western society, see Canterbery, 1976, *op. cit.*, pp. 28–34.

Not surprisingly, and as Galbraith notes, the enemy of the conventional wisdom is not ideas but the march of events. As the world moves on, the conventional wisdom is always in danger of obsolescence. As with automobiles, obsolescence is not necessarily or immediately fatal. Rather, the fatal blow to the conventional wisdom comes when the conventional ideas can no longer deal with some contingency to which obsolescence has made them palpably inapplicable. This is the fate of ideas which have lost their relation to the real world. Quite often, their irrelevance will be dramatized by some individual. To that individual, credit for the overthrow of convention will be accrued, and fame may ensue, though it may be tantamount to breaking through an already rotting door. John Maynard Keynes' *General Theory of Employment, Interest and Money* in 1936 could not be ignored because it was published during the midst of the Great Depression. This does not make Keynes's achievement any less remarkable, only more predictable. The conventional wisdom of the balanced national budget survived both. During the Great Depression, nonetheless, circumstance triumphed over the conventional wisdom, as by the second year of the Hoover administration, the federal budget was irretrievably out of balance.

Policy changes or recommendations often precede paradigm changes. That is, the conventional wisdom often progresses ahead of theory. Keynes's new ideas steadily evolved from 1931 to 1934, as capitalism was devolving. In the earliest months of the 1930s, Keynes expressed his belief that the fundamental cause of the slump was a lack of new plants and equipment, a result of the "poor outlook" for capital investment. To improve the outlook, profits must not be achieved by cutting costs; that would be deflationary. Keynes decided that profits could be raised either by inducing the public to spend a larger share of their income or by inducing business to convert a larger portion of its revenue into investment, but not by both.

At this point, Keynes was still relying in part on a failing paradigm, neoclassical thinking, mostly that of Alfred Marshall. In the old paradigm, an increase in consumption required sacrificing savings otherwise available for business investment. Keynes did not yet envision the pleasurable possibility of both total consumption spending and total investment spending growing simultaneously.

Even so, Keynes told his British radio audience in 1931 that heightened spending was necessary to counteract the Depression, an intuition that proved to be more useful than the advice of the neoclassicals. Keynes attacked thrift, a Victorian virtue, because he saw the fallacy of expecting large savings to be offset by investment when there were virtually no investment opportunities in sight. By 1932, for example, American industry was selling less than half of its 1929 output. Supra-surpluses are not a new or rare thing.

Keynes urged families to spend more and the government to increase its public works expenditures. Notably, he rejected Arthur Pigou's suggested wage reductions; that would, Keynes felt, only make matters worse. (This has not prevented some policymakers in the industrialized world for calling for wage slowdowns in the face of economic stagnation in recent years.) In 1931, Keynes also served on the Macmillan Committee to investigate and make recommendations about economic conditions in Britain. Anticipating his later theory of the multiplier, Keynes and other dissenting (from the neoclassicals) members of the committee argued that with private unemployment already high, public spending by government would not divert resources away from private investment but would rather have a compounding effect.

Although Keynes admitted that public-works programs might dampen business confidence for a short time, he thought that, on balance, increased government spending would be helpful, even desirable. Keynes was beginning to suggest that, if free markets did not produce working people and humming factories, then it would be necessary for the government to intervene to restore higher levels of economic activity.

And, so, one person can be very important in attacking the conventional wisdom. Until Keynes, critics of the neoclassicals were easily dismissed; they simply did not understand. But Keynes obviously did, and given his credentials, he had to be taken seriously when he condemned *laissez-faire*. This he did in an essay in 1926 called *"The End of Laissez Faire,"* in which he denied Adam Smith's principle of natural liberty and the close relationship of private and social interest with enlightened self-interest. Keynes doubted that that there would always be enough expenditure to stabilize the economy — that is, he questioned J. B. Say's law that supply always created its own demand. But at this point he lacked a counter theory to Marshallian economics. He had only a fuzzy vision. Still, the conventional wisdom was under assault. The polished Keynesian paradigm has been widely discussed, but is not without its critics.[6]

Keynes was an optimist; he had high hopes for capitalism, as practiced in the United Kingdom and in the United States. While his critics thought otherwise, he was trying to save capitalism from its worst enemies. Unlike Karl Marx, he did not envision capitalism as doomed. In this respect, if in no other, he joined hands with Adam Smith (1723–1790), the first great figure in economics, who also was a hopeful figure. Smith's vision was of an advancing national community, not a stagnant or declining one. His *An Inquiry into the Nature and Causes of the Wealth of Nations* had the unmistakable ring of affluence and well-being. He seemed to offer an all but certain formula for economic progress for humans. He envisioned a liberal economic society in which regulation was by the invisible hand of competition. The hope was for aggregate wealth, whereas he had little hope that the distribution of wealth between merchants, manufacturers and landlords on the one hand, and the working masses on the other, would be such as to benefit the latter. The advantage in relative bargaining power went to the holders of capital. In the normal course of events, the income of the working masses would be pressed down and then some. *Comes the optimism*, there was a floor below which working wages would not fall. Since a person lives by their work, and their wages must at least be sufficient to maintain life, the wages must upon most occasions be somewhat more; otherwise the family could not survive. Upon such thin hope the power of positive thinking would nearly wither. The USA optimist has always been able to concentrate their mind on other elements of Smith's thought.

The optimistic economist sees a connection between Isaac Newton, Newtonian mechanics, and Adam Smith. About 50 years after the death of Galileo, Newton stated the *law of universal gravitation*, which led to a new paradigm in natural science. According to the new paradigm, the planets move through space around the sun in Kepler's ellipses and in

---

[6] For the polished version, see E. Ray Canterbery, *The Making of Economics*: *Volume*. I, *The Foundation*, 4th edition (World Scientific: Singapore/New Jersey/London, 2003), Chapter 12.

conformity to Galileo's law of falling bodies. The Newtonian system put in concrete form the idea that all phenomena, all experience, consisted of the arrangement of atoms following mechanical mathematically regular laws. Now, in his theory of gravitation, Newton had found a cosmic law subject to precise mathematical proof and as applicable (he thought) to the smallest object as to the entire universe. Though Kepler was the first to note it, Newton's interpreters saw the universe as if it were a divine clock that kept perfect time. Indeed, with this mechanical world view emerged a God derivable from natural law and in harmony with the order of the universe. God, like His universe, was rational and dependable. This optimistic conception of reliability — intensified by the conviction that the Creator was kind and charitable — produced a profound sense of relief. The American clergyman Cotton Mather (1663–1728) could argue: "Gravity leads us to God and brings us very near to Him." To understand the forces of gravity was to better comprehend God's wondrous ways.

It was just a short step for Adam Smith to believe that once the economy had been set in motion by the hand of God, there was no need for any improvements. Repairmen would only upset the mechanism and disturb its ability to function in an orderly way. Smith was no doubt driven by a desire to emulate the most widely respected scientific system of his time, and the effects of Newton on social science and society continue to this day. Smith's market mechanism remains a large part of conventional wisdom in economics. The present volume contains mostly **unconventional** wisdom.

Chapter 4

ECONOMICS AND THE TRADITIONS OF SCARCITY AND DESPAIR

Besides *laissez faire*, a second, not necessarily conflicting tradition, deflected off Adam Smith. Smith had noted how wages had to be somewhat above subsistence for the family to survive. Smith was not categorical about this iron law. He conceded that a scarcity of workers might keep wages above the subsistence level for an indefinite time. Also, wages would rise along with economic growth, a very new concept. While England, according to Smith, was a much richer country (had more wealth) than North America, the wages of labor were much higher in North America than any part of England. Smith's association of high wages with rapid economic growth was largely lost to the conventional wisdom of scarcity.

The Nearly Holy Trinity in Economics

With Adam Smith, the founding trinity of economics included David Ricardo (1772–1823) and Thomas Malthus (1755–1834). It narrowly missed being a *Holy* Trinity, what with Malthus being a non-practicing Pastor. Ricardo gave economics its modern micro-structure by identifying the elements determining prices, rents, wages, and profits that continues to serve the conventional wisdom. However, Ricardo bent the branch of economics with Marxians and non-Marxians in his debt. We will find a reason to return to this connection.

With Ricardo and Malthus, Smithian optimism began to fade. They brought with them the idea of massive privation and great inequality. Because of Ricardo and Malthus, the eminent British historian Thomas Carlyle (1795–1881), later would refer to economics as the "dismal science," a name it has not entirely escaped for various reasons.[1] The fame of Thomas Malthus rests on his dark theory of population growth, nearly as dark as Hollywood's *Frankenstein*. In 1798, in the culmination of a dispute with his father [who sided with Utopian William Godwin (1756–1836)], the 32-year-old Malthus published anonymously "An Essay on the Principle of Population, as It Affects the Future Improvement of Society: with Remarks on the Speculations of Mr. Godwin, M. Condorcet, and Other Writers" Lengthy titles were popular, even expected. At the time Malthus's thesis was unconventional. From the great altitude of Godwin's optimism, we find Malthusian pessimism.

Malthus's Doomsday Scenario

Malthus devised an illustration for his argument that people tend to increase in number beyond their means of subsistence. His illustration involves two numerical progressions. If there were no limit to the food supply, the population of a country would easily double every 25 years, at a geometric rate of increase. The increase in food production under ideal conditions would be, as Malthus put it, "evidently arithmetical." Thus we see the humans in the cities increasing in the ratio of 1, 2, 4, 8, 16, 32, 64, 128, 256, 512, and so on, and subsistence increasing as 1, 2, 3, 4, 5 ,6, 7, 8, 9, 10, and so on. And so be it. As Malthus put it, "In two centuries and a quarter, the population would be to the means of subsistence as 512 to 10: in three centuries as 4,096 to 13, and in two thousand years the difference would be almost incalculable."[2]

---

[1] Thomas Carlyle, "Occasional Discourse on the Negro Question," *Fraser's Magazine for Town and Country*, Vol XL, 1849, p. 672.
[2] Thomas R. Malthus, *On Population*, Gertrude Himmelfarb ed. (New York: Random House, Modern Library, 1960), p. 13.

But people had lived in cities for centuries already. Why had the population explosion never come? Malthus had a gruesome answer: the tendency of the population to exceed food production was restrained by the "positive" checks to population — those events raising the death rate — in the form of famine, misery, plague, and war. Poverty and regret, he concluded, are the natural punishments for the "lower classes." Relief for the "unworthy" poor, such as provided by the English poor laws, only made matters worse, as more children would survive. Only the "class of proprietors" could be trusted with fecundity. The conclusion is as obvious as it is gloomy: poverty is inevitable. Malthus's ideas about the moral inferiority of the poor were adopted in the Poor Law Amendment of 1834. All relief outside the prison-like workhouses was abolished for able-bodied people. Relief applicants had to pawn all their possessions and enter the workhouse. Women and children usually were sent to work in the cotton mills, away from the temptations of the nuptial bed. The intent of the law was to make quiet starvation more dignified than public assistance. This system remained the basis of British poor-law policy until the eve of World War I. Vindicated by human laws, Malthus was still subject to those of Nature, which subtracted him from the population four months after the passage of the Poor Law Amendment.

The Doctrine in the Real World

Data can be adduced both to substantiate and to refute the Malthusian population doctrine. The British data for 1750–1800 appear to fit the Malthusian model. The population of Great Britain increased only 8 percent between 1700 and 1750; between 1750 and 1800, it was 50 percent (an enormous leap by the standards of the time). Declines in mortality and increases in productivity raised population growth, the swollen labor supply then lowered real wage rates. Then, population increased an incredible 100 percent between 1800 and 1850. By 1860, however, the teeter-totter of population-up and living standards-down was no longer in play because productivity was rising so rapidly. Eventually, the Industrial Revolution broke the old cycle. Modern statistics on population growth in Western Europe, the United Kingdom, North America, and Japan show the theory to be less than universally true.

Even so, certain poor areas of the world resemble the more agrarian society of Malthus's day and tend to support his theory. Humanity is threatened by its own replication in parts of Africa, Latin America, and rural India. Although these conditions support Malthus's views, he failed to anticipate some important connections. First, humans can reduce their fertility through modern birth-control methods. Second, advances in agricultural technology such as the development of new grain varieties (the Green Revolution) has resulted in increased yields in food production. Granted, we cannot ignore the various neo-Malthusian theories predicting that the world's energy resources, which in part support agriculture, may someday become exhausted. But these theories may also underestimate our ability to create new technologies to meet such threats. Godwin, for one, had argued that technological inventions were susceptible to perpetual improvement. Third, and perhaps most important, the shift from an agrarian society to an urbanized supra-surplus society reduces the need for the family to reproduce its own labor. All this, and we will withhold for now the prospects for robots.

Speaking of surpluses, we need to mention briefly another contribution of Malthus, his *theory of gluts*. Malthus strongly dissented from the position of Smith and Say with regard to the possibility of unsold goods. He saw a human desire for goods exceeded only by a passion for sex. However, he suggested that, if the individual who wished to buy had nothing to sell that others wanted, goods would remain unsold. A manufacturer will not hire a worker unless the laborer produces a value greater than the laborer's wage — a surplus equaling the employer's profit. Obviously, the worker is in no position to buy back the surplus, so others must. Hence, the dilemma: full employment is ensured only if all output is bought. Malthus worried about who would buy the surplus.

Adam Smith and Malthus had an instinct for national aggregates — for the forces which acted to enrich or impoverish a nation. While Malthus was concerned with showing how increased national wealth might be squandered by the explosive impulse to procreate, neither was particularly concerned with how different individuals and classes might share in what an economy produced. This was left to David Ricardo. What, he asked, were the laws which governed the distribution of product or income among the landlords, entrepreneurs and workers who had a claim to it?

He thought political economy was an inquiry into the laws which determine the division of the product of industry amongst the classes who concur in its formation. As to the laws formulated by Ricardo, they worked with vicious inequality. As with Malthus, poverty was a by-product of the economic system and it was inevitable.

The Iron Law of Wages

Ricardo and Malthus were friends who engaged in friendly disputation, mostly in letters.[3] In one such letter Ricardo argued that population regulates itself by the funds which are to employ it, and therefore always increases or diminishes with the increase or diminution of capital. Thus, increased wealth and productivity bring more people; but they do not bring more land from which to feed these people. Therefore, those who own land are able to command an ever greater return, given its quality, for what is an increasingly scarce resource. Meanwhile, profits and wages were in conflict for the rest of the product. An increase in profits meant a reduction in wages; an increase in wages must always come of out of profits. At the same time, every rise in profits is favorable to the accumulation of capital, and to the further increase of population, and therefore would, in all probability, ultimately lead to an increase of rent. This is a profits-driven theory: in order for a nation to have increasing capital and product, it must have rising profits. Then comes the Malthusian rub. As product expands, population will increase. Food requirements of the population will press on the available land supply and force up rents to the glorious advantage of the landowner. Capitalists must prosper through profits if there is to be progress and landlords just get the way of progress. Whither labor? Labor may be increased or diminished in quantity and has its natural and its market price. The *natural price of labor* is that price which is necessary to enable the laborers, one with another, to subsist and perpetuate their race, without either increase or diminution. This was the *iron law of wages*.

---

[3] The letters are reprinted Piero Sraffa, Editor, *The Works and Correspondence of David Ricardo*, Vols. I and II (Cambridge, England: Cambridge University Press, 1951).

The iron law of wages was not without qualification, for there was such as thing as a *market wage rate*. In an improving society, the market wage might be above the natural wage for an indefinite period. The qualification was quickly forgotten. The iron law of wages prevailed. It became part of the intellectual capital of the global economy. Like Malthusian poverty nothing could be done about it. These were the laws by which wages were regulated. Like all contracts, social or otherwise, wages were left to the free and fair competition of the market, and should never be controlled by the interference of the legislature. While the landlords were never considered by Ricardo as enemies of the state, they were merely the passive and natural beneficiaries of their great good fortune. For some 30 years following the death of Ricardo, economics continued in the tradition he had established. Throughout economic life was to be regulated by the magic of the market and not by the state. While on the continent, persons talked about socialism, in England and in the Anglo-Saxon tradition, the market was very nearly taken for granted.

The Lingering Despair

Left to Malthus and Ricardo, the economic prospect for the ordinary individual was remarkably dim. The normal expectation was to live at the clawing edge of starvation. For the few in which it was better, it also was abnormal. While the landlord was considered simply lucky, progress for the rising industrial class was for the already wealthy, not for the maddening masses. Worse, no remedy was in sight; nothing could be done amidst the despair. This was a general conclusion that laid claim to the propositions on which modern economic thought was founded.

As ever, only events could change minds. Beginning in the middle of the 19th century, England began a great era of commercial and industrial expansion. Real wages rose above mere subsistence, so the iron law of wages was overthrown. The Malthusian horror was also receding in Western Europe and America. Still, in the back of many minds was the idea that such progress was temporary. In time, population would again press upon the food supply. This fear eventually receded, especially in the world of surpluses. The worry shifted toward the surpluses of farm products and away from the idea of shortages. While the specter of Malthus still hangs over India, Bangladesh, and other countries of the Third World, other concerns abound in the supra-surplus nations. For some good reasons to be explored later, not everyone is assured that the rich nations will have enduring abundance. The remains of the dismal pall are there for everyone to see. Amidst surpluses, the fear of scarcity prevails in economic thought. What prevails in economic thought is quite different from what follows.

Chapter 5

POST GREAT RECESSION EXPECTATIONS

The most recent event to alter the way the ordinary person thinks about economics was the Great Recession. The National Bureau of Economic Research (NBER) has long served a useful purpose as the arbiter of recessions — when they begin and when they end. As prestigious as it is, the Bureau erred when it "officially" declared the end of the Great Recession as June 2009. Even by this overly conservative ending date, the 18-month duration greatly exceeded the post-WWII average of 10 months. There was one other remarkable episode, the sharp and deep 1981–1982 decline of Ronald Reagan's first term. At the time, I called it the "Great Recession," not without cause. As it turns out, I was among the first (if not the first) to call the more recent decline "*the* Great Recession." At the time I wrote,

> As the Dow became more and more volatile, the National Bureau of Economic Research officially declared a recession beginning in December 2007. Most likely, the long recession would be named the second Great Recession of the post-WWII era or the Great Recession of 2007–2010, the longest and most worrisome since the Great Depression of the 1930s. Today the 2010 ending date is a provisional one.[1]

---

[1] E. Ray Canterbery, *The Making of Economics*, Vol III, 4th edition (Singapore/New Jersey/London: World Scientific, 2010), pp. 216–217.

A year later, I amended the name of the latter episode to the "Global Great Recession."[2] The Great Recession had circled the globe. Besides "Global," you naturally raise the question of why the Bureau and I are at odds. The short answer is found in the magnitude of the unemployment rate that continued to bedevil policymakers for many years. It remained disturbingly high, reaching 10.2 percent in October 2009, followed by 10 percent rates. Dreadful numbers spilled over into 2010 and got stuck at 9.6 percent in August, September, and October. Worse, the possibility of a significant decline remained remote. Economists were referring to "the jobless recovery" when indeed economic growth remained at a snail pace. The economy had stagnated, awaiting more stimulus from monetary policy, as fiscal policy was taken off the table because of that old visceral fear of federal deficits and debt.

The Great Global Recession was preceded by the Great Depression, Reaganomics, the rise of the Casino Economy, and a housing market conundrum. Until Alan Greenspan altered the landscape, housing needed a healthy stock market to prosper. The conundrum occurs when house prices are driven by historically low long-term interest rates while other forms of investment flounder. By sometime in 2005 the housing industry and construction became by far the driver of Gross Domestic Product (GDP), the broadest measure of economic activity. At a time when short-term interest rates were at historical lows, long-term rates were dominating the economy via the housing-construction nexus. A bubble was inflated, only to be pricked by Greenspan's reversal. In the meantime the wealth distribution became more lopsided.

The Global Great Recession, 2007–2010

The George W. Bush administration saw two official downturns, though the Global Great Recession spilled over "officially" for 6 months into the Obama administration. For many months thereafter, President Barack Obama continued to refer to the "recession we are experiencing." There also was the Great Money and Banking Panic of 2007–2009, with 2008 as

---

[2] See E. Ray Canterbery, *The Global Great Recession* (Singapore/New Jersey/London: World Scientific. 2011).

the year of its greatest intensity. Within this span *The Wall Street Journal* and Maria Bartiromo have the financial insider's turning point as September 15, 2008, when Lehman Brothers filed for Chapter 11 bankruptcy.[3] But there was much more. Inside the recession came the debacle of the auto industry, which was essentially taken over by the government.

Unemployment and underemployment has proven to be the Achilles heels of the global economy. The problem did not end with the Global Great Recession. Voters — be they Republicans, Whigs, Democrats, Germans, Greeks, Italians, or whatever — want to hear more about how governments are going to reduce unemployment without burdening them with higher taxes and fewer benefits. There have been episodes of ups and downs in federal budgets, at home and abroad. Still, from about 1970 until the beginning of the Great Recession, the U.S. federal budget was unbalanced (on average) only by about 2 percent. Similarly, sustainable budget deficits characterized many nations in Europe and Asia. This all changed during the Global Great Recession. In 2010 the U.S. budget deficit was about 10 percent of Gross Domestic Product (GDP). Huge budget deficits emerged in the USA and elsewhere because of rising unemployment and falling national income; tax revenue fell and government spending rose in attempts to stabilize economies in the face of the worst economic climate since the 1930s. Easy money policies accompanied the fiscal ease in most instances. National budget deficits have been a by-product of financial crisis and they continue after the crisis has cooled. Were the remedies sufficiently radical, especially in the United States? Any fiscal policies to deal with national debt over the long run must be made in the face of weak employment and the threat of deflation.

The great recession left in its wake some major problems for the industrialized nations. During the 3 years following the recession, the U.S. economy grew slowly. That is, from the third quarter of 2009 though the second quarter of 2012, the economy's output grew at less than half the rate exhibited, on average, during other recoveries in the United States since the end of World War II. All told, between the "official" end of the recession and the second quarter of 2012, the cumulative rate of growth of

---

[3] See Maria Bartiromo (with Catherine Whitney) *The Weekend That Changed Wall Street* (New York: Penguin, 2010).

real GDP was nearly 9 percent points below the average for previous recoveries. Economists continue to grapple with understanding the roles that steep declines in house prices and financial crises play in slowing economic growth. Financial crises in the past had been the stuff of legends during the pre-industrial eras. But this was something relatively new.

During those 12 quarters, both potential GDP, a measure of the underlying productive capacity of the economy, and the ratio of real GDP to potential GDP grew unusually slowly. Potential GDP is the amount of real GDP that corresponds to a high rate of use of labor and capital and is not typically affected very much by the up-and-down cycles of the economy. In contrast, the ratio of real GDP to potential GDP depends on the degree of the economy's use of resources and therefore captures cyclical variation in real GDP around its potential trend. In the first 12 quarters after the Great Recession, both potential GDP and the ratio of real GDP to potential GDP grew at less than half the rate that occurred, on average, in the aftermath of other recessions since World War II. The Congressional Budget Office's (CBO's) analysis shows that that pace is mostly owing to the slow growth in the underlying productive capacity of the economy and to a lesser extent, to slow growth in real output relative to that productive capacity.

Put differently, the CBO estimated that about two-thirds of the difference between the growth in real GDP and the average for other recoveries can be attributed to sluggish growth in potential GDP. This sluggish growth reflected weaker performance than happened on average following other recessions by all three of the major determinants of potential GNP: potential employment (the number of employed workers, adjusted for variations over the business cycle; potential total factor productivity (average real output per unit of combined labor and capital services, adjusted for variations over the business cycle); and the productive services available from the capital stock in the economy. While some of the sluggishness of potential GDP can be traced to unusual factors in the Great Recession cycle, much of it was the result of long-term trends unrelated to the cycle, including the nation's changing demographics.

The remainder one-third of the unusual slowness in real growth can be explained by the slow pace of growth in the ratio of real GDP to potential GDP — which is attributable to a shortfall in the overall demand for goods and services in the economy. Compared with past recoveries, this recovery saw especially slow growth in four of those components:

(1) purchases of goods and services by state and local governments; (2) purchases of goods and services by the federal government; (3) residential investment (mostly the construction of new homes, home improvements, and brokers' commissions; and (4) consumer spending. Among these, the cutbacks by state and local governments account for the largest portion of the unusual weakness. In contrast to these four components, two other components of demand — investment by businesses and net exports — grew faster relative to potential GNP than was the case, on average, in past recoveries.

These differences from past growth experiences were captured in three charts by the CBO.[4] Plotted are relative real rates of growth in GNP as well as relative real rates of growth in potential GNP. The "current cycle" refers to the Great Recession in the USA as it extended to 3 years after the "official" end of that recession. As noted, the difference in growth after 12 quarters was 9 percentage points (see Figure 5.1 (top)). The two-thirds of the slower growth in the underlying productive capacity of the economy was explained as a deficiency in Keynesian aggregate demand (see Figure 5.1 (middle)). The remaining one-third is displayed in the bottom chart.

Before, during and after this period, there was over-reliance on monetary policy. Because the interest rate that the Federal Reserve generally uses to conduct monetary policy (the federal funds rate) was already low at the start of the recovery, the central bank could not lower it much further even as the gap between real GDP and potential GDP failed to close quickly. Besides, the economy has been less responsive than usual to low interest rates because of the oversupply of homes, the desire of households to reduce their indebtedness, and credit restraints imposed by lenders, among other reasons. As noted, however, investment by businesses and net exports grew faster than normal. While low interest rates (near zero for the federal funds rate) probably aided private business investment, housing remained moribund. The consequence was, during the recession and the early part of the recovery, the unemployment rate increased by 5 percentage points as real GDP fell relative to potential GDP, while during the rest of the recovery, the unemployment rate declined somewhat as real GDP stabilized (and edged up slightly) relative to potential GDP.

---

[4]Congressional Budget Office (CBO), "What Accounts for the Slow Growth of the Economy after the (Great) Recession?" 2012, p. 2.

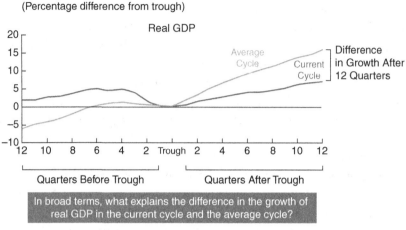

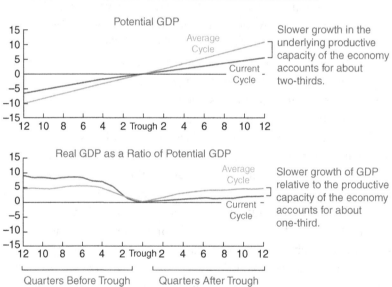

Figure 5.1 Gross Domestic Product Before and After Recessions

Notes: Real gross domestic product (GDP) is the total amount of goods and services produced in the United States, adjusted to remove the effects of inflation. Potential GDP is CBO's estimate of the level of GDP that corresponds to a high rate of use of labor and capital, adjusted to remove the effects of inflation.

The average cycle, or the pattern of economic growth before and after a trough, is the average for cycles since 1945 that were not followed by another recession within 12 quarters.

Source: Congressional Budget Office; Department of Commerce, Bureau of Economic Analysis.

More should be said about the apparent recovery in business investment. In part, this relative good performance reflects how far nominal business investment had fallen during the Great Recession,[5] which means that even brisk growth in investment during the recovery left the level of net business investment (investment minus depreciation) fairly low relative to potential GDP. Subdued business confidence during the recovery months and stricter standards and terms for borrowing explain part of the relative under-performance of investment. Indeed, during the first nine quarters of the recovery months, the ratio of real business investment to potential GDP grew more slowly than in the average cycle.

The Federal Reserve's ability to spur economic activity also was hampered by the stress on U.S. financial markets caused by financial problems in Europe. Some banks tightened standards on loans to non-financial firms that have operations in the United States and significant exposure to European economies. This constraint continued during 2014 and 2015.

According to its Board of Governors, the main operating tool of the Federal Reserve before, during, and after the Global Great Recession was the effective federal funds rate. Figure 5.2 traces this rate during these periods, with the ending date being March 11, 2016. The gray, shaded area highlights the "official" Great Recession. While the Fed began lowering the effective federal funds rate before the official beginning of the recession, it had been above 5 percent. An aggressive move was made on October 31, 2008, when the rate was lowered to 0.22 percent. Since, and until the first quarter of 2016, the effective rate has hovered just above zero. Until sometime in late 2015, Janet Yellen, the head of the Fed, had presumed that this interest rate and others like it abroad could not effectively become negative. This belief, like so many others, was altered by events.

A Negative Interest-rate World

Beginning in October 2014, the Riksbank, Sweden's central bank, cut its rates below zero, where they remained as recently as March 2016. This

---

[5] "Great Recession" refers only to the U.S., as opposed to the Global Great Recession.

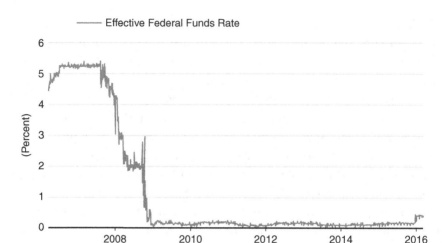

Figure 5.2   Effective Federal Funds Rate
Source: Board of Governors of the Federal Reserve System (US) research.stlouisfed.org.

has changed the way central bankers think about fighting recessions. It has long been believed that when it comes to interest rates, zero is as low as you can go. Who, it was asked, would choose to keep their money in the bank if they had to pay for the privilege? By now, many central banks have pushed their rates into negative territory and yet the financial system has still to come to an abrupt end. For central bankers, this has come as a relief. They had long believed that they had run out of room to support their respective economies, with interest rates pushed like a brake pedal close to the floor. There was believed to be a zero lower bound: cut rates too deeply, and savers would end up facing negative returns. In that case, it was thought, people would be encouraged to take their savings out of the bank and hoard them in cash. In turn, this would slow, rather than boost, the economy. What is now happening, according to the conventional wisdom, is not possible.

Sweden, the first country to dabble with negative interest rates, is perhaps the best candidate to start such an experiment. Sweden has the third highest savings rate in the developed world (OECD). Moreover, unemployment is unusually high: the unemployment rate reached 8.5 percent in June 2015, fell below 7 percent for several months, then bounced up to 7.5 percent in 2016. Worse, pre-crisis levels of the unemployment rate were below 6 percent. Along with high unemployment rates has been the battle policymakers have been having with deflation since late 2012, with inflation at *minus* 0.2 percent in August 2015. The Riksbank target inflation rate is a positive 2 percent, similar to that of the Federal Reserve Board of Governors. The Riksbank interest target has been forced by the plight of the euro-zone, where a tepid recovery has required the European Central Bank (ECB) to engage in ever-easier policy.

As ever, there is a tight connection between interest rates and exchange rates. The ECB's actions, which is a one-size-fits-all policy, weakened the euro against Sweden's krona. As a result, the cost of importing goods into Sweden fell, and contributed to deflation. The Riksbank had no choice except to cut its own interest rates to avoid deeper deflation. At the same time, the Riksbank introduced quantitative easing (QE). Meanwhile, Denmark and the euro-zone have joined hands with Sweden as members of the negative zone. Switzerland's rate is deeper still, at minus 0.75 percent at the end of 2015. The 3 month LIBOR rate was also at minus 0.75 percent on March 15, 2006.[6] The Bank of Japan is the fifth central bank to join the negative interest-rate club. Negative interest rates comprise a historically interesting event, which could have society-wide implications. Later, we will return to this world.

For now, let us return to the CBO analysis of the behavior of potential GDP and actual GDP. Figure 5.3 shows CBO estimates of the rate of

---

[6]LIBOR or the London Interbank Offered Rate is the average of interest rates estimated by each of the leading private banks in London that it would be charged were it to borrow from other banks. It is the primary benchmark, along with the Euribor, for short-term interest rates around the world. LIBOR rates are calculated for 5 currencies and 7 borrowing periods ranging from overnight to 1 year and are published each business day by Thomson Reuters. Many financial institutions, mortgage lenders and credit card agencies set their own rates relative to LIBOR. An estimated $350 trillion in derivatives and other financial products are tied to LIBOR. The Euribor is the daily reference rate based upon the averaged interest rates at which Eurozone banks offer to lend unsecured funds to other banks in the interbank markets.

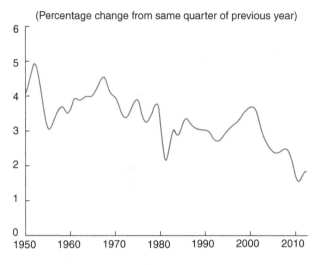

(Percentage change from same quarter of previous year)

Figure 5.3 Potential GDP

Notes: Potential gross domestic product (GDP) is CBO's estimate of the level of GDP that corresponds to a high rate of use of labor and capital, adjusted to remove the effects of inflation.

Data are quarterly and are plotted through the second quarter of 2012.

Source: Congressional Budget Office.

change in USA potential GDP from 1950 through the second quarter of 2012. The growth of potential GDP has been trending downward since the late 1960s. The initial slowdown reflected a reduction in the growth of total factor productivity and then, beginning in the mid-1970s, a reduction in the growth of potential employment. There was a sharp decline during the Reagan recession and during the Global Great Recession. Since the official end of that recession, the relatively slow growth of potential GDP has reflected slower growth of all three of its major determinants than happened, on average, following other recessions. To repeat: these are potential employment, potential total factor productivity, and the productive services available from the capital stock in the economy. It is not quite this simple. Potential output also depends on the average number of hours worked per worker and shifts in the number of workers among sectors of the economy that have different levels of productivity. But CBO argued that these elements played a small role in this slow recovery.

Employment, among other things, again appears to be an Achilles heel. The slower growth of potential employment directly accounts for more than a third of the slowdown in growth of potential GDP since the end of the Great Recession. It is thought that this slower growth in potential employment is the result of demographic trends that have slowed the growth of population that is of working age and, therefore, the growth of the potential labor force. The potential labor force is the labor force that exists at a labor force participation rate adjusted for the effects of fluctuations in aggregate demand. Put differently, the baby boomers that were entering the labor force in the earlier recoveries are now beginning to retire. The slowdown in population growth has not helped. A contributing element is an apparent end to the long-standing increase in women's participation in the labor force, which had boosted the growth of the labor force in the recoveries before 2000. Moreover, the number of people who would be unemployed if output was at its potential level has risen in the current recovery. Workers' skills and connection to the workforce have eroded because of the the length of their unemployment.

Slower growth in total factor productivity directly accounts for about one-fifth of the slowed pace of growth of potential GDP since the end of the Great Recession, according to the CBO. The financial crisis and the recession reduced the growth of potential total factor productivity in the non-farm business sector by about 0.2 percentage points during the 12 quarters following the end of the recession. The pattern in other sectors of the economy was similar to the non-farm sector.[7]

Like potential employment, the slower growth of capital services accounts for more than a third of the slowness in the growth of potential GDP during the "recovery." The slowdown reflects a much lower amount of net investment (investment minus depreciation) compared to the existing capital stock in this recovery. Several forces contributed to this outcome. One was the nature and severity of the recession when net business investment fell to unusually low levels. This can be attributed to the weak demand for goods and services and the relatively high cost of capital. Moreover, the housing slump sharply curtailed growth in the stock of

---

[7] For much more detail on rates of change in the various data series, see CBO, "What Accounts for the Slow Growth of the Economy After the Recession?" *op. cit.*, pp. 5–6.

housing capital. A second force restraining investment was the slower growth of potential employment, which meant that smaller increases in the stock of structures, equipment, and software were needed to equip the workforce with the same amount of capital per worker. A third force was the slower growth of total factor productivity, which reduces the growth of the productivity of capital and in this way diminishes real investment per worker.

The expectation is that the effects of the Global Great Recession and the slow recovery on potential output will persist and reduce the level of potential GDP.

Contributions to the Cyclical Variation in Real GNP

We come full circle to consider the effects of the cyclical variation of GDP around potential GDP (See Table 5.1). Among the major components of GDP, four have been especially weak relative to past recoveries. They are: (1) purchases of goods and services by state and local governments; (2) purchases of goods and services by the federal government; (3) residential investment; and (4) consumer spending. While the explanation is complicated, in contrast, investment by businesses and net exports grew faster relative to potential GDP in the first 12 quarters of the recovery from the Great Recession compared to past recoveries. There are some interdependencies. Depressed housing prices reduced the growth of property tax revenues, which combined with falling revenues from income and sales taxes restrained state and local governments' purchases. However, we should not understate the effects of ideology on state and local austerity measures. While federal purchases rose immediately after the official end of the Great Recession, they peaked after five quarters, but began falling after that point because of reductions in purchases for national defense. The decline in national defense purchases was temporary.

Global Prospects

This is the stuff from which projections are made. Based on the foregoing, we would not expect to see robust projections. The USA real GDP growth rate summarizes what was to follow, as well as indicating what was past

Table 5.1 Contributions to the Cyclical Variation in Real GDP, 12 Quarters Following Recessions Percentage Difference from Trough for Components of Real GDP as a Ratio of Potential GDP

Component	Current recovery(a)	Average recovery	Difference	Major factors contributing to the difference
State and Governments Purchases	-11/4 percent	-1/4 percent	-1 percent	Slow growth in tax revenues and federal grants
Federal Government's Purchases	-1/2	1/4	-3/4	A decline in defense purchases
Residential Investment	0	3/4	-3/4	Overbuilding during housing boom; weak household formation
Consumer Spending	1	13/4	-3/4	Loss of wealth; a bigger decline in share of national income going to labor; weak confidence
Business Investment (b)	23/4	21/2	1/4	Rebound from unusually weak investment during the recession
Net Exports	-1/2	-1	1/2	Slow growth in the USA; strong growth in emerging markets
Total	1 1/2	4 1/4	-23/4	

Notes: The average recovery is the average after recessions since 1945 that were not followed by another recession within 12 quarters. Numbers are rounded to the nearest one-quarter of a percentage point and, hence, do not add to totals. (a) From the Great Recession. (b) Includes investment in nonresidential structures, equipment, software, and inventories.
Sources: CBO; Department of Commerce, Bureau of Economic Analysis; and the author.

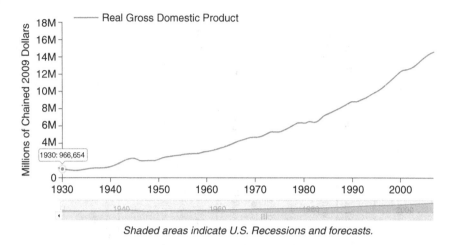

Shaded areas indicate U.S. Recessions and forecasts.

Figure 5.4 Real Gross Domestic Product (GDPMCA1)

Source: US. Bureau of Economics Analysis.

and prologue. Figure 5.4 shows the zigs and zags of real GDP growth since 1935. The Global Great Recession is notable for its depth and breath. Thereafter, the growth rate settled at about 2 percent yearly, dropping to only 1.8 percent in February 2016. In October 2015, the International Monetary Fund updated its forecasts for the USA, the Euro Area, Emerging and Developing Asia, and Latin America and the Caribbean. These forecasts go through 2016. (The shaded area highlights what is forecast.) These IMF forecasts are shown in Figure 5.5.

The IMF is surprisingly optimistic regarding USA prospects, where the recovery is expected to continue. The support for GDP growth comes from lower energy prices, strengthened balance sheets, and an improving housing market. These forces are sufficient to counter the drag on net exports from the strengthening of the dollar. However, longer-term growth prospects are weaker with potential growth estimated to be only about 2 percent, weighted down by the aforementioned aging population and low total factor productivity growth.

A moderate euro area recovery is projected to continue in 2015–2016, again sustained by lower oil prices, monetary easing, and the depreciation of the euro (see panel 2 of Figure 5.5). Potential growth nonetheless remains weak — a result of crisis legacies, but also of demographics and

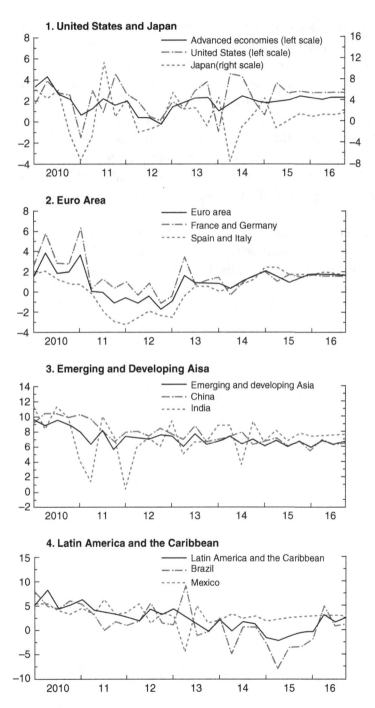

Figure 5.5 GDP Growth Forecasts (*Annualized quarterly percent change*)

Source: IMF staff estimates, October 2015

a slowdown in total factor productivity that predates the Great Recession. Expect moderate growth and subdued inflation. Still growth is forecast to pick up modestly for 2015 and 2016 in France and less so in Italy, but more so in Spain. In Germany, growth is expected to remain at about 1 1/2 percent. Greece remains a basket case.

In Japan GDP growth is projected to rise out of negative territory (−0.1 percent in 2014) to 0.6 percent in 2015 and 1.0 percent in 2016. Private estimates for Japan and Japan's own projections are not as "rosy." The IMF's relative optimism is based on additional quantitative and qualitative easing by the Bank of Japan, as well as (again) lower oil and other commodity prices.

Expectations have been altered by the underlying conditions of the Great Recession. While the presumption is that high levels of production are paramount, the reality in the USA, most of Europe, and Japan border on despair.

Part II
THE NECESSARY ECONOMY

Chapter 6

A NEO-RECARDIAN VIEW OF SURPLUSES AND BUDGET SHARES

Piero Sraffa: A Life in the Slow Lane

Piero Sraffa (1898–1998) was a shy, lovable Italian economist whose life was as dramatic as his best-known theory. He was born in Turin, Italy, to Angelo Sraffa (1865–1937) and Irma Sraffa (née Tivoli) (1873–1949), a wealthy Italian Jewish couple. His father was a Professor in Commercial Law and later Dean at the Bocconi University in Milan. Despite being raised in a Jewish family Sraffa later became an agnostic. He studied in his home town and graduated at the local university with a work on inflation in Italy during and after World War I. His tutor was Luigi Einaudi, one of the most important Italian economists and later a President of the Italian Republic.

From 1921 to 1922 Piero studied at the London School of Economics. In 1922, he was appointed Director of the provincial labor department in Milan, then Professor in Political Economy first in Perugia and later in Cagliari, Sardinia. In Turin he met Antonio Gramsci, the most important leader of the Italian Communist Party. They became close friends, partly due to shared political beliefs. Sraffa was also in contact with Filippoti, perhaps the most important leader of the Italian Socialist Party, who he met and frequently visited in Rapallo, where his family had a holiday villa.

Sraffa's friendship and influence with Antonio Gramsci continued in 1927 and was increasingly risky and compromising because of Gramasci's connection to the Italian Fascist regime. Gramsci had been previously imprisoned and Sraffa supplied him with pens and paper to write his *Prison Notebooks.* Sraffa was instrumental in securing Gramsci's prison notebooks from the Fascist authorities after the latter's death in 1937. Gramsci brought John Maynard Keynes together with Sraffa, who prudently invited Piero to the University of Cambridge, where he was initially assigned a lectureship. Sraffa has been sometimes considered a "closet Marxian" and would sometimes be quite explicit about his loyalties even though the 1920s England was not exactly welcoming to Marxian radicals. Still, Sraffa became a fixture in the Cambridge world. He was part of the legendary "cafeteria group" with Frank Ramsey and Ludwig Wittgenstein which explored the 1921 probability treatise of Keynes. Sraffa joined Keynes to bury Friedrich Hayek in the famous business cycle debates.

Sraffa's shyness in front of his few students made lecturing a hellish experience. Ever resourceful and loyal, Keynes arranged for Sraffa to be appointed as a librarian of King's College and, to keep him busy, got the Royal Society to hand over the task of editing a new collected edition of David Ricardo's works. Sraffa's painstaking and meticulous collecting and editing of Ricardo's works, begun in 1931, turned out to be a 20-year task. It was a formidable edition. As George Stigler put it later in a review, "Ricardo was a fortunate man. And now, 130 years after his death, he is as fortunate as ever; he has been befriended by Sraffa."[1] John Eatwell wrote of Sraffa's work on Ricardo:

> [Sraffa's] reconstruction of Ricardo's surplus theory, presented in but a few pages of the introduction to his edition of Ricardo's *Principles,* penetrated a hundred years of misunderstanding and distortion to create a vivid rationale for the structure and content of surplus theory, for the analytical role of the labor theory of value, and hence for the foundations of Marx's critical analysis of capitalist production.[2]

---

[1] George Stigler (ed.), Review of Piero Sraffa, *The Works and Correspondence of David Ricardo, Econometrica* 20, 504–505.

[2] John Eatwell, "Piero Sraffa: Seminal Economic Theorist," *Science and Society,* 48(2), 1984, 211.

Among these efforts came one of the longest-gestating works in economic theory. Begun in the 1920s Sraffa's *Production of Commodities by Means of Commodities*, a terse, 100-page text finally emerged in 1960. This book solved and restated Ricardo's theory for the moderns — inspiring the "classical Revival" spearheaded by the neo-Ricardians at Cambridge and elsewhere in the 1960s and 1970s. He was also the first to depict the famous "re-switching" problem in capital theory for an industry as well as an economy, which led to the Cambridge Capital Controversy and fueled further the Neo-Ricardian School.

The little book was an attempt to perfect classical economics' theory of value, as originally developed by David Ricardo and others. He aimed to demonstrate flaws in the mainstream neoclassical theory of value and develop an alternative analysis. In particular, Sraffa's technique of aggregating capital as "dated input of labour" in what led to the famous Cambridge Capital Controversy.

While economists disagree on whether Sraffa successfully refuted neoclassical economics, it cannot be denied that he virtually destroyed marginal product analysis as it relates to production. Others still argue that the importance of Sraffa's economics is that it provides a new framing for how we understand capitalist economies that does not fall back on the unrealistic assumptions of neoclassical economics. It is in this latter context that we engage Sraffa.

Sraffa had other famous connections. He is credited with providing Ludwig Wittgenstein with the conceptual break that founded the Philosophical Investigations, by means of a rude gesture on Sraffa's part. Wittgenstein was insisting that a proposition and that which it describes must have the same "logical form," the same "logical multiplicity." Sraffa made a gesture, familiar to Neapolitans as meaning something like disgust or contempt, of brushing the underneath of his chin with an onward sweep of the finger-tips of one hand. And he asked: "What is the logical form of that?" In 1946 after many years of weekly discussions, Sraffa broke with Wittgenstein. When the philosopher said he would talk about anything Sraffa wanted, "Yes," Sraffa replied, "but in *your* way."

As one might gather by now, Sraffa was a very intelligent man with a real devotion for study and books. His library contained more than 8,000 volumes, now partly in the Trinity College Library.

Sraffa made successful long-term investments in Japanese government bonds that he bought the day after the nuclear bombing on Hiroshima and Nagasaki. He could not imagine bond prices going any lower, and he was convinced that Japan would honor its obligations. In 1961, before the Sveriges Riksbank Prize in Economic Sciences in Memory of Alfred Nobel had been created, Sraffa was awarded the Soderstromska Gold Medal by the Swedish Academy. In 1972, he was awarded an honorary doctorate by Sorbonne, and in 1976 he received another one from Madrid's Complutense University.

Origins of Surplus Value

Notions of "surplus produce" have been used in economic thought and commerce for a long time (notably by the Physiocrats), but in *Das Kapital*, *Theories of Surplus Value* and the *Grundrisse* Marx gave the concept a central place in his interpretation of economic history. Today the concept is mainly used in Marxian economics. The German term Mehrproduki meant surplus product, where the translation of "Mehr" as "surplus" is in a sense unfortunate, because mehr can be taken to suggest "unused," "not needed" or "redundant," while literally it means "more" or "added" so that "Mehrprodukt" really refers to the additional or "excess" product produced. It is the later usage that we will deploy. In German, the term "Mehrwert" simply and literally means value added, a measure of net output. However, in Marx's specialist usage, it means the surplus-value obtained from the use of capital, that is, it refers to the net addition in the value of capital.

In *Theories of Surplus Value*, Marx says classical economics "surplus" refers to an excess of gross income over cost, which implied that the value of goods sold is greater than the value of the costs involved in producing or supplying them. That was how you could "make money" or profits. The surplus represents a net addition to the stock of wealth. This was theoretically a confusing issue, because sometimes a surplus arose out of clever trading, in already existing assets, while at other times it seemed that surplus arose because new value was added in production. One could get rich either at the expense of someone else, or by creating more wealth than there was before, or by a mixture of both. How, then, could one devise a system for grossing and netting incomes and expenditures to estimate only the value of the new additional wealth created by a country. The Physiocratic school, for example, believed that all wealth originated from the land, and their social accounting system was designed to show this clearly.

In *Das Kapital*, we will find a distinction that is especially useful. Therein, Marx divides the new "social product" of the working population (the flow of society's total output of new products in a defined time-interval) into the necessary product and the surplus product. The "necessary" product refers to the output of products and services necessary to maintain a population of workers and their dependents at the prevailing standard of life (effectively, their total reproduction cost). This is similar to the idea of subsistence production. The "surplus" product is whatever is produced in excess of those necessary. Socially speaking, the division of the social product reflects the respective claims which the laboring class and the ruling class make on the new wealth created.

These definitions are not completely satisfactory for three reasons. (1) A fraction of the new social product usually is held in reserve at any time-interval. That is, there is what we call inventories, a form of residual investment. (2) A growing population requires that more product must be produced to ensure the survival of the population. (3) At any time a fraction of the adult working-age population does not work at all; yet these people must somehow be sustained as well. They have to be sustained from communal or state resources or by some other means.

To what use is the social surplus product put? It can be destroyed or wasted, held in reserve as wealth, or hoarded, consumed, traded or otherwise transferred to others, or reinvested. As a simple example, surplus seeds could be left to rot, stored, eaten, traded for other products, or sown on new fields. Only if the surplus product is traded or reinvested does it become possible to increase the scale of production. If the seeds are sown, economic growth ensues. Surplus product does require surplus labor.

Human needs are not a simple matter. Marx distinguishes between the physical minimum requirements for the maintenance of human life, and the moral–historical component of earnings from work, In this respect, it is difficult to distinguish a luxury from a necessary good. Owning a car may be considered a luxury, but if owning a car is indispensable for traveling to work and to shops, it is a necessity. If, in an affluent society, households spend only about a quarter of their income on consumer goods and services, the rest goes to interest, rents, taxes, loans, retirement provisions, and insurance payments.

For most of human prehistory, there was no economic surplus product of any kind at all. This changed with the English Industrial Revolution. Once a social surplus product existed, conflict arose over its distribution. The corollary of the enormous increase in physical productivity (output of goods) is that a larger and larger component of the social product, valued in money prices, consists of the production and consumption services. This leads to a redefinition of wealth; not just a stock of assets, but also the ability to consume services that enhance the quality of life. By their nature, services cannot be accumulated. The services of a physician cannot be congealed.

Going from the Necessary to the Surplus Economy

Now we can understand Sraffa's necessary economy. Sraffa's invocation of Ricardo is an abstraction of the system of production only and of the way that the real value of goods is decided.

After introducing a classical subsistence model in Chapter 1, Sraffa (1950) moves on to a production surplus economy, one that produces commodities in excess of labor's physiological necessities plus actual depreciation of all the means of production. In Sraffa's model of the surplus economy basic commodities or goods that appear as inputs and outputs are necessities only in a technological sense.

Demand, although (abstractly) affecting the level of production, plays no role in deciding prices. Prices are production prices or physical costs, not market prices. A move in the wage (and profit) rate, one of which is given leaves the ratio of net output or economic surplus to means of production unaltered because productivity is determined solely by the technical conditions of production rather than from the distribution of product or income between wages or profits.

In the surplus economy non-basic commodities or goods and services entering only into final demand include both consumer necessities and luxuries. Only in Sraffa's subsistence model are basic commodities necessities in consumption as well as in production. In his surplus economy, Sraffa makes no attempt to separate the allocation of the extra-subsistence wage between necessary and "luxury" consumer goods. Moreover, Sraffa's treatment of labor as neither a basic good or non-basic service in the surplus economy raises additional serious questions about the nature of demand. Nonetheless, his notion of a standard commodity group comprised of those basic commodities that enter into production in the same proportion that they exit production drives a wedge in the neoclassical system sufficiently wide to allow room for a new theory of demand and of income distribution.

What then are the central propositions from Sraffa that are going to be useful to us? Sraffa's production system is an input–output matrix. In an industry in which equal amounts of, say, labor are always combined with a unit of capital, the marginal product of capital evaporates. Profits can no longer be said to be a return on capital. (In an interindustry model the value of heterogeneous capital cannot be determined anyway.) Moreover, this neo-Ricardian theory tells us that relative production price movements are driven by changes in the income distribution and technology rather than by demand movements. Finally, the income distribution can be altered without changes in the economic surplus relative to the available means of production. There is little room for the usual supply-and-demand considerations so central to neoclassical price theory, because the wages-to-profits relation becomes a social-political question to be answered elsewhere (possibly by relative power relations).

Sraffian prices of production can be shown in a simple equation. The equation says that the value of a product is the sum of the costs in terms of wages and profits on capital. The equation is

$$p = wn + rMp,$$

where p is a column vector of prices, w is the wage rate, n and M are a vector and a matrix of technical coefficients representing respectively labor per unit of output and the amounts of each kind of machines per unit of output. And, finally, r is the uniform profit rate. The equation can be solved for prices by rewriting it as

$$p = wn \, [I - rM]^{-1}.$$

This model can be contrasted with Robert Solow's neoclassical growth model. In Solow, labor and capital are freely substitutable and there is a marginal product of capital and of labor. However, techniques and input–output coefficients are fixed in the long run. As in Sraffa, technology plays a major role in deciding output and thus surplus value.

Once we enter the world of necessities and luxuries as well as basic and non-basic goods, there arises the need for a new set of statistics, statistics which are cross-sectional in nature. We recognize that standards of living change over time. For example, during the 19th century, the upper classes in Britain and Europe viewed Americans with unease. At its recent growth rate in population, the United States would soon have a population greater than the United Kingdom (including the whole of Ireland). This happened in 1857 and the U.S. population exceeded that of the newly united Germany in 1873. A still more serious challenge for the Europeans was the set of manufacturing skills that the United States steadily developed in the mid-19th century, as exemplified in the 1851 Crystal Palace reaction.

Alexis de Tocqueville and James Bryce were the two most famous European observers of America in that century. Most relevant for our purposes is Bryce's *The American Commonwealth*.[3] It raises the question of whether in 1870 the American standard of living was pathetic and pitiable, or was it agreeable and pleasant. Bryce had the acute eye of an English Professor of History and Law. He thought the American standard of living was high, and he made invidious comparisons with England and the European continent. In particular, he observed that the life of the American working class was better than that of counterparts in England and France. Indeed, living conditions for a substantial share of Americans living in small towns and rural areas were actually much better than in Europe. The picture is not entirely rosy. Blighted conditions existed in the Eastern cities and 26 percent of the 1870 U.S. population lived in the states of the old Confederacy where living conditions had deteriorated because of the Civil War. Bryce could retain his optimistic outlook because he traveled mostly in the North and apparently not at all in the South.

---

[3] James Bryce, *The American Commonwealth*, Louis M. Hacker, ed. (New York: Capricorn Books, G.P. Putnam's Sons, 1888/1959).

Budget Shares, 1870–2013

Consumption expenditures in 1870 were about 75 percent of GDP. This implied consumption expenditures per capita of $2,808 in 2010 prices. With an average household of five members, the average household consumption was $998 per year.[4] We wonder how families could have lived on so little. Consumer expenditures were almost entirely for the three necessities of food, clothing, and shelter, with virtually nothing left over for discretionary items. 1870 was Sraffa's necessary economy. Robert Gallman found that in 1859, 51.9 percent of consumer expenditures were for perishable goods 14.7 percent for semi-durable goods, 9.3 percent for durable goods and the remaining 24.1 percent for services, mainly rent. This in an economy in which manufacturing was a small share of GNP.[5]

Detail regarding expenditure shares in each category for 1969, 1940, and 2013 is provided in Table 6.1. Over the years the shares of semi-durable goods changed little in composition, though the sources of some shifted to overseas. Shares of expenditures for clothing and footwear did decline by 2013. As to durable goods, horse-drawn vehicles had disappeared by 1940, on the eve of WWII. Motor vehicles, not invented in 1869, dominated durable goods expenditures by 2013. The love affair of Americans with the automobile has yet to much abate. Shares for furniture, floor covering, and house furnishings had declined somewhat by 2013. The giant leap in health care is the main change in services by 2013. Many goods and services abundant in 2013 had not been invented in 1869. Among items either not invented or not purchased in 1869 are household utilities, health care, transportation services, recreation services and financial services, as well as "other services." Even New Yorkers could not hail a taxi. Of course, important changes had happened generally to the economy between 1869 and 2013. By 1940, the USA was an economy of

---

[4] This $983 figure is confirmed by a 1874–1875 budget study by the Massachusetts Bureau of Labor Statistics. This survey of 397 wage-earner families reports an average consumption level of $738.

[5] For these details and much more, see Robert Gallman, "Economic Growth and Structural Change in the Long Nineteenth Century," in Stanley L. Engerman and Gallman, (eds.). *The Cambridge Economic History of the United States*, Vol. II (Cambridge, UK/New York: Cambridge University Press, 2000), pp. 1–55.

Table 6.1   Consumer Expenditures by Category, Percent Shares, 1869, 1940, and 2013

	1869	**1940**	**2013**
Perishable goods	51.9	28.2	9.2
Food, alcohol for off-premises consumption	44.3	22.3	7.6
Tobacco, printed material, heating/lighting fuel	7.6	5.9	1.6
Semi-durable goods	15.7	17.3	13.4
Clothing and footwear	9.9	10.1	3.1
Dry goods for making clothing at home	5.0	0.0	0.0
House furnishings, toys, games, sports equipment	0.8	0.8	1.2
Not invented yet, including motor vehicle fuels, pharmaceuticals, recreational items, and housing supplies	0.0	6.3	9.1
Durable goods	9.3	11.5	10.9
Furniture, floor coverings, house furnishings	4.5	2.8	1.4
Glassware, tableware	0.9	0.7	0.4
Sporting equipment, guns, ammunition	0.0	0.3	0.5
Books, musical instruments, luggage	0.9	0.8	0.6
Jewelry and watches	1.5	0.6	0.7
Horse-drawn vehicles	1.3	0.0	0.0
Not invented yet, including motor vehicles, appliances, video and IT equipment, recreational vehicles, therapeutic appliances, telephone equipment	0.0	6.3	7.3
Services	24.1	43.1	66.5
Rent including imputed rent on owner-occupied dwellings		13.2	15.5
Food services and accommodations		6.2	6.2
Contributions		1.5	2.7
Not invented or not purchased	0.0	22.2	42.1
Household utilities		2.7	2.7
Health Care		3.1	16.7
Transportation Services		2.7	2.9
Recreation Services		2.2	3.8
Financial services		3.4	7.2
Other services (communication, education, professional, personal care, household maintenance)		8.1	8.8
Summary			
Share of spending on categories that existed in 1869	100.0	65.2	41.5
Share of spending on other categories	0.0	34.8	58.5

Source: 1869. Major categories from Gallman (2000, Table 1.10, p. 30), allocated into subcategories with data from Shaw (1947, Table II-1, pp. 108–52).

Reprinted from Robert J. Gordon, *The Rise and Fall of American Growth* (Princeton and Oxford: Princeton U. Press, 2016), pp. 38–39.

surpluses; by 2013, it was a supra-surplus economy. Later, we will have more to say about the characteristics of the supra-surplus society.[6]

The most important thing about food consumption in 1869 was the dominance of home production in a mostly rural nation. Diets were tied to what farmers could raise on their own land, and the diets were monotonous. Preservation was made by salt and smoking so that smoked pork was the dominant meat. Pigs needed little attention and could be allowed to roam freely, eating acorns and other vegetation in forests. Likewise, corn was easy to grow everywhere, and the ubiquity and cheapness of cornmeal made products baked from corn the dominant starch, along with corn derivatives such as hominy or bread made from a mixture of corn and wheat flower. In a Sraffian sense these were basic goods that exited production in almost the same ratio that they had entered production. "Hog'n'hominy" still was the chief fare in the southern and western communities not yet serviced by railroads. Southern planters subsisted mainly on bacon, corn pone, and coffee sweetened with molasses.

Chocolate, tea, and especially coffee were the beverages of choice almost everywhere. The coffeepot could almost stand beside the six-shooter or the covered wagon as a symbol of the Old West, as was later told in American Western movies. Malnutrition was limited to individuals or families living in poverty, mainly in large cities, where crops could not be grown. Yet immigrants had to adjust to the monotony of food available on the frontier and missed many of their traditional foodstuffs. Because most European immigrants had lived closer to the sea in Europe than in America, they missed fish. For example, the Swedes missed salt herring, and those from central Europe missed sweet-sour rye bread. Closely related to food consumption was another perishable commodity, tobacco. Production of manufactured cigarettes was only 13 per capita in 1870 and brand names were few, with only 120 trademarks in 1870, as compared with more than 10,000 registered in the 1906. The first trademark of all, adorned with a flaming mustachioed devil, was granted in 1867 for Underwood's deviled turkey and deviled ham.

The icebox had been invented in the 1860s but did not become commonplace until the 1880s. The refrigerated rail car was invented in 1871,

---

[6] See especially Chapter 11.

and greatly expanded the variety of available food items in the last part of the century. Midwestern beef was sent to the urban northeast and California-grown lettuce was shipped everywhere. Indeed, the standard source of food and dry goods (i.e., fabrics for making clothes) was the closest country store. Colorful packaging of consumer goods was still in the future in 1870 and goods were displayed primarily in bulk in barrels, jars, bins, and sacks. Customers had to wait while clerks spooned out and weighed the coffee, tea, sugar, and other bulk products. The lack of central heating meant that fuel, whether wood or dirty coal, had to be hauled into the dwelling unit and the ashes removed. Despite this, the dwelling of 1870 remained cold in the winter. Open fires for heating, open-flame gas or oil lamps for illumination created the constant danger of fire. An oil lantern kicked over by Mrs. O'Leary's cow was the often credited (and often disputed) source of the Great Chicago Fire of 1871.

As ever, the upper class lived different lives compared with the lower class. There was a substantial urban middle class and a small but very prosperous urban upper class in 1870. There are many examples of 1870-era middle-class houses in cities of the northeast, from Cambridge, Massachusetts to Washington DC. Blocks of architecturally significant houses can be viewed on house tours in Charleston, South Carolina, and Savannah, Georgia. Obviously these houses were built to last and many are currently for sale, built in 1870–1875 in states ranging from Maine to Arkansas to California and in between, now viewable online.[7] Though much more expensive today, these houses cost roughly $3,000 to $10,000 to build in nominal dollars of the time. The occupational distribution tells us that 8 percent of households were classified as managers, professionals or proprietors. These were the initial occupants of the iconic 19th-century brownstones of New York City and the substantial Queen Anne houses built in cities and towns throughout the northern tier of states.

One definition of the middle class in the late 19th century encompassed any household that kept a servant. In 1870, some 7.8 percent of the work-force was classified as "domestic service workers." Roughly 15 percent of urban families employed a service worker. Thus about 15 percent of the

---

[7] In 2016, under oldhouses.com we found an 1825 Colonial in Wales, Maine listed for $225,900 and an 1870 Victorian: Queen Anne in Burton, Texas, at $375,000.

households of 1870 were middle class. Little more could distinguish the middle class since virtually all the progress of the late 19th century was still in the future — gas fires would become common in the 1880s and gas cookers in the 1890s, and the electric light bulb would become available in the 1880s. Inventions defined progress.

In 1870 there did not exist what Thorstein Veblen would later describe as a leisure class. The American invention of the telegraph had announced the joining together of the transcontinental railway, which had in 1851 made the Pony Express technologically obsolete. It also had allowed local print newspapers to report the events of national and world affairs on the day that they happened, including daily chronicles of the carnage of the Civil War. But the great surge of popular journalism came in the late 19th century, while few people read newspapers in 1870. The telephone, phonograph, motion picture, and radio had not yet been invented.

Thus, there was little entertainment in 1870 in working-class households. What entertainment there was consisted mainly of the male head of household drinking with friends in the local saloon. Females were not invited and were accustomed to a secondary rank within the family. The saloon as a leisure space clearly distinct from home thus gave workers a more comfortable and appealing place to spend their leisure time. The relatively small urban middle class began to earn vacation time, but, because of primitive transportation, had few places to visit beyond local parks and attractions. A notable early source of working-class entertainment was the Coney Island amusement park in Brooklyn, New York, and was connected with central New York City by streetcar by the 1860s. Similarly, Chicago's Riverview opened in 1904.

As noted, income and budget studies become important in a Sraffian view of the economy. The first known budget study for the United States was conducted by the Massachusetts Bureau of Labor (MBLS) in 1874–1875. Inspired in part by the MBLS study, the newly formed U.S. Bureau of Labor (BLS) undertook large-scale studies for 1888–1891, 1901, 1917–1919, and 1934–1935, the results of which are summarized in Table 6.2. Since incomes increased from year to year, we would expect the share spent on food to gradually decline, but this is not what happened. From 1888 to 1919, there was virtually no change in the expenditure **shares** across categories, and particularly no shrinkage in the expenditure

Table 6.2 Four Consumer Budget Studies, 1888–1936

	Workers in nine cities in U.S., 1888–91 (1)	Working families in 1901 (2)	Urban familes in 1917–19 (3)	Consumption expenditures of urban families, 1935–36 (4)
Sample Size	2562	11156	12896	14469
Average Family Size	3.9	4.0	4.9	3.6
Income before Taxes	573	651	1505	N.A.
Expenditures				
Total	534	618	1352	1463
Food	219	266	556	508
Clothing	82	80	238	160
Rent	80	112	224	259
Fuel	32	35	74	108
Sundries	121	124	260	428
Percent Expenditures				
Food	41.0	43.0	41.1	347
Clothing	15.4	12.9	17.6	10.9
Rent	15.0	18.1	16.6	17.7
Fuel	6.0	5.7	5.5	7.4
Sundries	22.7	20.1	19.2	29.3
Total Expenditures in Prices of 1901	491.6	618.0	739.7	873.6

Sources: Columns (1)–(3) from HSUS Cd465–Cd502. Column (4) from HSUS Cd540–557.
Note: "Rent" in column (3) includes "household operation."
Reprinted from Robert J. Gordon, *The Rise and Fall of American Growth* (Princeton and Oxford: Princeton University Press, 2016), p. 65.

share of food. With such a pattern of spending, three is little room in this interval for a major improvement in the standard of living, unless it occurs in the variety and types of food consumed. There was an enormous increase in manufactured (i.e., processed) food in the first three decades after 1870, which might have allowed for some variety. Clothing and rent round out the traditional three necessities, and fuel for heat and light qualifying as a fourth necessity.

It was not until the 1935–1936 survey that food consumption declined below 40 percent. This allowed room for an increase in miscellaneous "sundries" from 19.2 percent in 1917–1919 to 29.3 percent in 1935–1936. Such items included spending on insurance, medical care, tobacco, haircuts, meals away from home, furniture, union dues, church contributions, and public transit fares. To the extent these items were discretionary, they represented surplus-value. This happened despite 1935–1936 being the mid-years of the Great Depression, suggesting the persistence of such spending.

We can use the share of consumer expenditures on food as an index of subsistence. Table 6.3 shows not only the percentages spent on food, but on alcoholic beverages and tobacco as well, for a large sample of countries for 2013. While alcoholic beverages and tobacco may not be considered by some as "necessities," they nonetheless are habitual for part of the population. Besides, such expenditures are part of the measure of standard of living. The top 15 countries can be classified as supra-surplus countries, spending less than 13 percent of their consumer budget on food. At the top is the USA and Singapore, each spending just 6.7 percent of their consumer budgets on food. Switzerland actually spends a greater share for food than does the U.S. Moreover, its total consumer expenditures are $45,308, suggesting that Switzerland enjoys a higher standard of living than the USA. Switzerland is followed by the United Kingdom, Canada, Austria, Australia, Ireland, Germany, Denmark, Qatar, Netherlands, Sweden, Norway, and Finland. Oil-rich Qatar is the only non-Western nation in the supra-surplus category. The next 20 countries, beginning with South Korea, are clearly economies of surpluses — that is, beyond subsistence. Their shares of consumer expenditures going for food range from 13.4 percent to 17.9 percent for Slovakia and Poland. They are "advanced" economies but not supra-surplus countries. The next 17 countries have smaller surpluses and can be categorized as less developed or newly industrializing. Their share of consumer expenditures for food ranges from 17.9 percent for Columbia to 23.4 percent for Mexico. Among the nations in this list are Portugal, Kuwait, South Africa, Turkey, and Venezuela. Below Mexico are the economies operating at a

Table 6.3 Percent of Consumer Expenditures Spent on Food, Alcoholic Beverages, and Tobacco that were Consumed at Home, by Selected Countries, 2013[1]

| Country/Territory | Share of consumer expenditures | | Consumer expenditures[3] | Expenditures on food[2] |
	Food	Alcoholic beverages and tobacco		
	Percent		*U.S. dollars per person*	
USA	6.7	2.1	35,448	2,362
Singapore	6.7	2.0	20,892	1,410
Switzerland	8.9	3.7	45,308	4,052
United Kingdom	9.1	4.0	25,797	2,345
Canada	9.4	3.5	27,798	2,617
Austria	9.9	3.5	27,545	2,717
Australia	10.0	3.4	36,005	3,583
Ireland	10.3	5.2	21,833	2,242
Germany	10.4	3.3	24,504	2,551
Denmark	11.2	3.8	28,337	3,182
Qatar	12.0	0.3	12,278	1,473
Netherlands	12.1	3.1	22,592	2,742
Sweden	12.2	3.6	27,632	3,378
Norway	12.3	4.0	37,844	4,641
Finland	12.8	4.7	25,905	3,319
South Korea	13.4	2.2	12,420	1,664
France	13.4	3.5	23,709	3,185
Japan	13.6	2.6	22,946	3,116
Taiwan	13.6	2.1	11,866	1,617
Bahrain	13.7	0.4	11,396	1,567
Belgium	13.8	3.5	23,343	3,225
United Arab Emirates	14.1	0.2	22,705	3,201
Italy	14.3	4.2	21,940	3,138
Hong Kong, China	14.3	1.9	26,309	3,765
Spain	14.4	2.9	18,058	2,597
Israel	15.2	2.5	20,208	3,068
New Zealand	15.3	5.0	23,425	3,575
Slovenia	15.3	5.5	13,434	2,060
Chile	15.6	3.0	9,917	1,546
Brazil	15.7	2.3	7,202	1,131

(*Continued*)

Table 6.3 (*Continued*)

Country/Territory	Food	Alcoholic beverages and tobacco	Consumer expenditures[3]	Expenditures on food[2]
	Percent		*U.S. dollars per person*	
Czech Republic	16.2	9.9	10,153	1,640
Greece	16.6	4.4	16,115	2,670
Hungary	17.8	7.9	7,228	1,285
Slovakia	17.8	5.0	10,041	1,789
Poland	17.9	7.6	8,251	1,476
Colombia	17.9	3.0	4,761	854
Portugal	18.0	3.4	14,437	2,598
Uruguay	18.4	1.2	11,274	2,079
Kuwait	18.5	0.5	7,775	1,438
Bulgaria	18.7	6.7	4,997	935
Latvia	18.8	8.1	9,323	1,751
South Africa	19.2	6.0	4,292	825
Estonia	19.6	9.0	10,112	1,979
Venezuela	19.9	3.6	4,693	935
Costa Rica	20.1	0.9	7,290	1,469
Montenegro	20.5	3.6	7,123	1,460
Argentina	20.7	4.5	9,878	2,043
Malaysia	20.7	1.8	5,662	1,172
Turkey	22.0	4.9	8,088	1,782
Tunisia	22.7	3.3	3,007	682
Ecuador	23.1	0.8	3,757	869
Mexico	23.4	2.6	7,304	1,708
Lithuania	23.7	7.4	9,876	2,341
Dominican Republic	24.1	4.2	4,907	1,183
Thailand	25.0	3.2	3,409	851
Iran	25.0	0.4	2,640	661
Saudi Arabia	25.5	0.6	7,134	1,822
China	26.1	3.6	2,506	654
Serbia	26.6	5.7	4,753	1,263
Romania	28.3	3.5	5,805	1,640
Bolivia	28.7	1.9	1,767	506

(*Continued*)

Table 6.3   (*Continued*)

Country/Territory	Food	Alcoholic beverages and tobacco	Consumer expenditures[3]	Expenditures on food[2]
		Share of consumer expenditures		
		Percent		*U.S. dollars per person*
Russia	29.1	8.7	7,295	2,125
India	29.6	2.8	900	266
Uzbekistan	30.8	2.5	1,068	329
Croatia	31.1	3.7	9,650	3,003
Bosnia-Herzegovina	31.3	6.3	4,076	1,275
Indonesia	33.2	5.4	2,116	703
Georgia	33.2	5.2	2,692	894
Macedonia	34.2	3.4	3,872	1,325
Vietnam	35.6	2.8	1,185	421
Morocco	35.8	3.8	2,130	763
Peru	36.5	6.0	4,143	1,510
Belarus	37.3	7.7	3,757	1,401
Egypt	37.4	4.0	2,810	1,052
Jordan	37.5	6.2	4,680	1,756
Ukraine	37.7	7.8	2,894	1,090
Turkmenistan	38.8	2.2	3,182	1,234
Guatemala	40.1	1.7	3,046	1,221
Philippines	42.4	1.2	2,052	871
Algeria	42.6	2.2	1,919	818
Pakistan	42.7	1.0	846	361
Kazakhstan	43.5	1.3	6,237	2,713
Azerbaijan	45.3	1.6	3,276	1,483
Cameroon	45.8	2.1	1,073	491
Kenya	46.9	3.5	792	371
Nigeria	56.7	1.4	2,132	1,209

[1] The data were computed based on Euromonitor International data extracted May 2015.

[2] Includes nonalcoholic beverages.

[3] Consumer expenditures comprise personal expenditures on goods and services. Consumption expenditures in the domestic market are equal to consumer expenditures by resident households plus direct purchases in the domestic market by non-resident households and minus direct purchases abroad by resident households.

subsistence level, beginning with Lithuania with 23.7 percent of the consumer budget going for food and ending with Nigeria, with 56.7 percent of its consumer budget allocated to the basic, food. These shares alone do not reveal anything about the variety in the diet of these countries. Yet, we know also that countries such as Mexico, Turkey, Brazil, Venezuela, Argentina, and China have a rich variety in their diets.

These categories are not without paradoxes. In the budgets of nations such as Mexico, Greece, Turkey, Brazil, Hungary, Saudi Arabia, and China are outlays for automobiles, though they are mostly used ones.

There is a small upper class in these countries that drive BMWs and Mercedes Benz's or other luxury cars. Still, much of their populations depend on public transportation. We should emphasize that food budget shares comprise just one measure of economic development and affluence. The level of education expenditures would be another indicator of well-being. Even GDP or total expenditures hide a great deal. They say nothing about the distribution of incomes and wealth. Also, a happiness index would give us a different rank order for these countries. Finally, we should note that the International Monetary Fund (IMF) classifies these economies differently.[8] Its "advanced economies" include supra-surplus and surplus economies, without distinguishing between the two. Moreover, the IMF classifies Qatar as an "emerging market or a developing economy." The IMF goes beyond food budget shares to consider other factors (perhaps education) that place Qatar in this category. Later, we will return to these matters.

Next, we will merge Sraffa's subsistence model with the work of Michal Kalecki. This merger was not approved by the Italian economists. Hopefully, the American Economic Association will not file anti-trust actions against me.

---

[8] See Tables A2.1, A2.2 and A2.3 in Appendix 2 to view the IMF classifications.

Chapter 7

THE IMPORTANCE OF THE KALECKIAN INCOME DISTRIBUTION

While at Cambridge, Marxist economist Michal Kalecki (1899–1970), was befriended by John Kenneth Galbraith. "A small, often irritable, independent, intense man," Galbraith relates, "Kalecki was the most innovative figure in economics I have known, not excluding Keynes."[1] Like Sraffa, Kalecki seldom put pen to paper. But when he did, the clarity and depth of his thoughts were powerful.

In 1933, Kalecki had developed a Keynes-style theory of the level of employment, prior to and independent of Keynes's General Theory. Kalecki's income distribution views, however, were more in tune with the Ricardian and Marxian chorus about income classes. In fact, Kalecki's theory can be summed up in the adage, "The workers spend what they get; the capitalists get what they spend." It would have made a marvelous line for one of George Bernard Shaw's plays.

In Kalecki the national income is divided between profits received by capitalists and wages received by workers. The national product is divided among the investment and consumption spending of the

---

[1] John Kenneth Galbraith, *A Life in Our Times: Memoirs* (Boston: Houghton Mifflin, 1981), p. 75.

capitalists and the consumption expenditures of the workers.[2] If we simplify by saying that all profits are diligently plowed back into the business to purchase new investment goods, saving, as well as investment, is equal to profits. The capitalist is the lone saver in this simple economy.

A Kaleckian view of production can be made to conform with Sraffa's subsistence model, if we divide Sraffa's output sector into two distinct industries, one producing necessary consumption goods, the other producing necessary investment goods. Although Sraffa does not prefer his model of physiological subsistence, in it nonetheless the amount of business investment in capital and the prevailing production technology would decide the level of employment as well as the division of labor between the production of consumption necessities and production necessities (investment goods). This technology and the prevailing level of production capacity (of the vintage technology) also decide the total amount of each class of good produced.

The introduction of subsistence wages into Sraffa's subsistence model transforms it into a Kaleckian world of income distribution. Subsistence wages decide the quantity of consumer necessities manufactured. Since investment goods are combined with labor at a given technology, the demand for consumer necessities and investment goods determines the employment level. The distribution of income between workers and capitalists (between wages and profits) becomes the mirror image of the distribution of national output between consumer necessities and investment goods. We nonetheless wonder what happens to Kalecki's theory when Sraffa's production system produces surpluses and (with a demand theory addendum) the "working class" receives a larger share of the national income than required for subsistence. When wages (perhaps bolstered by interest and rents) become substantially greater than those required for subsistence, the surplus economy is on the way to becoming a supra-surplus system.

---

[2] See Michal Kalecki, *Selected Essays on the Dynamics of the Capitalistic Economy* (Cambridge, England: Cambridge University Press, 1971).

While the national income accounts had yet to be developed, Kalecki's system can be expressed in national income and product terms, so:

> *Income*
>
> Profits (capitalist's income)
>
> + wages (workers' income)
>
> ———————————————
>
> National Income
>
> *Expenditures*
>
> Investment
>
> + capitalists' consumption
>
> + workers' consumption
>
> ———————————————
>
> National Product

Although "investment" here is expressed as a by-product of consumption, it can also be defined in the standard national income accounting way — purchases of fixed capital (tools, machinery, buildings, etc.) and changes in inventories or unsold finished goods. In Sraffa, these are the commodities used to produce commodities. In this schema, all workers' wages are spent entirely on necessary goods, so wages must equal the workers' expenditures on consumption goods — the food, clothing, shelter, and transportation required for life and for work. Kalecki is using Marx's and John Stuart Mill's notion of cultural subsistence. Sraffa's system reveals the inputs necessary to produce particular outputs in an input-output sense; Kalecki's defines the amounts of necessary consumption goods (demand), including the consumption of "luxury goods" by the capitalists. The capitalist hires maids while the workers *are* maids.

As noted, all profits can be plowed back into the business to purchase new investment goods. Surprisingly, capitalists can add to their current share of the national income (profits) by having increased their investment spending in a prior period. Investment, Keynes-style, is multiplied in terms of total output. Out of a larger output come greater profits. Moreover, even if the capitalists consume their profits in the style of the savings and loan executives of the 1980s — buying yachts, building vacation homes, supporting lovers — they experience no decrease in profits income. This is because investment and profits are equal. Capitalist profits are like the water of the artesian well: no matter how much water is taken out, the well never empties.

The accumulation of capital is both the rainbow and the pot of gold! If a greater share of national output is devoted to investment goods, the level of employment in the investment sector will be greater and (given that investment equals profits) a greater share of the national income will go to the capitalists. Conversely, if a greater share of output is devoted to consumer necessities, the workers snatch a larger piece of the national income pie.

This is not the end of it. Although the capitalists are masters of their own universe in this sense, Kalecki (apparently under Keynes's influence) saw outside elements, such as uncertainties regarding profitable investment, causing unavoidable fluctuations in profits. We see this in the real world where profits move up and down monthly.[3] Investment is that spending which is devoted to increasing or maintaining the stock of productive capital, which is comprised of factories, machines, and other durable products that are used up in the production process. Both Kalecki and Keynes saw a close relationship between business investment and GNP. The connection of the two ran through profits in Kalecki. That is to say, gross business profits and gross business investment are highly correlated. In Kalecki and Keynes's accelerator model of investment, increases in GDP lead to increases in the desired stock of capital (denoted K^*). To get to the desired stock of capital, business investment out of profits must be increased. In turn, increased investment leads to a further rise in GDP. Thus, we can define the desired capital stock as:

$$K^* = vY,$$

where the fixed multiple, v is the desired capital to output ratio (K/Y). This means that to produce, Y firms have to have K/v in place. For example, if the K/Y ratio is 2 and output is expected to increase by \$10 billion, then firms would revise their desired capital stock upwards by \$20 billion to

---

[3] Much of the above paragraphs is based on E. Ray Canterbery, "Galbraith, Sraffa, Kalecki and supra-surplus capitalism, *Journal of Post Keynesian Economics*, 7(1), 1984, pp. 79–80. The article is reprinted in E. Ray Canterbery, *Beyond Conventional Economics* (Singapore, London, New Jersey: World Scientific, 2016), pp. 502–515.

ensure they have enough productive capacity to meet the expected increase in demand for goods and services. In order to increase the capital stock to meet the change in desired capital stock, firms will invest. From this, we would expect to see a close connection between changes in GDP and changes in gross investment. This is shown in Figure 7.1, where a tight connection between profits and investment holds for a long period 1947-2000. Thereafter, the connection is broken during the dot-com crisis of the early 2000s and the financial crisis of 2008-2009. The departures are dramatic as profits flow much faster than investment. Later, we will explain the connection of profit excesses to the Casino Economy.

We would expect to find countries which spend a lot on investment to have high levels of GDP and that economic growth is tightly tied to business investment. Table 7.1 shows total investment as a percent of GDP for selected countries for different times. Except for Australia, the investment ratios have been falling. Australia is experiencing a high rate of economic growth relative to these other nations. Japan's investment to GDP ratio has

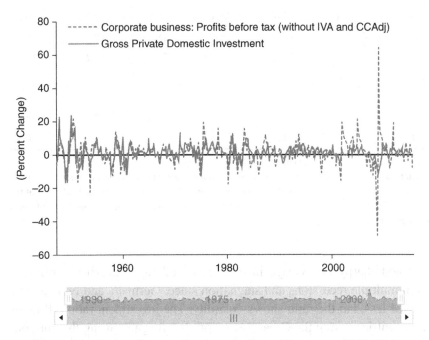

Figure 7.1   Percent Changes, Corporate Profits and Investment, 1947–2015

Source: research.stlouisfed.org.

Table 7.1   Total Investment Ratios for Selected Countries, Percent of GDP

Year	Australia	France	Germany	Japan	United Kingdom	United States
2000	24.7	19.9	22.3	25.1	17.7	20.9
2001	23.2	19.6	20.3	24.3	17.4	19.3
2002	24.9	18.6	18.1	22.5	17.1	18.7
2003	26.6	18.5	17.9	22.4	16.8	18.7
2004	27.2	19.1	17.6	22.5	17.1	19.7
2005	28.0	19.9	17.3	22.5	17.1	20.3
2006	27.3	20.8	18.1	22.7	17.5	20.6
2007	28.6	21.9	19.3	22.9	18.2	19.6
2008	29.0	21.9	19.4	23.0	17.0	18.1
2009	27.3	19.0	16.5	19.7	14.2	14.7
2010	26.8	19.2	17.3	19.8	15.4	15.8
2011	27.2	20.1	18.0	19.9	14.8	15.9
Average						
1980s	26.8	20.9	24.5	29.6	18.5	20.5
1990s	24.6	18.9	22.6	28.8	17.4	18.7
2000s	26.7	19.9	18.5	22.3	16.7	18.5
CV						
1980s	7.3	6.4	6.0	5.9	10.5	4.9
1990s	5.7	10.2	6.1	8.5	7.0	6.5
2000s	6.3	5.8	8.6	7.7	7.3	10.9

Source: IMF World Economic Outlook Database, April 2012.
The total investment ratio is expressed as a ratio of total investment in current local currency and GDP in current local currency. Investment or gross capital formation is measured by the total value of the gross fixed capital formation and changes in inventories and acquisitions less disposals of valuables for a unit or sector.

declined sharpy on average in the 2000s and Japan has been suffering from multiple recessions and stagnation since. Germany and France have slowed less, but the ratio shows volatility. The investment ratio fell in all the countries during the Great Recession. It fell again during the dot-com and financial crises in the U.S., dramatically in 2009.

The investment decision by the firm is not quite this simple. The firm must also take into account expectations of future economic conditions and the current interest rate. Notably, in the U.S. and Japan the interest rate has hovered around zero during the past decade. It has even gone negative in Japan. This, of course, makes investment much cheaper.

As noted above, in Kalecki's simplified model the economy was comprised of two groups:

1. Workers who earned wages and did not save; and
2. Capitalists who produced and earned profits.

He also assumed that the economy was closed (no foreign trade) and there was no government sector. In this model profits are determined by investment, not the other way round. Still, in Kalecki there are two profits equations, a simplified and generalized equation. Table 7.2 illustrates these two approaches.

In the generalized profits model, workers have positive savings (taking away from profits), an export surplus (foreign investment) can add to overall investment, and a budget deficit (government investment) can add to overall investment. This, of course, is the more realistic model.

Table 7.2   Kalecki's Simplified and Generalised Profits Equations

Income	Spending
Simplified Profits Model	
+ Gross Profits	+ Gross Investment
+ Wages and Salaries	+ Capitalist's Consumption
	+ Workers' Consumption
= Gross National Product	= Gross National Product
Generalised Profits Model	
Gross Profits net of taxes =	+ Gross Investment
	+ Export Surplus
	+ Budget Deficit
	− Workers' saving
	+ Capitalist's Consumption

From the simplified profits model, we would expect to see a high correlation between gross business investment and gross profits. Figure 7.1 shows the percentage changes in these two variables from 1947 to October 2015 for the USA. The two are so closely connected that it is difficult to tell one from the other. A different view of the same two variables is displayed in Figure 7.2. For a long period of time, from about 1929 through 1960, real gross domestic investment and corporate profits after taxes followed the same trend line. Thereafter, profits began rising faster than business investment, with the gap widening toward 2015. This may be better represented by the generalized profits model of Kalecki. The rise in the importance of the trade surplus and budget deficits may account for the widening disparity between the two variables. To see the whole picture, we need to consider what is happening in the financial sector. As we will come to note, as profits outran real capital investment, just beginning in

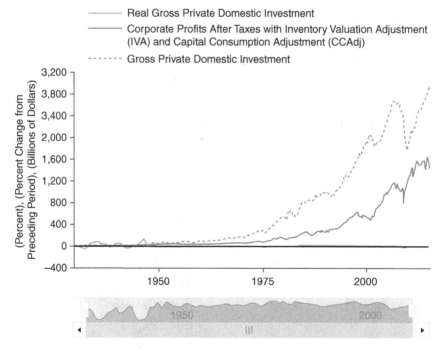

Figure 7.2   Percentage Changes, Investment and Profits, 1929–2015

Source: research.stlouisfed.org.

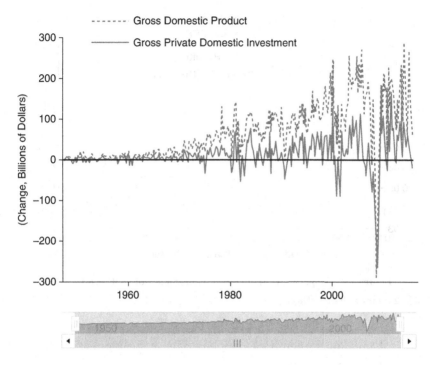

Figure 7.2 Variations in investment and GDP, 1947–2016

Source: research.stlouisfed.org.

the early 1970s and accelerating during the 1980s and even beyond, the financial sector grew rapidly. Note that in price-adjusted terms, real business investment is a flat-liner.

The simplified profits model also contains other information — about wages and salaries. Since income is divided between gross profits and wages/salaries, we would expect a trade-off between the two. Figure 7.3 shows the relationship between gross corporate profits and wages as shares of GDP. We note particularly the widening gap between the two in favor of profits before and after the Great Recession. Profits are outracing wages except during the Great Recession when gross business investment is also falling. Since the mid-1970s, wages as a percentage of GDP have fallen 7 percent while corporate profits have risen 7 percent. That's a pretty compelling relationship. Since most of income is from wages, the

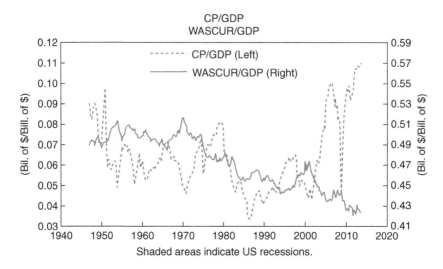

Figure 7.3   Wages vs. Corporate Profits, as Shares of GDP 1940–2015

Source: 2014 research.stlouisfed.org.

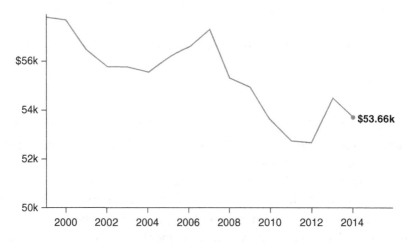

Figure 7.4   Median Household Income, in 2014 Dollars

Source: Census Bureau.

median household income is a good measure of the well-being of the middle class; half of all households have higher incomes and half have lower incomes. So, this is the middle. Figure 7.4 illustrates what has been happening to the middle class since the year 2000. As wages have declined relative to corporate profits, real household income has declined. The decline accelerated during the Great Recession.

The middle class is making less money than it was 15 years ago. Median family income in 2014 was 6.5 percent lower than it was in 2007. It's 7.2 percent below 1999 levels.

Kalecki and a Minsky Moment

Hyman Minsky explicitly incorporated the Kaleckian result in his simplest model. In it, aggregate profits equal private investment plus the government's deficit. In an investment boom, profits would be increasing along with investment, helping to validate expectations and encouraging even more investment. The fundamental instability in capitalism is upward — toward a speculative frenzy. Moreover, the government budget deficit would grow in a downturn and would help to prop up profits — reducing downside risks even more. Minsky argued that private sector-led expansions tend to be more unsustainable than government-led expansions because private deficits and debt are more dangerous than government deficits and debt. The countercyclical movement of the government's budget would automatically stabilize profits — limiting both the upside in a boom and the downside in a slump. Government is a stabilizing force.

With the Kalecki view of profits incorporated within his investment theory of the cycle, Minsky argued that investment is forthcoming today only if investment is expected in the future — since investment in the future will determine profits in the future. Moreover, since investment today validates the decisions undertaken "yesterday," expectations about "tomorrow" affect the ability to meet previous commitments undertaken when financing the capital assets in place today. This has a banking and financial system corollary. In Minsky, banks are a source of funds for investment. As Minsky put it,

> Not only must the banking and financial system maintain favorable asset prices and conditions for investment financing now, but the banking and financing system also must be expected to maintain favorable asset prices and conditions for investment financing in the future. Because

such normal functioning of banking and financial system is a necessary condition for the satisfactory operation of a capitalist economy, disruption of the system will lead to malfunctioning of the economy.

Minsky links this circularity to the price of capital. Anything that lowers expected future profitability can push today's demand price of capital below the supply price, reducing investment and today's profits below the level necessary to validate past expectations on which demand prices were based when previous capital projects were begun. In Chapter 16 we will return to Minsky and the Minsky moment.

Kalecki and the Markup

We next turn to Kalecki again, and his theory of pricing at the firm level. Each firm in an industry fixes the price for its product by "marking up" its average unit prime cost in order to cover overheads and to achieve profits; that is, prices are formed by adding a proportionate markup on the prime cost. In simple algebra,

$$p = \text{price per unit of output}$$

Unit prime cost consists of:

m: raw materials cost per unit of output
w: wage costs per unit of output
o: overhead per unit of output
r: profit per unit of output
s: gross profit per unit of output.

Then,

$p = m + w + o + r$, where $m + w = u$ (unit prime costs) and $o + r = s$ (unit gross profits),

and

$$p = u + s.$$

The markup is measured as the excess of price per unit of output over unit prime costs divided by unit prime costs, or

$$(p - u)/u.$$

The markup is also equal to the gross profit margin to cover overhead and achieve profits in relation to prime costs, or

$$(o + p)/u.$$

Alternatively, the markup may be conceived in the form of a coefficient k by which unit prime cost is multiplied to obtain price ($p = ku$), where k is generally larger than unity, or

$$k = 1 + (p - u)/u.$$

The relationship between the markup on prime costs and k is simply

$$(p - u)/u = k - 1.$$

The simplicity of the mathematics is deceptive, for the implications are powerful. The markup depends on a number of things: (1) the process of industrial concentration and weaknesses in competition; (2) on the structure of markets; (3) on the degree of freedom and constraints in price setting; (4) and on the income distribution. The markup is governed by a firm's price fixing policy in relation to price formation in an industry. Its determination is a key to arriving at class shares of national income, in turn affecting spending propensities and the degree of utilization of resources. The markup is a powerful force. It is determined by and reflects semi-monopolistic and monopolistic influences resulting from imperfect competition or oligopoly.

Closely related to Kalecki's degree of monopoly is the Lerner Index of a firm's market power. It is defined as

$$L = (P - MC)/P,$$

where P is the market price set by the firm and MC is the firm's marginal cost.[4] The index ranges from a high of 1 to a low of 0, with higher

[4]A. P. Lerner, "The Concept of Monopoly and the measurement of Monopoly Power," *The Review of Economic Studies* 1 (3), 1934, 157–175.

numbers implying greater market power. For a perfectly competitive firm (where $P = MC$), $L = 0$, and such a firm has no market power. The Lerner Index is equivalent to the negative inverse of the formula for price elasticity of demand facing a firm, when the price, P chosen is that which maximizes profits available because of the existence of market power. Thus,

$$L = -1/E,$$

where E is the elasticity of demand of the firm's demand curve, not the market demand curve. If the Lerner index can't be greater than one, then the absolute value of elasticity of demand can never be less than one (the elasticity can never be greater than -1). Put differently, the firm which is maximizing profits will never operate along the inelastic portion of its demand curve.

Surplus capacity characterizes oligopoly. With surplus capacity and constant prime costs over the relevant range of output, the firm fixes the price of the product taking into consideration mainly its prime costs per unit of output and the prices of other sellers in an industry, producing similar products (and only to a much lesser degree is price-fixing influenced by prices and expected reactions outside the product group or an industry). This departs from an orthodoxy in which prices are compared with dissimilar products. Prices are fixed by allowing for the mobility of customers (market imperfections) and the influence of their own prices and expected reactions on those of their rivals (oligopoly). The firm must be satisfied that the price fixed is more advantageous than a higher or lower one. For the firm "must make sure that the price does not become too high in relation to prices of other firms, for this would drastically reduce sales, and that the price does not become too low in relation to its average price cost, for this would drastically reduce the profit margin."[5]

Kalecki next links the ratio of proceeds to prime costs in an industry with the relative share of wages in the contribution to output by that industry. Then, he proceeds from a single industry to the manufacturing industry as a whole and generalizes the determinants of relative share

---

[5] Michal Kalecki, *Theory of Economic Dynamics* (London, 1954), p. 12.

of wages in the economy as a whole. He goes through successive stages of aggregation to a general macrodistribution theorem. He concludes that, broadly speaking, the principal determinants of the relative share of wages in gross domestically produced national income are: (1) the degree of monopoly; (2) the ratio of prices of raw materials to unit wage costs; (3) the structural composition of the value of the gross income of the private sector. The degree of monopoly is the central determinant of the distribution of national output between wages and profits.

The Profit Equation

Kalecki singles out the development of marketing and high pressure sales-manship as the second crucial factor underlying the rise in the degree of monopoly. Sales promotion campaigns create or maintain consumer demand, protect the seller, and lead to high prices and profits to the detri-ment of the public, and account for the bulk of wastefulness of market imperfections. In this he anticipates John Kenneth Galbraith. Kalecki considers two other factors influencing the degree of monopoly. The degree of monopoly may rise as a consequence of a rise of overheads in relation to prime costs incurring constriction of profits, unless the ratio of proceeds to prime costs is allowed to rise. Then there is the influence of the trade union's power.

All this can be summed up in Kalecki's most famous contribution, his **profit equation**. He divides the economy into two groups: workers, who earn only wages and capitalists, who earn only profits. Workers do not save. The economy is closed (there is not international trade) and there is no public sector. He relaxes these assumptions, as noted above, in a more complicated model. With these assumptions Kalecki derives the account-ing identity:

$$P + W = C_W + C_P + I,$$

where P is the volume of gross profits (profits plus depreciation), W is the volume of total wages, C_P is capitalists consumption, C_W is workers consumption and I is the gross investment in the economy. Since workers do not save ($W = C_w$), we have

$$P = C_p + I.$$

This is the famous profit equation, which says that profits are equal to the sum of investment and capitalist's consumption. The capitalist's investment and consumption decisions determine profits. If we move capitalist consumption to the left, the equation becomes:

$$S = I.$$

The causal relation goes from investment to saving, rather than the other way round. In an open economy with a public sector, we have

$$P_N = C_p + I + D_g + E_e - Sw.$$

In this model total profits (net taxes) are the sum of capitalist consumption, investment, public deficit, net external surplus (exports minus imports) minus workers savings. Investment is decided by a combination of many factors difficult to explain, which are considered given, exogenous. Regarding capitalist consumption, he considers that a simplified form is the following:

$$C_p = A + qP.$$

That is, capitalism consumption depends on a fixed part, the term A, and a proportional share of profits, the term q, which is called the marginal propensity to consume of the capitalists. Substituting the consumption function into the profit equation, we have

$$P = A + qP + I.$$

Finally, if everything is reduced to P, we have

$$P = (A + I)/(1 - q),$$

whereby profits are decided by investment, after all. If the capitalists are so greedy that they consume at the margin all of their income, then profits would be zero. This is an unlikely scenario. The marginal propensity to consume is more likely .5. Then, investment determines profits.

This bring us full circle to the overall income distribution. Firms set a markup on variable average costs (raw materials, wages of employees on the shop floor that are variable in order to cover their overhead cost (salaries to senior management and administration) to obtain a certain amount of profit. The markup fixed by firms is higher or lower depending on the degree of monopoly, or the ease with which firms raise the price without reducing the quantity demanded. This is summarized in the equation,

$$P + B = k(W + M),$$

Where P and W are again profits and wages, k is the average markup for the whole economy, M is the cost of raw materials, and B is the total amount of salaries (which must be distinguished from wages, since these are variables and salaries are considered fixed). The preceding allows us to derive the wage share in the national income. If we add $P + B$, and pass one to the other side, we have:

$$Y = k(W + M) + W.$$

Multiplying each side by W, we have

$$a = W/(W + k(W + M)$$

or, which is the same,

$$a = 1/(1 + k(1 + j),$$

where a is the wage share in the national income and j is the relation between the cost of raw materials and wages. It necessarily follows that the wage share in the national income depends negatively on the markup and on the relationship of raw material costs to wages. During recession, firms collaborate to cope with the fall of profits, so the degree of monopoly increases and this increases the markup. The k parameter goes up. Nonetheless the lack of demand during recession causes a fall in the price of raw materials, so the *j* parameter goes down. The opposite happens during the boom: prices of raw materials rise (*j* parameter increases) while the strength of unions causes the degree of monopoly to fall and thereby the markup level to decline. The *a* parameter is roughly constant over the cycle. We can further state

$$1 - a = (P + B)/Y,$$

which says that the share of profits and sales are the complement of the share of wages. Solving for *Y*,
we have

$$Y = (P + B)/(1 - a).$$

Now we have three components necessary to determine total product: an equation of profits, a theory of the income distribution, and an equation that links the product with profits and income distribution. Substitute the equation of *P* and

$$Y = [(I + A)/(1 - q) + B]/(1 - a).$$

The above equation shows the determination of income in a closed system without a public sector. It shows that output is completely determined by investment. Put the equation in terms of changes, and we have the multiplier:

$$dY = dI/(1 - q)(1 - a).$$

Changes in output and hence the business cycle is due to changes in the volume of business investment. We look to investment to find the reason for the fluctuations of a capitalist economy. Unlike Keynes theory, Kalecki's has the income distribution as an integral part of the story. The value of the multiplier is decided by the ratio of changes in GDP and changes in investment, so

$$dY/dI = (1 - q)(1-a).$$

Need we say it, investment plays a crucial role in a capitalist system. What determines investment? Kalecki's investment function is

$$D = aS + b(dP/dt) - c(dK/dt) + e,$$

where D is the amount of investment decisions in fixed capital, a, b and c are parameters that specify a linear relation, e is a constant which can vary in the long run, P are profits, S is the gross saving generated by the firm, and K is the stock of fixed capital. Thus, investment decisions are based on the savings generated by the firm, on the rate of change of profits and a constant subject to long-term change, and negatively on the increase of fixed capital. This equation is able to generate cycles. During booms, firms are able to generate more cash-flow and enjoy increases in profits. However, the increase in orders for capital investment increases the stock of capital, until it proves unprofitable to make more investments. Ultimately, the variation in the level of investment generates the business cycles. We would expect to find variations in gross business investment to be highly correlated with variations in GDP. This indeed is what we see for the USA in Figure 7.2.

The USA is clearly an economy of surpluses. Whether necessities are a constant or variable market basket of goods and services, their quantities and market prices will determine their value and the required value of the money wage bill. For example, in the autumn of 1978, the Bureau of Labor Statistics (BLS) estimated the annual cost of a "lower" consumption budget for a four-person family in the urban United States at $8,162. If $8,152 represented the cultural subsistence requirements for an average family in the urban United States, the wage bill paid to the household had to be at least $8,162.[6]

Although it cannot be denied that there are many American households that exist at the biological subsistence level, Galbraith's affluent society is indisputably an economy of surpluses. The estimate for the "higher" consumption budget for a four-person family in the urban United States in

---

[6]The content of the BLS budgets is based upon the manner of living and actual consumer choices in the 1960s. The nutritional and health standard, as determined by scientists and nutritionists, are used for the food-at-home and housing components.

Table 7.3 Income before Taxes: Average Annual Expenditures and Characteristics, Consumer Expenditure Survey, 2001–2002

Item	All consumer units	Complete reporting of income											
		Total complete reporting	Less than $5,000	$5,000 to $9,999	$10,000 to $14,999	$15,000 to $19,999	$20,000 to $29,999	$30,000 to $39,999	$40,000 to $49,999	$50,000 to $59,999	$60,000 to $69,999	$70,000 to $89,999	$90,000 and over
Number of consumer units (in thousands)	111,223	90,559	3,991	6,946	8,053	7,035	12,194	10,617	8,805	7,220	5,779	8,195	11,723
Consumer unit characteristics:													
Income before taxes 1	$48,484	$48,484	$1,640	$7,700	$12,403	$17,305	$24,495	$34,439	$44,431	$54,507	$64,478	$78,619	$140,150
Income after taxes 1	45,780	45,780	1,571	7,700	12,409	17,184	23,973	33,322	42,436	51,864	61,116	73,971	128,941
Age of reference person	48.1	48.0	39.1	52.6	55.7	53.0	50.0	47.2	45.8	45.1	45.0	44.7	46.0
Average number in consumer unit:													
Persons	2.5	2.5	1.7	1.6	1.9	2.1	2.3	2.5	2.6	2.8	2.9	3.1	3.2
Children under 18	.7	.7	.4	.4	.5	.5	.6	.6	.7	.8	.8	.9	.9
Persons 65 and over	.3	.3	.2	.4	.5	.5	.4	.3	.2	.2	.2	.1	.1
Earners	1.4	1.4	.8	.5	.7	.9	1.1	1.4	1.5	1.7	1.9	2.0	2.1
Vehicles	2.0	2.0	1.0	.9	1.1	1.5	1.6	1.9	2.1	2.4	2.6	2.9	2.9

(Continued)

Percent distribution:

Sex of reference person:													
Male	51	51	42	33	35	43	49	53	55	58	61	63	63
Female	49	49	58	67	65	57	51	47	45	42	39	37	37
Housing tenure:													
Homeowner	66	65	32	41	51	54	58	63	69	76	80	82	91
With mortgage	40	40	13	12	12	17	26	36	46	55	60	65	76
Without mortgage	26	25	19	29	39	36	32	27	23	20	19	17	15
Renter	34	35	68	59	49	46	42	37	31	24	20	18	9
Race of reference person:													
Black	12	12	16	19	15	15	13	12	11	10	8	8	5
White and other	88	88	84	81	85	85	87	88	89	90	92	92	95
Education of reference person:													
Elementary (1-8)	6	6	8	16	13	11	8	4	4	2	1	2	1
High school (9-12)	38	38	35	50	50	50	47	42	38	33	32	27	15
College	56	56	57	33	37	39	45	53	58	65	66	71	85
Never attended and other	(2)	(2)	(2)	(2)	(2)	1	(2)	(2)	(2)	(2)	(2)	(2)	(2)
At least one vehicle owned or leased	88	88	61	61	72	85	90	94	96	97	98	98	97

(*Continued*)

Table 7.3 (*Continued*)

Item	All consumer units	Total complete reporting	Complete reporting of income										
			Less than $5,000	$5,000 to $9,999	$10,000 to $14,999	$15,000 to $19,999	$20,000 to $29,999	$30,000 to $39,999	$40,000 to $49,999	$50,000 to $59,999	$60,000 to $69,999	$70,000 to $89,999	$90,000 and over
Average annual expenditures	$40,102	$41,988	$20,117	$16,562	$20,780	$25,033	$28,733	$35,262	$41,351	$47,668	$53,567	$60,740	$87,292
Food	5,348	5,637	3,490	2,963	3,323	3,765	4,423	4,976	5,703	6,395	7,087	7,736	9,805
Food at home	3,092	3,235	2,093	1,978	2,263	2,504	2,835	3,071	3,365	3,568	3,749	4,271	4,729
Cereals and bakery products	451	476	309	294	343	379	419	440	478	517	549	618	712
Cereals and cereal products	155	163	121	111	120	136	145	152	170	173	183	202	236
Bakery products	296	312	188	183	223	243	274	289	308	344	366	416	476
Meats, poultry, fish, and eggs	813	842	583	540	619	675	774	833	859	924	948	1,082	1,147
Beef	240	251	166	156	172	198	240	264	244	280	278	332	337
Pork	172	180	135	132	143	160	172	176	176	202	192	227	219
Other meats	102	105	65	68	80	85	99	101	105	111	127	138	141
Poultry	148	153	105	87	116	118	133	143	163	174	191	198	210

Fish and seafood	117	117	84	70	79	82	94	111	130	120	123	146	200
Eggs	34	36	28	26	30	32	37	37	40	37	37	40	41
Dairy products	330	348	213	213	225	275	304	325	375	385	404	484	504
Fresh milk and cream	131	140	96	93	102	122	133	136	150	150	157	180	179
Other dairy products	199	209	116	119	123	153	172	189	225	235	247	304	325
Fruits and vegetables	537	557	359	335	407	443	501	527	565	595	624	723	824
Fresh fruits	169	174	117	108	125	135	158	159	174	184	187	222	273
Fresh vegetables	168	175	111	99	129	137	159	169	177	187	199	227	258
Processed fruits	116	120	80	72	88	97	108	114	119	129	137	163	172
Processed vegetables	84	88	51	56	65	74	77	85	97	96	101	111	120

1975 was $17,048, more than twice the lower budget. In an affluent economy, we need to identify the hierarchy of absolute physical necessities and "wants." Society imposes a rank order, because satisfaction of a greater number of wants is usually associated with higher standard of living.

There is a certain regularity in the way that most household allocate expenditures on food, clothing, transportation, and other items. The poor, for example, spend their incomes primarily on physiological necessities. After these same needs are met by the nonpoor, the discretionary income remaining meets "needs' or wants that are difficult to pigeonhole. The uncertainty increases as we shift focus away from specific needs, such as the need to be clothed toward the particular way these needs and wants are met, such as attempts to be fashionably dressed. Though households tend to eat more (and sometimes better) as income increases, there is a limit to the amount of extra money that people spend on food as incomes rise. That is, beyond the income level that meets basic nutritional needs, food expenditures as a share of the household budget grows slowly. This general behavior was first identified as Engel's law.

Discretionary income is to consumption what physical surplus (overcapacity) is to production. Budget shares in Galbraith's system are to consumption what production prices are to production in Sraffa's system. Budget shares lead to an understanding of nonprice competition that is lost when disputes ae confined to market pricing. Snob appeal takes on concrete meaning in the face of the one-to-two ratio of the subsistence to the "higher" consumption budget. The large gap between the lowest and highest incomes inspires the corporate structure to transcend the role of simple producer of goods and services. Although the difference between the consumer's physiological necessities budget and the higher income budget could in theory be devoted entirely to savings, the corporation tries to divert these household dollars toward consumer goods and services. The producers create many of the wants they seek to satisfy, an economic phenomenon Galbraith (1958) calls the *dependence effect*. Not surprisingly, in such an economy, a large share of the GNP subsidizes salespeople, marketing efforts, and advertising. Only in the affluent society can wants be created in a Galbraithian manner. As Galbraith (1967, p. 207) notes, "Mass communication was not necessary when the wants of the masses were anchored primarily in physical need. The masses could not then be persuaded as to their spending — this went for basic foods and shelter."

All this is to say that the budget shares change across the income distribution. This is evident in Table 7.3. The income intervals vary from a low of less than $5,000 to $90,000 and over for 2001–2002. Those reporting income of $70,000 and over are clearly in the supra-surplus range. They enjoy more and a greater variety of foods in their diets. They are more likely to dine out in fine restaurants. They also are more likely to be a homeowner. For the $90,000 and above, their education likely includes college. Budget shares across the income distribution is a Sraffian–Kaleckian way of looking at the economy. And it is instructive.

Sraffa's and Kalecki's focus was on production and the income distribution. Demand generally was a "given." Next, we consider what demand would look like in a manner consistent with budget shares across the income distribution.

Chapter 8

VEBLENIAN DEMAND AND ENGEL'S LAW

Where demand is influenced by advertising, salesmanship, marketing and other forces, the orthodox theory of demand will not suffice. For help, we turn to Thorstein Veblen. Veblen has contributed such evocative terms as "conspicuous consumption, conspicuous emulation," "pecuniary culture," "vicarious consumption," and "the leisure class" to the language of economics. Though little noted, and not yet celebrated, important improvements in demand theory have emanated from *The Theory of the Leisure Class* (hereafter TLC). Since the enduring Veblenian contributions to our language are related to consumption it is hardly surprising that even the mainstream has ratified Veblen with "Veblen effects."

Several of the author's phrases have resurfaced in *Bartlett's Familiar Quotations*, greatly elevating their stature. Three lengthy Veblen quotations made the 1980 edition, all from TLC. Notable for the task at hand, all the quotations are relevant to demand theory at both the micro- and macro-levels Their worthiness bears reprinting: the first, "Conspicuous consumption of valuable goods is a means of reputability to the gentleman of leisure." The second, slightly longer, is: "With the exception of the instinct of self-preservation, the propensity for emulation is probably the strongest and most alert and persistent of the economic motives proper." Bartlett's devotes even greater space to the third citation.

> The requirement of conspicuous wastefulness is not commonly present consciously, our canons of taste, but it is none the less present as a constraining norm selectively shaping and sustaining our sense of what is beautiful, and guiding our discrimination with respect to what may legitimately be approved as beautiful and what may not.[1]

In addition to the exquisite styling, these quotations are remarkable, too, for the phrases Veblen bequeathed to the English language. I will show how they have instructed mainstream economics and economics against the stream, to use Gunnar Myrdal's facile expression. In great part, Veblen endured because he illuminated modern supra-surplus society, a society still very much intact, with evolutionary electricity. We first will walk through the mainstream and, then, seek alternative vistas.

On and Off the Bandwagon

Veblen entered the mainstream in a classic article by Harvey Leibenstein on "bandwagon, snob, and Veblen effects."[2] Leibenstein distinguishes between *functional demand* or demand for a commodity due to the qualities inherent in the commodity and *nonfunctional demand* or the portion of demand due to qualities external to it. In nonfunctional demand the utility derived from the commodity is enhanced or decreased because others are purchasing and consuming the same commodity or because the commodity bears a higher rather than a lower price tag.

The bandwagon, snob, and Veblen effects are due to external effects on utility. The bandwagon effect derives from the demand for

---

[1] The three quotations are from John Bartlett, Emily Morison Beck, ed. *Bartlett's Familiar Quotations*, 15th Edition (Boston: Little Brown and Company, 1980) [1855], p. 685.

[2] Harvey Leibenstein "Bandwagon, Snob and Veblen Effects in the Theory of Consumer's Demand," *Quarterly Journal of Economics*, 1950. The article was widely reprinted including its appearance in Edwin Mansfield ed. *Microeconomics: Selected Readings*, 3rd edn (New York and London: W. W. Norton, 1971), pp. 12–30.

a commodity increasing because others, too, are consuming the same commodity. Social taboos that effect consumption are bandwagon effects in reverse. When the wagon leaves the station, those practicing a social taboo forbidding that particular good will refuse to get on the wagon. The snob effect derives from the demand for a commodity decreasing because others are also consuming or increasing their consumption of the same commodity. The snob effect has an opposite but otherwise symmetrical relationship to the bandwagon effect. The snob jumps off the wagon because they do not want to associate with those jumping on. The "Veblen effect" refers to conspicuous consumption in which the demand for a consumer's good is increased because it bears a higher rather than a lower price (upward sloping demand segment).

Leibenstein advances the principle of diminishing marginal external consumption effect. This principle suggests that beyond a point, incremental increases in the demand for a commodity by others will have a decreasing influence on a consumer's own demand and, eventually, a zero influence. Not only do incremental increases in total demand command smaller and smaller shares of a larger and larger market demand but there are no cases in which an individual's demand for a good is infinite. Moreover, the income constraint guarantees that a consumer's demand increases eventually will cease. Taking all these influences into account, the most plausible demand curve is shaped like a backward *S* wherein the schedule is upward sloping against price in some range, a range exhibiting the "Veblen effect." At some higher price for the good, the budget constraint would preclude further amounts being demanded; at some low price the good's reason for conspicuousness disappears. From these behaviors emanate the backward S.

Veblen rides the bandwagon much further than Leibenstein. Emulation dominates Veblen's Chapter VII on "Dress as an Expression of the Pecuniary Culture," where he writes that "admitted expenditure for display is more universally practiced in the matter of dress than in any other line of consumption" (p. 167). We can imagine hundreds of thousands of women jumping on the shoe-store wagon, as Veblen writes, "the woman's shoe adds the so-called french heel to the evidence of enforced leisure afforded by its polish; because this high heel obviously makes any, even the simplest and most necessary manual work extremely difficult" (p. 171). Of course, much more complex and subtle sociology is at work in TLC, including the woman's service as a "chief ornament" around the house and an adequately-adorned "trophy" for her husband.

Emulation too, can explain why persons buy high-priced goods that otherwise might fail to be identified as those preferred by a higher social class. What Leibenstein calls the "Veblen effect" is only one element in the complex matrix of emulation. For a large set of reasons, persons buy more of some goods despite not because their prices are higher. In Veblen, the excessive expense of such goods comes from the cost of production side. As he writes "there are today no goods supplied in any trade which do not contain the honorific element in greater or less degree" (p. 157). "Honorific" refers to the amount of cost in excess of what goes to give goods serviceability for their ostensible mechanical purpose. The "proper honorific finish" is more important than price.

When it comes to emulation, the rich are more likely to take note of the higher prices of luxury goods than the middle-class emulator seeking status at any cost. In Veblen's perspective, too, "function" is in the eye of the beholder; a good conferring status serves a higher social purpose. Still, in Leibenstein's and his follower's interpretation, persons increase their demand for status goods only because they have higher prices. In this way Leibenstein set the standard for most of the mainstream contributions on prestige or status goods. There are those in the upper middle class or even middle class who want to emulate the rich leisure class but must do so by buying cheap imitations or by borrowing even at the risk of bankruptcy or worse, which might be called the "Gatsby effect." The Gatsby effect, of course, intimates disasters beyond bankruptcy from which recovery *is* possible.

The Great Gatsby: Parable of Conspicuous Consumption

F. Scott Fitzgerald's *The Great Gatsby* is the supreme Veblenan parable of conspicuous consumption, of conspicuous emulation, of pecuniary culture, and of vicarious consumption — even of waste and the leisure class itself. Jay Gatsby wants to live with Daisy because she is a member of the established American aristocracy of wealth. Gatsby lacks the maturity to realize that Daisy cannot be obtained by money alone. Therefore, Gatsby flaunts in a vulgar version of conspicuous consumption, his *nouveau* wealth. Despite Daisy's infinite price, Gatsby is most attracted to Daisy's voice (not the supra-price), which he describes as "full of money," because that is the most unrealistic thing about her. Then, too, Daisy is attracted to Gatsby because he reminds her of "an advertisement," the superficial illusion he represents. In the end of course, Daisy cannot leave the trappings of the old aristocracy and Gatsby cannot escape the greatest Gatsby effect of all — paying the final price with his life. As in Veblen's *TLC*, the cultural illusions are more important than wealth or money for Fitzgerald's central characters.

As to snobbery, Fitzgerald's Gatsby again provides instruction. Tom and Daisy Buchanan live in a Georgian Colonial mansion representing established wealth. Gatsby, not unlike the early Robber Barons, owns a pretentious, vulgar imitation of a European mansion, adorned even in brand-new ivy. Even Gatsby's ivy is not in the same league as the Buchanan's. It is clear to the establishment that Gatsby, having no sense of tradition, simply copies the style of others much as an American university erects a library based on a medieval Gothic chapel. Worse, Gatsby's sartorial choice is as vulgar and nouveau as his cream-colored car, his mansion and his lavish parties. Daisy could never leave Tom for Gatsby because she and Tom are partners in a "secret society" of wealth, one that Gatsby cannot enter because he does not know it Neither this cultural richness nor the culture of the rich can be entirely captured with Leibenstein's downward shifting demand curves of individual "snobs" reducing their demands for a good because too many others are buying it.

Deep into the mainstream, Bagwell and Bernheim deal with the Veblenian cases that Leibenstein excludes. "In a theory of conspicuous consumption that is faithful to Veblen's analysis," they write, "utility should be defined over consumption and status, rather than over consumption and prices." This does not make high price irrelevant, however, "the prices that one pays for goods may affect status in *equilibrium*."[3] Since individuals like Jay Gatsby consume conspicuously to advertise their

---

[3] Laurie Simon Bagwell and B. Douglas Bernheim, "Veblen Effects in a Theory of Conspicuous Consumption," *The American Economic Review*, 86(3), 1996, 350.

wealth, any relation between price and status should signal wealth. Otherwise "invidious comparison" and pecuniary emulation" cannot happen, terms insinuating a rank-order in the distribution of wealth. The upper class invites invidious comparison with the lower class whereas the lower class "emulates" the upper class. The upper class, of course hopes that its costs are sufficiently prohibitive to the lower class that emulation is discouraged, especially by the *nouveau riche*. Bagwell and Bernheim use game theory to explain the consequences of these upper-class and lower-class interdependences.[4]

Three findings from Bagwell and Bernheim are persuasive. First they show that some individuals might prefer to purchase a larger quantity of conspicuous goods at a lower price or a higher quality of conspicuous goods at a higher price. For instance, social climbers do not have to be rich to buy Ralph Lauren's Polo brand clothes; yet, the label signals exclusivity. Moreover, if luxury brand "knock-offs" such as fake Rolex watches, Polo shirts, and King Cobra golf clubs can be distinguished from the "real things," the thrifty rich can have it both ways by buying the cheaper fakes. Veblen who often strolled golf courses looking for golf balls, none the less would expect the King Cobra "knock-offs" to have the proper workmanship and polish.

Second, Bagwell and Bernheim rebut the "single-crossing property" of models with asymmetric information. If we define the benefit ratio as the ratio of the utility gains from another unit of a conspicuous good, to the utility losses from another dollar of conspicuous expenditure, the benefit ratio is always higher for the upper-class households under the single-crossing property. (The indifference curves depicting the substitutability between inconspicuous and conspicuous goods are, contrary to neoclassical theory, concave rather convex to the origin. The "single crossing" occurs where the higher-income individual's indifference curve crosses the lower-income individual's indifference curve from below,

---

[4] Much of the foregoing and what is to follow is based on E. Ray Canterbery, *"The Theory of the Leisure Class"* and the Theory of Demand, in Warren Samuels, ed. *The Founding of Institutional Economics* (London and New York: Routledge, 1998), pp. 139–256, reprinted in E. Ray Canterbery, *Beyond Conventional Economics* (Singapore/London/New Jersey: World Scientific, 2016), Chapter 24.

reflecting the possibilities for cheap emulation.) Contrary to the single-crossing property, Bagewell and Bernheim show that the upper-class households can increase their utilities, without causing imitation, by purchasing more of the conspicuous good at a lower price.

Third, they show that households' conspicuous consumption need not be affected by bankruptcy if the conspicuous good cannot be repossessed (normally, such is the case for a house even if it is ostentatious). There is a catch, a kind of "Catch 11:" If the lower class imitates the upper-class households by making their every luxury goods purchase, they would default on their loans foreclosing imitation and foregoing the property protection under Chapter 11. Such an ultimate, even irrational, economic loss — the failure to retain what was purchased as well as the means of pursuit — nonetheless does not exclude what I have called the Gatsby effect, wherein bankruptcy is its mildest manifestation. As it turned out, Gatsby could not preserve the Daisy he pursued nor the means of pursuit, himself.

Bagwell and Bernheim's use of game theory becomes an apt metaphor when we reconsider Fitzgerald's parable. Daisy's insincerity betrays her desire to play games with her husband, Gatsby, and others, rather than participate in life where she would be responsible for her actions. Empty gestures signal more to her than genuine emotions. At the center of the American dream as well as Gatsby's own is the belief that sufficient wealth can recapture and fix everything, even the ephemeral, illusory qualities of youth and beauty. Veblen, too, was writing about the great American chimeras.

Though Bagwell and Bernheim do not explore price elasticities, Leibenstein suggests important implications for the price elasticity of demand as well as the nonadditivity of individual into collective demand curves. If the bandwagon effect dominates, the demand curve is more elastic since reactions to price changes are followed by other reactions, in the same direction. If the snob effect dominates, the demand curve is less elastic since increases in total amounts consumed because of price reductions are countered by some snobs leaving the market. If Leibenstein's "Veblen effect" dominates, the demand curve is less elastic than otherwise, and in part may be positively sloping, making stable equilibrium improbable.

The more important implication — one that pervades Veblen, but eludes Leibenstein — is the critical role of household incomes or the ability to sustain a particular standard of living. If snob effects and conspicuous consumption are truly important, income elasticity overwhelms price effects and price becomes unimportant except as it effects relative real incomes. Moreover, the only constraints keeping persons off the wagon are income and social tabus. If price becomes sufficiently unimportant, the need for price theory (and neoclassical markets) evaporates. This conclusion was not lost on the neoclassicals during the early 20th century in their pursuit of hegemony or later, in their snubbing of Leibenstein, though he was closer to the mainstream than was Veblen. If income dominates and price is pushed into the background, than Engel curves began to replace orthodox demand curves.

Econometric Estimates of Elasticities

Going mainstream implies econometrics. Econometric tests claiming to estimate "Veblen effects," however, are sufficiently rare to be an endangered species. Nonetheless a small but substantial effort was made by Basmann, Molina, and Sloittje.[5] They employ Veblen's distinction between primary consumption and secondary consumption. Rather than functional and non-functional qualities of commodities, however, Basmann *et al.* define consumption effects in utility language. *Primary utility* comes from the direct enhancement of life and well-being on the whole though consumption; *secondary utility* comes from consumption that displays consumer's relative ability to pay, a feature of consumption they ascribe to "Veblen effects."

Primary utility is measured from own-use elasticities. Secondary utilities relate to total expenditures, a proxy for real income (that leads to Engel curves). Since ability to pay drives Veblen effects, such effects prevail over all social classes from the richest to the poorest. Otherwise, Veblenian emulation is not possible. Capturing both effects, according to Basmann *et al.* requires the use of a Fechner–Thurstone direct utility

---

[5]R. L. Basmann, D. J. Molina, and D. J. Slottje, "A Note on Measuring Veblen's Theory of Conspicuous Consumption," *Review of Economics and Statistics*, 77(3), 1988, 532–535.

function. Using this function, the authors can estimate both kinds of elasticities. A relatively large and statistically significant elasticity for durables with respect to total expenditures is found. We would expect this for automobiles. The lowest elasticity with respect to expenditures is for medical services. The results are consistent with Veblen effects since durables are the most visible items consumed and medical services the least visible. The greatest medical expenditures usually happen during the final 3 to 6 months of life. Since the rich cannot escape mortality, no matter how much they spend on medical services, even their expenditures are price inelastic. As categories, we would expect, even without the benefit of econometrics, that food and medical services would have lower price elasticities than durables (whose expected lives greatly exceed 6 months).

The Engel Curve

We have discovered that the total expenditures for a good or household income is important in determining demand. The Engel curve describes how household expenditure on a particular good or service varies with household income. There are two varieties of Engel curves. Budget share Engel curves describe how the proportion of household income spent on a good varies with income. Alternatively, Engel curves can describe how real expenditure varies with household income. They are named after the German statistician Ernst Engel (1821–1896), who was the first to investigate this relationship systematically in 1857. The best-known result states that the poorer a family is the greater the budget share it spends on nourishment.

In budget share form, the Engel curve can be expressed mathematically as

$$w_i = h_i[\log(y), z],$$

where w_i is the fraction of y that is spent buying good i and y is household income. Alternatively, the real expenditure equation would be

$$q_i = g_i(y, z),$$

where q_i is the quantity consumed of good i, y is income, wealth, or total expenditures on goods and services, and z is a vector of other characteristics of the consumer, such as age and household composition.

Using data from Belgian surveys of working class families, Ernst Engel (1857, 1895) studied how households expenditures on food vary with income. He found that food expenditures are an increasing function of income and of family size but that food budget shares decrease with income. This relationship of food consumption to income known as Engel's law has since been found to hold in most economies and time periods.

Engel curves can be used to calculate a good's income elasticity, which is roughly the percent change in q_i that results from a 1 percent change in y, or doing the math, $g_i(y, z)/d\log(y)$. Goods with income elasticities below zero, between zero and one, and above one are called inferior goods, necessities, and luxuries respectively, so by these definitions what Engel found is that food is a necessity. Elasticities can vary with income, for example, a good that is a necessity for the rich can be a luxury for the poor. The slope of the Engel curve also can tell us whether a good is inferior or normal. If the slope is positive, the good is a normal good; if the slope is negative, the good is an inferior good because consumption decreases as income rises.

Figure 8.1 shows how an Engel curve can be constructed from the income expansion path. Figure 8.2 shows an Engel curve for a normal good. Figure 8.3 is an example of an Engel curve with both normal good and inferior good segments. After income increases past 100, Good X shifts to being an inferior good. Movies might be an example of a good that becomes inferior at high income levels.

When we go from needs to wants, things can become complicated. Some expenditures do not serve their specific needs are incurred by consumers in the process of satisfying other needs. There exists an order amongst needs but also another type of order amongst goods: some goods directly satisfy the consumer's needs while others are used by consumers to satisfy needs in a more indirect fashion. Engel's expenditure categories are well-defined and rank-ordered; they are nourishment, clothing, housing, heating and lighting, tools for work, intellectual education, public safety, health and recreation, and personal services.

What shapes of Engel curves are found for different categories of products? Sulgham and Zapata have estimated six curves with U.S.

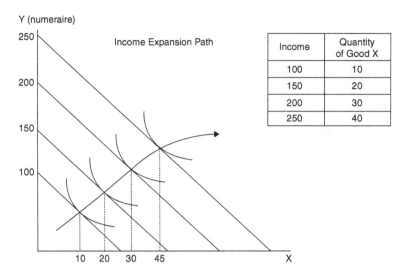

Figure 8.1   This shows an Income Expansion Path for Goods X and Y with four points of consumer's optimum shown. Good Y is a numeraire (priced at 1) and the relevant points for forming an Engel Curve are in the table to the right of the income Expansion Path.

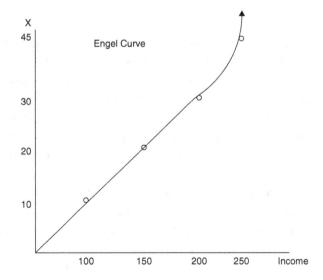

Figure 8.2   The Engel curve is formed plotting the quantities of Good X consumed at the varying incomes presented in the Income Expansion Path in Figure 7.b.1. As income increases, the quantity of Good X continues to increase. Good X is a Normal Good.

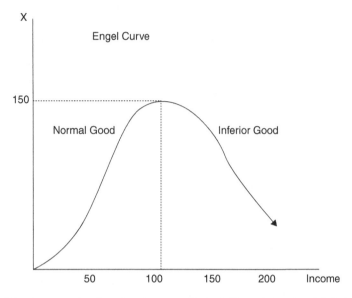

Figure 8.3 An example of an Engel curve with both Normal Good and Inferior Good segments. After income increases past 100, Good X shifts to being an Inferior Good.

micro data.[6] These curves are represented in Figure 8.4. The Engel curve for food shows it to be in all income ranges an inferior good. The shares allocated to food decline as income rises. For the other curves, there exists an inferior, normal, and luxury range. Alcohol begins as an inferior good, becomes a normal good and then a luxury good at high income levels. Clothing begins as a normal good and then at higher incomes is an inferior good. Transportation runs the gamut from normal good to inferior good at higher incomes. Recreation expenditures exhibit normal and inferior ranges, becoming an inferior good at high income levels. As to "Other Engel curves," these surprisingly are inferior goods except at very high incomes. As can be seen, there are some variations for a larger family (two kids).

Table 8.1 reveals budget shares in rank order for Belgian workmen's families in the original study by Engel. It shows that a hierarchy existed

---

[6] Anil K. Sulgham and Hector O. Zapata, "A Semiparametric Approach to Estimate Engel Curves Using the U.S. Micro Data," Paper at the American Agricultural Economics Association Annual Meeting, Long Beach, California, July 23–26, 2006.

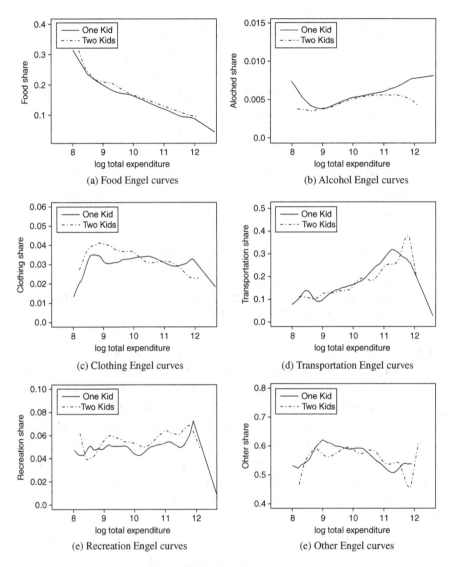

Figure 8.4   Other Engel curves.

Source: Sufis Home and Capita, *op. cit.*, p. 14.

amongst needs.[7] Orthodox neoclassical theory cannot account for how budget expenditure shares change in the face of rising income — as

---

[7] E. Engel, Die produtions- und coonsumtionsverhaltnisse des Konigreichs Sachsen, 1857. Reprinted in *Bull. Inst. Int. Stat* (1895).

Table 8.1   Budget Shares of Belgian Workmen's Families

Needs	Family type		
	On relief	Poor but independent	Comfortable
Nourishment	70.89	67.37	62.42
Clothing	11.74	13.16	14.03
Housing	8.72	8.33	9.04
Heating and lighting	5.63	5.51	5.41
Tools for work	0.64	1.16	2.31
Intellectual education	0.36	1.06	1.21
Public safety	0.15	0.47	0.88
Health and recreation	1.68	2.78	4.30
Personal services	0.19	0.16	0.40

Source: Lines 1–10: Table 6 in Engel (1857: 27) reprinted in Andreas Chai and Alessio Moneta, "At the Origins of Engel Curves Estimations", Research Gate, January 20, 2017, p. 154.

embodied in the basic shape of the Engel curve. Traditional theory deals only with infinitesimal changes and cannot be related to the general shape of Engel curves. Closely related to hierarchies is the idea of lexicographic ordering. Lexicographic preferences imply that the indifference curve is strictly vertical in certain regions, since consumers have no interest in substituting away from a certain good that serves first order needs until they have attained a critical quantity of this good. Only when this threshold is reached is it possible for consumers to substitute between this good and goods serving needs of a lower order.[8] We will return to this problem for an affluent society in Chapter 9.

Using UK household expenditure data spanning over four decades (1960–2000), Chai and Moneta use Engel's needs-based approach in analyzing household expenditure patterns.[9] The Chai–Moneta results

[8]A lexiographical system is developed in E. Ray Canterbery, "Inflation, Necessities and Distributive Efficiency" in J. H. Gapinski and C. E Rockwood, eds. *Essays in Post-Keynesian Inflation* (Cambridge, Mass.: Ballinger, 1979).
[9]Andreas Chai and Alesssio Moneta, "Back to Engel? Some evidence for the hierarchy of needs," *Journal of Evolutionary Economics* 22, 2012, 649–676.

Table 8.2 Budget Shares for the Lowest Income Decile, 1960–2000

Needs	1960	1970	1980	1990	2000
1. Nourishment	62	60	60	40	38
2. Clothing	8	9	10	9	9
3. Housing	1	1	1	13	17
4. Heating and lighting	6	5	4	6	9
5. Tools	7	7	7	7	6
6. Intellectual education	3	3	5 .	3	6
7. Public safety	1	0	1	0	0
8. Health and recreation	3	4	3	6	3
9. Personal services	2	2	1	1	0
10. All other	7	9	8	15	11

Note: Entries denote percent of total expenditure.
Source: Chai and Moneta, *op. cit.*, p. 661. See Footnote 9.

(in Table 8.2) are surprisingly similar to the Belgian results. These budget shares are for the lowest income decile, 1960–2000. Expenditure on nourishment for the poorest category of workers was roughly 71 percent of total expenditure in 1856, while in 1960 it was 62 percent of total expenditure. It took 104 years for the budget share to drop 9 percent — a century which witnessed unprecedented economic growth in Europe and an eightfold increase in world per capita income. The budget share for heating and lighting in the contemporary data also appears to be roughly the same of what it was in the 19th century, although more recently this has increased which reflects the rising price of energy services. This evidence suggests that a stable pattern of expenditure does exist at the lowest levels of household income, which has remained stable in spite of the growth in real household income, as well as the goods and services available to households. These results are highly correlated with those of 1870 in the USA as well (Table 8.1).

Table 8.3 shows budget shares for the *highest* income decile for 1960–2000. As predicted by Engel's Law, food expenditure is much lower relative to low income households. Also, in the lowest income decile there is a very uneven distribution of expenditure as most of the expenditure is

Table 8.3   Budget Shares for the Highest Income Decile, 1960–2000

Needs	1960	1970	1980	1990	2000
1. Nourishment	28	21	23	15	16
2. Clothing	15	9	10	8	8
3. Housing	17	16	18	15	25
4. Heating and lighting	2	2	1	0	9
5. Tools	17	7	10	14	10
6. Intellectual	3	3	4	5	3
7. Public safety	2	1	0	2	0
8. Health and recreation	7	11	9	7	9
9. Personal services	2	2	2	1	2
10. All other	8	29	24	33	18

Note: Entries denote percent of total expenditure.
Source: Chai and Moneta, *op. cit.*, p. 663.

concentrated in providing nourishment. At high income levels, household expenditure appears to be distributed much more evenly across the different expenditure categories. For both the lower and higher-income samples, the category, "All others," rises dramatically from 1960 to 2003. These represent truly discretionary expenditures and doubtless includes items that had not yet been invented in 1856. Otherwise the rank order of budget shares remains intact across Belgium, the United States, and the UK over time periods from 1856 through 2003. Engel's original categories show great intuition on his part.

All in all, these results reveal that income patterns of low income households are remarkably stable over several decades and across countries. This is a stability that could be attributed to the basic needs of the consumer which are the product of biological evolution. In particular, expenditure classified by Engel as being related to a group of needs that together constitute physical sustenance is significantly larger than expenditure on other lower order needs. In this regard Engel's law defines the basic needs of the poor. Moreover, lexicographic ordering is supported by these studies.

While biological needs always should be met, next we go beyond necessities to supra-surplus capitalism. We should not lose sight of Veblenian demand for it has a lot to do with prices and advertising.

Part III

SUPRA-SURPLUS CAPITALISM

Chapter 9

PRICES, ADVERTISING, AND POWER

Most economists would agree that Veblen's logical successor is John Kenneth Galbraith. Though Galbraith was a best-selling author, he is not mainstream among professional economists. Thorstein Veblen's influence on Galbraith's demand theory is most visible in *The Affluent Society*. Galbraith's "conventional wisdom," an established set of ideas used to explain the world and how it operates, providing stability, cohesion, meaning, and predictability in a highly complex environment parallels Veblen's "vested interests." Since, by its nature, the conventional wisdom denies a change in the environment, it always and everywhere lags behind the times. This "inertia and resistance" comprise Veblen's institutional lag.

In a sense, too, the wealthy had, in Galbraith's view, and despite institutional lag, eventually learned from Veblen. The power to redistribute wealth had shifted toward unions and government. This shift made it downright dangerous for the wealthy to flaunt their wealth by consuming conspicuously since such display increased the agitation by liberals to redistribute the wealth. Besides, the middle class now could emulate the rich in dress and even in automobiles especially as the rich downsized to Volvos. At the time, later to be recanted, Galbraith believed economic insecurity among the masses had greatly diminished.

Product Surpluses

Galbraith concealed behind the "much reduced urgency" of consumption the idea of economic surplus, the means whereby the remaining economic

137

insecurity could be banished. Production had now become the "solvent of the tensions once associated with inequality, and it has become the indispensable remedy for the discomforts, anxieties, and privations associated with economic insecurity." Enhanced production comes at the cost of paradox, or, in Galbraith's words, "as production has increased in modern times concern for production seems also to have increased."[1] We have become addicted to production, which goes a long way toward explaining supra-surpluses.

Galbraith invokes the image of a hierarchy of goods whereby those required for daily living are more important to the average consumer than luxuries. Such a view, long ago advanced by the Austrian Carl Menger and the German Ernst Engel, is a contradiction in neoclassical economics in which no rank ordering of goods according to biological need or psychological satisfaction is possible because cardinal utility is implied. Along with the hierarchy comes the Engel curve and Engel's Law in which consumption depends on income. The Engel curve replaces the Marshalian demand curve derived from price. As production surpluses mount (from rising productivity), consumers increasingly must be persuaded regarding adequate consumption. The producer must take on an ancillary role of synthesizing wants "by advertising, catalyzed by salesmanship." That wants are "shaped by the discreet manipulations of the persuaders show that they are not very urgent. A man who is hungry need never be told of his need for food."[2] Ostentatious display is impossible and advertising unnecessary without surpluses; in contrast, during the Gilded Age the rich engaged in self-advertisement.

The existence of economic surplus permeates Veblen's *The Theory of the Leisure Class* from beginning to end. "It has been customary in economic theory," writes Veblen, "to construe this struggle for wealth as being substantially a struggle for subsistence." However, he concludes, "industrial efficiency is presently carried to such a pitch as to afford something appreciably more than a bare livelihood to those engaged in the

---

[1] John Kenneth Galbraith, *The Affluent Society* (Boston: Houghton Mifflin, 1958), pp. 119–120.
[2] *Ibid.*, p. 158.

industrial process."[3] Without surpluses, of course, excesses — of which Veblen finds in themselves, a surfeit — cannot exist. The motive for wealth accumulation cannot be only the satisfaction of physical comfort but must evolve from pecuniary emulation. Put differently, a Jay Gatsby in pursuit of a Daisy must distinguish himself in money terms, even if it is money disreputable for its newness, if not for its source.[4]

In the end even "higher learning" is an expression by, of and for the pecuniary culture. Scholastic discipline conserves the habits of thought believed suitable by the leisure class. Only a leisure class can develop and pursue "esoteric" as well as "exoteric knowledge." The former comprises, as Veblen puts it, "such knowledge as is primarily of no economic or industrial effect, and the latter comprising chiefly of knowledge of industrial processes and of natural phenomena which were habitually turned to account of the material purposes of life." Esoteric knowledge becomes part of the surplus, in a sense being surplus knowledge. It serves the agenda of the leisure class by demarcation "between higher learning and the lower." Galbraith has followed Veblen's lead in his critiques of "higher learning" in economics. Veblen and Galbraith alike have viewed the economics orthodoxy as a system of pecuniary belief suffering serious institutional lag.

Veblen and Galbraith's animus is not so much for the classicals, but for the neoclasicals. After all, the classicals had workers being paid subsistence wages with subsistence often defined culturally. Wage goods provided subsistence. For those political economists, necessity was the mother of convention. The neoclassical economists, to the contrary, presume all income to be discretionary. Relieved of the burden of purchasing necessities, the imaginary consumers are "free to choose" any set of goods and services. Most important for the mathematics (and the theory) the assumption that necessities are unnecessary and luxuries are a special case, guarantees the convexity of indifference curves on which adequate budgets always yield marginal utility ratios.

---

[3] *Ibid.*, pp. 24–25
[4] For much more on Jay Gatsby and Daisy, see E. Ray Canterbery, *Scott: A Novel of F. Scott Fitzgerald* (London: Austin-Cauley, 2017).

Still, the idea that discretion is the better part of value is an incomplete account of supra-surplus capitalism. In a theoretical system of perpetual scarcity, the capitalist can barely be a prime mover. Any self-respecting capitalist is rightly embarrassed when they fail to produce a net surplus. Since the upper 1 percent now control nearly 40 percent of the USA's total household wealth a surplus must exist on the income side either in a reflection of production surplus or as rentier income. Though many American households exist at the biological subsistence level, American capitalism is indisputably an economy of surpluses. In the supra-surplus economy, a hierarchy of absolute physical necessities and "wants" coexist. "Higher standards of living" usually are associated with the satisfaction of a greater number of wants, not the satisfaction at the margin from one more unit of the same good. The wants of least urgency can be met only by those with incomes or credit sufficient to buy more than basic necessities, a hierarchy of needs and wants implying a lexicographical utility function in which budget constraints for lower-income persons eliminate lower-order goods.

Neoclassical economics has difficulty assimilating Veblen and Galbraith not only because utilities are interdependent or social, but also because surplus production pitted against the income and wealth distributions drives their economics. To the extent that prices are important to Veblen, their role is likely to be perverse; the amounts demanded of a luxury often rise with its price and the incomes of those who purchase it, though the causality need not run from higher price to greater consumption. Since emulation and display need not require a high income the purchases of "fakes" or labels imply inexplicable waste amid a neoclassical sea of undeniable efficiency. Still, the prices of authentic luxury goods are beyond the means of the middle class. For the neoclassicals poverty, like richness, cannot be explained except by marginal revenue products, which is not an explanation applicable to either extreme since the importance of the absolutes overwhelm that of the increments. Surpluses of course cannot exist in a system in which the quantities that producers are willing to supply exactly match those that consumers are willing to buy. For that matter, surpluses cannot exist where scarcity is the operative assumption defining economic theory. Neoclassical theory is about scarcity and the necessity of parsimony; Veblen and Galbraith's economics is about surpluses and the necessary implications of dreadful waste.[5]

Kalecki is primarily responsible for the introduction of imperfect competition into macroeconomic theory in Europe, a role performed by Sidney Weintraub in America. Galbraith's conception of the New Industrial State is consistent with both notions of pricing behavior. Kalecki's and Weintraub's vision of pricing in the manufacturing sector can be dramatized in one word: *markup*. The markup plays a strategic role in supra-surplus capitalism

The Markup and the Degree of Monopoly

According to Galbraith, firms in the manufacturing sector have sufficient market power to pass on to the consumer most cost increases as well as price increases required by investment needs. Somewhere between 75 and 90 percent of gross (including placement investment) fixed capital investment in the United states is financed from retained profits, the discretionary income of corporations. The giant firm has the power to select a percentage markup over production costs (mostly wages) that is sufficient to complete its investment plans most of the time without going hat in hand to a banker. This configuration serves the same purpose as Kalecki's capitalist plowing all profits back into the firm but, in Galbraith, the capitalist is replaced by the technostructure, that amorphous committee.

Capacity utilization may move up and down with the demand for products but the corporation will stick with the markup that will provide its target level of retained profits. This target depends upon its dividend payout ratio to stockholders, the amount of debt relative to its equity and most importantly its perceived investment needs. As long as the firm's capacity is sufficient to meet demand for its products and as long as production costs do not vary greatly from expectations, the firm will cling to that old rugged price derived from its careful planning. The margin of

---

[5] See especially John Kenneth Galbraith, *The Affluent Society* (New York: Houghton Miffliin Company, 1958, 1969, 1976, 1998) and Thorstein Veblen, *The Theory of the Leisure Class* (New York: Macmillan Company, 1899).

prices over current costs already reflects the market power of the giant corporation. This power is formidable.

Kalecki's measure of the "degree of monopoly" of the firm conforms neatly with Galbraithian power. The essence of the degree-of-monopoly formula is that a firm can raise its own price in proportion to its increase in production costs, if other firms in the industry do likewise. Non-price forms of competition displace price competition so that supply-side economics cannot remain simply the theory of price. As noted in Chapter 7, the markup formula is

$$k = 1 + (p - u)/u,$$

where k is the markup, p = price per unit of output, and u = unit prime costs. A brother or sister of Kalecki's degree-of-monopoly is Lerner's index of market power, or

$$L = (P - MC)/P,$$

where MC = the firm's marginal cost.

The Lerner Index is equivalent to the negative inverse of the formula for price elasticity of demand facing the firm, or

$$L = -1/E,$$

so there is some comfort here for the orthodox or Marshalian economist. At last, they can breathe easy because elasticities comprise much of the lifeblood of neoclassical economics. Besides, the concept is useful beyond conventional economics.

The markup and investment plans are inexorably linked. Because of the degree-of-monopoly influence, actual prices charged by the industrial firms do not reflect current demand conditions; they more closely mirror the funds requirements for the planned investment expenditure the technostructure deems sufficient to increase capacity (plant size or number of machines) to meet expected future demand. There is more to it than that. Such a markup serves the technostructure's affirmative purpose of growth; when costs of production rise the firm protects its profits-for-investment by raising prices according to its established markup over costs.[6] A fixed markup serves the technostructure's protective purpose. At times the capacity accumulated with these retained profits will be in excess of that needed to meet current demand but this situation is no problem for an oligopoly. Just as for the monopoly, the oligopoly wants to be ready to meet the wants of any purchasers. Supra-surplus capitalism also enjoys supra-surplus capacity. The technostructure, this shapeless organization, savors the bureaucratic advantage of over-capacity and hence power.

What of the overall price level and inflation? If money wages are administered by union-management agreements, the balance of income is provided by the markup over wages, most of which will be retained profits (profits plus depreciation) and dividend payouts. Once again, we are reminded that markup pricing typifies the supra-surplus economy. If this markup remains constant throughout the economy and productivity remains unchanged any cost increase from a boost in average wages will be reflected as an increase in the price level. A sustained period-over-period increase will comprise inflation. While inflation has not prevailed in recent times, it is always in the back of the mind of the central banker. In any case, in Galbraith there is a revised sequence in which the price level and the rate of inflation are resolved *after* the money wage rates and increases in prices are determined. Money wages — exogeneous or "outside" the theory in Sraffa — are endogenous in Galbraith but decided by social-political conditions, not by the technology of production. That the decisions are social or political make orthodox economists wince. Still, at this juncture, if Galbraith did not exist, he would have to be invented.

What is next required is the establishment of a connection among personal incomes, demand and production. In Galbraith, demand is, for the most part, managed by the corporation and the industry. Nonetheless, when demand shifts up or down since the neoclassical response of rising and falling

---

[6] The motivation for investment "needs" have been variously attributed to market share, growth and power goals. These explanations have been put forward, respectively, by Alfred S. Eichner, *The Megacorp and Oligopoly: Micro Foundations of Macro Dynamics* (Cambridge: Cambridge University Press, 1976); Robin Marris, *The Economic Theory of "Managerial" Capitalism* (New York: Basic Books, 1964) and John Kenneth Galbraith.

prices is absent, adjustments made by the firm are in *output* levels. If GM is not selling its inventory of cars at the current prices (based upon markup over unit prime costs) GM produces fewer Chevrolets next month and eventually may even lay off production workers. Rather than responding to lower demand by reducing prices giant producers reduce production levels.

Cultural Subsistence in Supra-surplus Capitalism

Where corporate and union powers exist in supra-surplus capitalism and are symbiotic, physiological subsistence for the labor class expands into cultural subsistence. Cultural subsistence becomes paramount when corporate power supersedes a weakening union movement. The notion of cultural subsistence brings the personal income distribution in line with a Galbraithian estate of consumption. The technology of production and the prevailing level of production capacity will decide the total potential output of two types of goods: now culturally "necessary" consumption goods and the requisite investment goods. The sales force and advertising of the corporation and retailers help to define culturally necessary goods. The requisite investment goods, given technical coefficients, are dictated by technology. However, realized output still depends upon effective demand and the income distribution.

The distribution of income between workers and "capitalists" reenters the picture, but in a more complex way than Kalecki would lead us to believe. There are two tugs-of-war between the manufacturers and the consumers–workers; producers seem unaware of one of them and workers of the other. Displaying the instincts attributed to corporate management by Galbraith, corporations create and stimulate new demand for their goods and services. However, in the planning system, the wherewithal to fulfill both the manufacturers' and the workers' dreams is decided at the labor-management bargaining table. Even when labor is weak, management still must negotiate wages and hours. Only in the guise of consumers are there any losers. Goodbye Adam Smith, in which consumers wear crowns.

The planning system has succeeded all too well in convincing consumers that they should expand the number of goods and services they consider necessary. In response to these culturally determined desires the giant labor union demands higher wages so that the workers can pay for the newly defined standard of living. Again, when labor unions are relatively weak, the corporation may have the upper hand. In any case, the corporation capitulates, knowing that anyy higher cost of production from a larger wage can be passed on to consumers. The illusion that a higher wage is always a good thing — a money illusion — is enjoyed by the workers, who don't quite sense the fallacy of composition in their dual role as both laborers and consumers. These increases merely cover the "cost of living." As Galbraith suggests, it is not mere historical accident that the highest paid workers reside in the protected part of the economy, the planning system.

If the process stopped at this point, the working class would increase its share of national income, at least in money terms, but the defensive power instrument of the manufactures is the markup. The concentrated industries can use the markup amplified by ready access to the largest banks and the lowest rates of interest, to generate funds for investment purposes. Throughout the history of capitalism, the idea that workers have to be employed in order to purchase the producers' goods often has eluded manufacturers. Though it is in the interest of any single producer to minimize his total wage bill, all producers succeeding in that calculus will find there is no outlet for their products. Henry Ford used this arithmetic when he paid his workers $5 an hour so that they could buy his automobiles.

Galbraith's technostructure replaces the Smithian market mechanism in the setting of prices. Now we know that prices comprise a markup on primary costs, mostly wages. The degree of monopoly power depends upon the ability to set this markup. The elasticity of the markup replaces the elasticity of price. Price, so essential to neoclassical economics, is displayed by the power of the technostructure in setting the markup. At last, with elasticity, we have a useful economic tool. While supply and demand curves, while conceptually elegant, populate microeconomics, it is the elasticity of supply or demand that compels out interest. Since elasticities involve ratios of percent changes, they have some universal value. So, the elasticity of the markup can displace the elasticity of price.

The Economics of Manipulation and Deception

George A. Akerlof and Robert J. Shiller, two Nobel Prize-winning economists, challenge the long-held belief that free markets provide us with material well-being, as if by an invisible hand. They argue that free markets harm as well as help us. As long as there is profit to be made, sellers will systematically exploit our psychological weaknesses and our ignorance through manipulation and deception. Rather than being benign and always creating the greater good, markets are filled with tricks and traps and "phish" us as "phools."[7] The 19th century was so busy for inventors — of the automobile, the telephone, the bicycle, the electric light — that the slot machine received very little attention. Akerlof and Shiller use the history of the slot machine to illustrate the dual view of the market economy. The market gave us something we always wanted but also gave us the slot machine with an addictive turn of the wheel that takes your money for the privilege. Most of their book is about slot-machines-bad, rather than about slot-machines-good, because as reformers both of economic thought and of the economy they seek to change not what is right with the world, but rather what is wrong.

First come the definitions. Rather than viewing phishing as illegal, they present a definition for something that is much more general. Phishing is about getting people to do things that are in the interest of the phisherman. Angling has a lot to do with it, about dropping an artificial lure into the water and waiting as wary fish swim by, make and error, and get caught. Of course, we the people are the fish. A phool is someone who is successfully phished. In one instance, the emotions of a psychological phool override the dictates of his common sense. In another case, cognitive biases, which are like optical illusions, lead him to misinterpret reality, and he acts on the basis of that misinterpretation. One may be self-aware of the situation at the slots, but unable to help oneself. As we might have guessed, Akerlof and Shiller are among the behavioral school of economists, and outside the mainstream. They are among those rejecting the "conventional wisdom," while they embrace "two great classics, Thorstein Veblen's *The Theory of the Leisure Class* and John Kenneth Galbraith's *The Affluent Society*."[8]

Not surprising, advertising plays a major role in "phishing for phools". Advertisers aim to enhance the sales of companies that hire them,

---

[7] George A. Akerlof and Robert J. Shiller. *Phishing for Phools: The Economics of Manipulation and Deception* (Princeton and Oxford: Princeton University Press, 2016).
[8] *Ibid.*, p. 230.

even if those sales reduce customers' well-being. I know this first-hand, having misspent part of my youth in the business (which included advertising Budweiser Beer and Jack Daniels Bourbon). Taken in moderation, of course, they may be no adverse side-effects from advertised products. Buyer, nonetheless, should beware. Besides, advertisers over the past century have developed scientific, statistical methods for measuring their effectiveness. Just as even Thomas Edison tested more than 1,600 materials for the filament for the light bulb, advertisers use trial and error to find out what causes people to buy what they are selling. For example, I used to sip Jack Daniels Black Label to make sure it was mellower than the Green Label. Of course, we backed up my sipping with that of many other sippers statistically.

I was a minor player compared with Albert Lasker, Claude Hopkins and David Ogilvy, whose storytelling is related by Akerlof and Shiller. Lasker rescued the Wilson Ear Drum Company with "DEAFNESS AND HEAD NOISES RELIEVED BY USING WILSON'S COMMON SENSE EAR DRUMS." This was accompanied in small print "New scientific invention, entirely different in construction from all other devices." This was soon followed by even bolder claims.[9] This device, while not quite invisible in the ear, was intended to replace a trumpet or tube. It was claimed that Wilson, himself deaf, now could hear as well as anyone. The improved copy for the advertising now included a man cupping his ear with his hand, with the expression of "the deafest man you ever saw." While Lasker's career was made, in 1913 the distinguished *Journal of American Medical Association* announced that "as a cure for deafness [a pair of Wilson Ear Drums was] not worth 5 cents."[10]

Claude Hopkins was more distinguished; he expanded the scope of advertising into modern-day marketing. In 1907 Hopkins was hired by Lasker and soon became the star of Lord and Thomas. Together, Lasker and Hopkins took many advertising campaigns. The successfully promoted Schlitz beer as being brewed uniquely, though it used the same

---

[9] *Ibid.*, pp. 47–48. My brief encounter with advertising was with Gardner Advertising Company, in their St. Louis office. They also had offices in New York City, as did Ogilvy.
[10] "The Propaganda for Reform," *Journal of the American Medical Association* 61(18), 1913, 1648.

process as other brewers. They invented the "beauty soap," advertising Palmolive as the one soap that dubiously could make women beautiful. They created the famous "Sunkist" orange, under a new trademark. Lord and Thomas and the California Fruit Growers Exchange developed, and distributed, electric and hand-glass juicers, direct from Sunkist, that pioneered orange juice.

David Ogilvy, after some successful advertising campaigns, founded his own agency, Ogilvy and Mather, which had clients such as General Foods, Bristol-Myers, Campbell's Soup, Lever Brothers, and Shell. Ogilvy is best known for "the man in the Hathaway shirt" campaign from the 1950s to 1970s. "The man" always had an eye patch and would be featured in different settings and different guises in *The New Yorker*, every week for several years. The sale of Hathaway shirts soared with the ads. Were they the best shirts on the market? Probably not, but men didn't care. Another famous Ogilvy campaign advertised the Rolls-Royce Silver Cloud as "At sixty miles an hour the loudest noise in this new Rolls-Royce comes from the electric clock." After that, clocks became a feature in "luxury" autos before seat belts became commonplace. The clocks were safe at any speed.[11]

Albert Lasker has the dubious distinction of being responsible for the election of Warren G. Harding as President of the United States. Going along for ride was Calvin Coolidge as Vice President, catapulting him into a subsequent failed presidency. Since Harding was a horrific on-the-stump campaigner, Lasker developed the strategy of keeping Harding in small-town Marion, Ohio, literally in his big white house with its wide front porch. The porch would be the stage playing on the public's exhaustion from Woodrow Wilson's "foreign entanglements." Better, a vote for Harding was a vote to "return to normalcy" after the Great War and the Depression of 1920–1921. The new normal was this friendly Republican on his comfortable front porch. It was a time when front porches were not only common but a popular place to commune with neighbors. His speeches concluded with "Let's be done with wiggle and wobble," which

---

[11] I have taken some liberties with the discussion in Akerlof and Shiller. For a complete account of the Lasker, Hopkins, and Ogilvy advertising stories, see, Akerlof and Shiller, *op. cit.*, pp. 46–52.

became a campaign motto. The new media played a role, as Lasker sent film clips to movie houses across the nation. Lasker brought the Chicago Cubs to Marion for an exhibition game, where Harding threw the first three pitches. If you build a big front porch for the Cubs, they will come.

What is so bad about a successful advertising campaign for President? According to anybody who counts, Warren G. Harding (during his short term of 1920–1923) was one of the worst Presidents in history, followed closely by Calvin Coolidge, on his coattails. Scholars rank Harding around 40th among 42 ranked Presidents. A recent CNN poll ranks him slightly better at 38th. For economists there is some irony in all this. A tax cut during the Harding administration helped to end the 1920–1921 Depression. Harding didn't have much to do with it. The tax plan was engineered by Secretary of the Treasury Andrew W. Mellon; Harding said he had no clue as to whether a tax increase or tax decrease was called for. As serendipity would have it, the misery index, which combines the unemployment rate and the inflation rate, had the greatest fall in its history during 1920–1923. The economy was growing at a robust 5 percent rate.

It has been said that the manipulations of one man, Michael Milken, in the 1970s and 1980s changed the face of USA finance forever. The leveraged buyout, where a raider's company could amass cash by taking on enormous debt (through high-yield, or "junk," bonds developed by Milken) to acquire, usually, a much larger company. The leveraged buyouts increased everything related to corporate mergers and acquisitions, notably risks, and potential payoffs. For example, in the leveraged buyout of RJR Nabisco, a $45.7 million golden parachute was given to Edward Horrigan, the CEO of the tobacco subsidiary; and a reputedly yet more capacious takeaway for Ross Johnson, the CEO of the whole company. An age of excess had begun. Many of the junk bonds of Milken failed later, resulting in what is now known as the junk bond crisis of the 1980s. Part of what happened is related to the role of misleading financial ratings, especially of corporate bonds.

This is but a narrow but important slice of the manipulation and deception uncovered by Akerlof and Shiller. The economic cases are related to the effect of illusions on price. The markup over "unit costs" can be greater, the bigger the illusion. Such pricing is not independent to the income distribution and inequality.

Chapter 10

THE VITA THEORY OF THE PERSONAL INCOME DISTRIBUTION AND POWER

Industries' ability to pay a demanded wage is enhanced by its ability to impose price markups on the consumers. The industrial union's power tool is the wage rate rather than the labor supply.[1] This means that, in the short run, employment is not related to the wage rate and the wage rate is related to employment only if full employment extends across all labor. Therefore, a high wage can be associated with a high unemployment rate, because employment is decided by technology and effective demand rather than by the marginal product of labor. This process was so deeply imbedded in the economic system that it too a four-year global recession (1979–1982) to slow wage (and price) inflation in the United States. History went into reverse beginning with the Great Recession (2007–2009), from which we have yet to experience a full recovery. Power was ceded by labor unions to the giant corporation.

---

[1] The modeling of economic power is practically nonexistent. Howard P. Tuckman and I made our attempt in E. Ray Canterbery and Howard P. Tuckman, "Toward a Theory of Power," American Economic Association Meetings, Washington DC, December 1974. It puts John Kenneth Galbraith's countervailing power into matrix algebra.

Wage Differentials

In the unskilled, non-organized labor market, there is little incentive or ability to substitute capital goods for labor as expected wages rates are low, and unskilled workers cannot operate complex machines. The long-run supply of unskilled workers is determined by non-wage elements. Few individuals actively strive to achieve characteristics that would yield low wages. Indeed, the unskilled might be viewed as failures so their long-term supply is a kind of residual unrelated to the current wage rates, a pool of waste. An unused supply of unskilled labor is a characteristic of recent experience in the industrialized countries of the USA, UK, France, and Japan. The wage differentials between skilled and the unskilled is the consequence of (at least) dual labor markets that reflect the duality between the planning system and the competitive system. At one extreme handling involves performing routine, non-machine tasks with little or no latitude for judgments. Physical stamina is required. The work is usually so elemental in nature that no previous training is required. Wages are rock-bottom.

Technological change — unpredictable and not widely understood — plays a major role. Its impact is readily seen once we accept the wage settlement as largely a political solution based upon the relative power of organized labor and planned production. It is precisely the more advanced secondary or planning sector of the economy that, in the long-run shifts toward more and more complex, automated ways of delivering its product. However, there is no guarantee that productivity will grow steadily faster than the wage rate. Moreover, we cannot expect the slow productivity growth in services to offset any such tendency. Stagnation and negative short-term interest rates are the secular consequence.[2]

---

[2]In this and the following paragraphs, Canterbery's vita theory is used to amend Galbraith and Kalecki. It was first published as "The Vita Theory of the Personal Income Distribution," *Southern Economic Journal*, 46(1), 1979, 12–48. Shortly thereafter, I wrote of the implications of the theory for welfare economics in E. Ray Canterbery, "Welfare Economics and the Vita Theory, "*Eastern Economic Journal*, VI(1), 1980, 1–20. Both papers are reprinted in E. Ray Canterbery, *Beyond Conventional Economics* (Singapore/London/New Jersey: World Scientific, 2016, Chapters 10 and 11.

Even though the primary sector may constrain competitive industries, the planning system of the advanced economy is in charge, wielding its power in the marketplace to control production and pass on rising costs (including money wage increases) to all of us. Its symbiotic relationship with big labor and big government gives giant business an almost inexhaustible supply of funds for investment. The usually benign countervailing power of an earlier Galbraith (1952) gives way to non-benign compensatory power (1983). The well-funded investments in new technology that replace workers have the effect of redistributing income away from the working class, particularly away from the least skilled. Although the working class receives a share of profits, most "non-earned" income from high technology is accumulated by the entrepreneurial, managerial, and professional classes.

The Effects of Technological Progress

Technological progress alters the demand for a particular labor type in two ways. First, it can change the technical coefficients and thus labor-quantity requirements. Though capital goods and labor services complement each other in the short run (two workers may be needed for each new machine), they can become substitutes for each other in the longer run. The long-run trend of wages in the planning sector is known to be upward, and it is hardly surprising that the main purpose of new equipment in industrialized economies is to reduce labor requirements. Machines do not talk back or go on strike, not even robots. Technological change also exerts a more indirect effect on labor demands. A new, more complex technology can cause a shift to labor of a different type altogether. Workers who once combined the ingredients for frozen cakes may be unqualified to monitor the automated machines that now perform this task and unemployment of these workers results. "Let them eat cake!" is an inappropriate policy response.

We have no assurance that displaced labor will be hired elsewhere. The rehiring of such labor requires the coincidence of new products and new industries emerging quickly enough to absorb the labor reserve. Even then it is the more skilled reserve that is needed. Meanwhile the life plans of the more advantaged workers move inexorably toward collectively increasing their numbers and the skilled labor supply. From the viewpoint of those who wish to have the highest possible personal income this collective response is unfavorable. Rather than "rationality" being a way out of poverty or low-income predicaments, it can be a way in.

In the traditional world of economics wages and profits are factor payments to labor and capital. In the more advanced economy we have been describing, this isn't so. Income payments are made to persons, not stereotypes, and therefore we are concerned with the personal income distribution.

Beyond his subsistence model wherein labor requires a subsistence wage to meet basic physiological needs, Sraffa provides no guide to the distribution of surpluses. What happens then to Sraffa's and Kalecki's theories when — as in the modern economy — we find some "workers" with sufficient incomes to indulge in non-spending, that is, savings? If such persons purchase income producing financial assets, they can then share (*albeit* indirectly) in total profits. The incomes of such persons then include labor earnings plus some capitalistic profits. In this case, of course, the working "class" receives a larger share of the national income than that derived from their labor efforts alone.

The Diversity of Incomes and Jobs

Because such persons also receive some non-wage income — interest on savings accounts, rent, or profits — more than two income classes exist, and the simple distinction between "workers" and "capitalists" dissolves; such income intervals would identify the personal income distribution. However, this refinement of the income distribution does not alter Kalecki's general conclusions as long as there is one group that receives only profit income. Such a group of income receivers does exist (coexist?) in modern capitalistic societies.

In short, the reliance on a stereotyped income division between workers and capitalists is an inadequate explanation for the income distribution of an affluent society. Moreover, it tells us little about the characteristics of the labor receiving differential income payments beyond the color of their collars. We need to know more about why different households occupy varied places in the income distribution. Our concerns go beyond the extremes of Tiger Woods $110 million for *not* playing golf, Jay Leno's $32 million as a talk-show host (now retired), or Taylor Swift's $80.0 million for singing. These numbers fade when compared with Donald Trump, businessman, who made enough deals to net him $380 million. Kim Kardashian received $85 million for simply being famous. Ordinary people received ordinary incomes. Edward L. Jones Jr, 39, earned $103,514 selling automobiles in St. Charles, Missouri. Samantha Ann King, 55, a romance novelist, earned $34,400, hunched over a computer in Albuquerque, New Mexico. A pharmacist in El Paso, Texas earned $143,000 while a library Director in Springfield, Illinois earned $36,000. Meg Whitman, 59, the CEO of Hewlett Packard Enterprise earned $17.1 million while the owner of a recycling company in Cadet, Missouri earned only $36,800. A real-estate appraiser in Vail, Colorado earned $215,000 while a copyeditor in Corvallis, Oregon earned only $25,000. A family physician averages about $160,000 a year; a specialist averages $267,000.[3] Generally, the more specialized the occupation the higher the income.

At the other extreme from the handler in the occupational spectrum is the surgeon. Work activities primarily involve diagnosis and treatment of disease, injury, and deformity by manual or instrumental operations. A significant combination of intellectual capacity to comprehend a wide variety of subjects in basic medical sciences and college-level courses in humanities and social sciences is required. Preparation to practice requires 8–9 years of pre-medical and medical training leading to the doctor of medicine degree, followed by 3–5 years of advanced training and experience directed toward development of specialized skills required in the operating room. Incomes are high. Incomes vary with a myriad of occupations, gender and location. Unionized workers generally earn more than like-occupied non-union workers. The members of these diverse income classes end up spending their incomes in equally distinct stores, restaurants, and nightclubs. My vita theory provides a more eclectic explanation. Sraffa and Kalecki leave open the possibility of a new theory of the personal income distribution.

---

[3] For these incomes and for many occupations, see *Parade* April 11, 2010 and *Parade*, April 10, 2016.

A vita is a brief summary of the main attributes and events of one's life, a kind of autobiographical sketch. The vita theory is a way of saying that an individual's life history is important in deciding their income and that income is important in deciding the person's lifestyle.

An Introduction to the Vita Theory

The main thrust of a vita theory can be simply stated. Imagine that one labor market exists for each general class of labor, such as plumbers, medical doctors, electricians, or elementary school teachers. The individual's quantity as a productive member of the economy determines which labor market that person enters. A person "qualifies" for a particular labor market by the state of his or her vita at the time. For example, a PGA golfer can qualify to play in a tournament by shooting a low score on Monday. His vita includes a list of prior wins on the Tour. The vita theory begins with birth, when race, sex, religion, national origin, inherent or initial mental and physical capacities, inheritances, and family background (endowments) are duly noted. The PGA golfer, for example, may have been born with golfing genes.

The autobiography is added to over the life span by education, other training and experience. An individual does have some control over the length and depth of his autobiography. However, production "recipes" change in the long run. Because labor demand is related to technology as well as to product and services demand, only the rarest of individuals can predict with any accuracy the amount of future demand for workers with his or her own emerging or mature autobiography. Beyond this, specific labor supply conditions are a collective outcome that is beyond personal control.

Thus, given the vita and the characteristics of the applicable labor market, the individual's basic wage rate depends upon the average wage for such services. Upon closer examination, however, the individual's personal income exhibits differentials from potential labor market earnings. The differentials — occupational, geographic, inter-industry, union–non-union, discriminatory and so on — often can be traced back to the first vita stage, the birth vita. Second and third stages are the pre-career vita, and the career or mature vita. Life stages highlight those events and times in which the individual often loses control over important choices. At birth, the genetic code has already determined one's initial or innate IQ, sex, race, and initial state of health. The pre-career vita is the time for education, when earning qualities can be enhanced. For example, 35 percent of all white householders earned $30,000 or more in 1981 while only 15 percent of black householders earned as much. Of the above average whites, 47 percent were college graduates whereas 7 percent had completed elementary school. Education adds substantially to the income of blacks, though not nearly as much as to that of whites. Education beyond that which is mandatory and free normally depends heavily upon parental contributions. Individuals thus have only moderate control over their pre-career vitae because voluntary schooling and training is often directly related to inherited material endowments. By maturity, the options of the individuals are greatly narrowed. From the view of earnings prospects, the autobiography is for the most part written, although one new consideration enters at this life stage — years of experience. The new worker faces a dilemma: he or she lacks experience.

The labor force, the supply side of the labor market, consists of those people who are of working age who wish to work, and who have either pre-career or mature vitae, which identify the persons' occupational characteristics. In the short run, individuals can enter only that labor market they "fit"; in the long run they potentially can change their characteristics and qualify for a different labor market, perhaps one with a higher wage rate. In general, however, the number of vitae directly applicable to the labor market decreases with increases in skills, special aptitudes, and required credentials. For example, the number of people who qualify as unskilled labor greatly exceeds the number who qualify as medical doctors. Similarly, the possibilities for substitution of different types of labor are greater among occupations with unskilled labor markets. The least labor substitution occurs within the most specialized occupations. At the higher skilled extreme, in fact, the professional occupation is the labor market. Such would hold for lawyers as members of the legal profession and golfers who are members of the PGA or LPGA.

There is no assurance that all vitae will be employed at any particular time for employment levels depend upon demand. However, it is presumed that, wherever involuntary unemployment exists, it involves those of lowest ranked employment vitae including young people with pre-career vitae who lack job training or being newly considered for on the job training.

During production and employment expansion, upward occupational mobility can occur. However, labor institutions — craft unions and industrial unions — are a major part of the real-world conditions for mobility. Industrial unions, for example, organize entire industries. They consist of persons with diverse autobiographies and occupations, including both the unskilled and the semiskilled. The main economic effect of the industrial union is the negotiation of a wage floor for its members. However, the industrial union tries to gain some of the advantages of the craft union through apprenticeships, regulations, seniority practices, and (in some cases) discrimination. These practices alter the mobility conditions for union workers as they attempt to change occupations within the unionized plant.

The vita theory points toward a structural view of labor demand. In the short run, employment and wages are not always determined by the same forces. In describing such a process, we lose the determinism of the neoclassical labor market but gain some realism

In the short run, product prices, the state of technology, and industrial competition are Givens. Employment is a fixed proportion of production so the quantity of labor demanded is tied directly to the production level. With fixed capital-to-labor combinations, employment levels are unrelated to the wage rate and therefore vary with output levels.

Technological progress can alter demand for a particular labor type in two ways. First, it can change labor-quantity requirements. Though capital and labor complement each other in the short run or even the intermediate run (two workers may be needed for each new machine), they can become substitutes for each other in the longer run. The long-run trend of wages in the concentrated sector is known to be upward, and it is not surprising that the main purpose of new equipment in the industrialized economies is to reduce labor employment. Robots are replacing people on assembly lines in the auto industry. Technological change also exerts a more indirect effect on labor demand. A new, more complex technology can cause a shift to labor of a different stripe altogether. Workers who once combined the ingredients for frozen cakes may be unqualified to monitor the automated machines that now perform this task and unemployment of these workers results.

The labor markets dominated by industrial unions are akin to "administered" wages and prices. If the labor union is powerful, industry's ability to pay the demanded wage is enhanced by its ability to impose price markups on the consumer. The industrial union's tool is the wage rate rather than the labor supply. This means that in the short run employment is not related to the wage rate and the wage rate is related to employment only if full employment extends across all labor. (At full employment wages can be bid up by Keynesian excess demand.) Therefore, a high wage can be associated with a high unemployment rate because employment is decided by the level of production.

Union labor sets the pace for the wage structure across the industrial economy. Moreover the price markup is not limited to concentrated industries. Competitive industries producing industrial or consumer necessities can pass along rising costs because the industry or consumer supplied does not have an alternative to the product. Oil is an example of such a good: it is a necessity in both consumption and production.

The long-run labor supply is related to what individuals expect the wage rate to be, because the supply over time represents the maturing of vitae that have been directed along a career path designed years earlier. In the long run increases in the expected market wage rate, for whatever reason are likely to attract new entrants and the labor supply for that class of worker is increased. Even in this longer run it is probable that the labor supply will be controlled in craft union areas. It is not mere historical accident that skilled workers were the first to organize in craft unions and successfully raise wage rates.

The actual and expected wage rates may tend to converge for industrial labor but this by no means assures a full employment equilibrium for such labor. The substitution of newer industrial processes that require less labor may have advanced to the point that long periods of idleness are traded off for high wages. Full employment under such conditions might require extraordinarily high production levels and glut of goods — a supra-surplus. An unused supply of unskilled labor is characteristic of recent experience in the United States, England, Japan, and Western Europe.

The vita theory explains several kinds of wage differentials. If we invoke the assumption of "rational man" or "super-rational man" with respect to income, these differentials represent an opportunity for a worker to move from a low-wage market to a high-wage market. Unfortunately, the mobility of labor is a complex, difficult, and cumbersome process. Studies attribute only 53–69 percent of migration to purely economic motives, leaving considerable room for the motivations of regional preferences, health, education, housing, marriage, lifestyle, and so on.

Nonetheless, according to the vita theory, a higher wage rate for individuals depends upon their mobility. Significant upward mobility requires the acquisition of a "higher quality" set of skills, whether in response to changing technological requirements or because of the individual's desire to increase income and status. Despite the training and education that require a substantial amount of time and personal investment this search for higher earnings may end with still another barricade. The individual may not receive the wage rate of the labor market and occupation of his choice because of genetic characteristics — race, sex, nationality. Even age is a source of discrimination that can bar a worker from receiving the desired wage. Studies suggest that more than half of the earnings differential relates to racial discrimination. In short, earnings and income differentials are wider than wage differentials. Under such circumstances the best advice is that children be very selective with regard to their parentage.[4] Parents have a lot to do with the education of the young. The importance of the pre-career vita is highlighted by the distribution of unemployment in September 2010. For those with less than high school education the unemployment rate was 15.4 percent; with high school completed, 10.0 percent; some college 91 percent; bachelor's degree or higher, 4.4 percent.

In the light of the vita theory, an economy of workers demanding only minimal necessities cannot be described as robust. If we are looking for an "invariant" measure of value from the demand side, the quantity of necessities per worker seems a better candidate than Sraffa's composite standard commodity. Nevertheless, in the long run just as the standard commodity must change with new technology, the quantity of

---

[4] For support of this view, see John Brittain, *The Inheritance of Inequality* (Washington, D.C.: The Brookings Institution, 1977).

"necessities" will change as workers redefine what is necessary. Whether necessities are a constant or a variable market basket of goods and services, their quantities and prices will determine their dollar value and the required dollar value of the wage bill. From here, we move, as before, to consumer budgets and Engel curves.

The Vita Theory — Just Do the Math

The following section is mostly for those with mathematical endowments. In it, I go through several selected equations from the original exposition of the vita theory. At the end of this sometimes bumpy ride is the national income accounts, which most everyone can understand.

As before, initially assume a one-to-one correspondence between general human capital classifications (HCs) and labor market types. We can think of the members of the labor supply of a human capital type as being in rank order (for example, $1, 2, \ldots n$) from most to least preferred employee characteristics, a labor force queue at either a local or national level. It is presumed that whatever involuntary unemployment exists it will involve the persons ranked lowest within the HC classification. In the short term the wage rate and the employment level are decided by different forces. Let e_j be the labor hours required of the ith human capital type (HC_i) per unit of physical output in a selected geographical area. As employment is a fixed proportion of production, the quantity of labor demand is

$$z_i = a_i q_j$$

where q_j is the total output of product j, which is assumed to be homogeneous across the labor market.

If labor is paid its value in production, the wage rate would be

$$w_i = a-1_i p_j$$

where p is the price of the product or service produced by this labor type. No union worker alone can influence this price. Technological progress or change in the production process can alter the demand for a particular labor type directly by changing labor-quantity requirements.

When we look at individuals, we find many wage differentials. The individual achieves a higher wage rate via his or her labor mobility, either through time (temporal) or across space (spatial). The high wage worker would look into the labor market of licensed professionals with monopolistic supply control over high-priced series of inelastic demand with little prospect for capital intensive technological advances located in a traditionally high-wage geographical area.

Significant upward temporal mobility requires the acquisition of a greater quantity of human capital (moving from HC_n and toward HC_1. Whether it be a response to changing skills requirements from technological change or a result of the person's desire to increase status and income, the training and education augmentation requires substantial blocks of time and, unless the employer offers a training program, a substantial personal investment commitment.

Unfortunately, low levels of capital which inhibit upward temporal mobility also slow spatial mobility. Such transfers are related to desire, ability, and prospects for success. Although social barriers to labor migration no doubt vary with the quantity of human capital, the main economic inhibitor to successful migration is the cost of physical transport, financed from one's capital stock, and the level of capital itself. Still, the individual may not receive the wage rate of the labor market and occupation of choice because of characteristics decided by his or her birth vita. Discrimination, be it racial, sexual, age, ethic, or whatever can preclude a particular individual from receiving the wage rate of central tendency. We expect, therefor, to find earnings differentials are wider than wage differentials.

A general personal income function for the ith individual is

$$y = y(h, k_1, k_2, p, m, \theta, M, R),$$

where the subscript, i, is deleted, y = before-tax personal income, h = hours worked, k_1 = the ith individuals' human capital, k_2 = the ith individual's nonhuman capital endowment, p = the average price of the product or service produced by this individual's labor, m = an index of mobility, θ = a variable that measures risk and uncertainty regarding income opportunities at alternative geographical locations, M = an index of monopolistic power that would equal zero for individuals with "ordinary" or average human and nonhuman capital endowments under free entry conditions in groups of large numbers, R = a discrimination (racial, sexual, ethnic, and other) index that is negatively related to income for those who suffer economic effects from discrimination.[5]

Whereas temporal mobility is a direct function of the quantity of human capital (k_1), worker spatial mobility is a direct function of k_1, k_2, and, so $m = m(k_1, k_2)$. The monopolistic power function is $M = M(EN, k_1, k_2)$, where EN is an index of entry in which larger values of EN represent greater ease of entry. The value of EN for most blue-collar occupations is described by the type and level of unionization. Finally, there is a labor demand shifter (professional) or wage rate shifter (union or unskilled) associated with product price changes. The main impact of technological improvements is upon employment, that is, upon h, which becomes zero unless the individual becomes underemployed. Generally, the individual responds by attempting to increase his or her human capital. Let the function W be the human or personal capital rate and we now have

$$y = h \times W[k_1, k_2, p, m(k_1, k_2), M(EN, k_1, k_2)\theta].$$

The wage rate is the entire function W.

The earning function is not at "first causes" in terms of birth, precareer, and mature vitae. The mature vitae are represented as

$$k_1 = F(G, h_1, s_2, s_3, E, t)$$

and

$$k_2 = H[I_0, F(G, h_1, s_2, E, t)],$$

where I_0 is the initial nonhuman capital endowment, G is the genetic code, E represents family environment conducive to earnings potential, s_1 is the

---

[5] The partial derivatives for the variables are provided in Canterbery, "The Vita Theory of the Personal Income Distribution," *op. cit.*

hours of education within the sole control of the individual, s_3 is the number of hours of State-required formal schooling, s_3 is the hours of initial on-the-job training within sole control of private industry, and t is years of experience. Net additions to total capital can be derived from an increase in the hours devoted to human capital accumulation. Assume that G and E are indices that take on larger values when they are favorable for augmenting human capital (earnings capability) at birth.

The income distribution is a rank-order vector of all persons' before-tax personal incomes, that is,

$$y = [y_1, y_2, \ldots y_n].$$

Such a distribution can be arrayed in the usual ways. (We are reminded that y_n through y_x may be zero because some population members may be unemployed and have no nonhuman capital). Beginning with y_n, the poor can be identified as those with a food budget share at subsistence. Our rank ordering of human capital quantities does not exactly match our rank ordering of personal incomes.

The aggregate personal income is the sum of

$$y_1 + y_2 + y_3 + \cdots + y_n.$$

From this, we can derive the other national income accounts.

National Income = Total Personal Income + Corporate profits

Net National Income = National Income + Transfer payments + Indirect business tax (less subsidies and surplus of Govt. enterprises)

Gross National Product = Net National Product + Consumption of fixed capital

Gross Domestic Product = Gross National Product − Net factor incomes from rest of world

From the expenditure side of the accounts,

> Gross Domestic Product = Personal consumption expenditures +
> Gross private domestic investment +
> Government purchases of goods and
> services

Personal income is closely related to personal consumption expenditures.

Concluding Remarks

The weakness of individual control over certain human capital variables leads to policies often urged collectively by society to satisfy social goals. A number of studies find that inherent capabilities and family environment have important impacts upon life plans that culminate in occupational selection and personal incomes. The advantageous birth vita starts the individual on the optimum vita path, aiding the selection of the "optimum" years of schooling and other training. Genetic and family endowments directly and indirectly affect occupational choice and thus earnings. In the mature vita, the genetic code can impinge again in the way of job and wage discrimination.

The acceptance of the vita theory raises profound social and economic questions. The crucial and cumulative impacts of the initial state conditions suggest that a program of equal schooling for "equal opportunity" may leave the income distribution virtually unaltered even while contributing to economic growth. Are economic and social policies aimed indirectly at reducing income and wealth inequalities effective? Can job training programs and migration subsidies succeed where education might fail?

The distributional issue, of course, is of concern only to those in the society who find the existing income distribution unacceptable. However, if unequal birth vita in a society of ideally equal opportunities leave the society with unacceptable income and wealth inequalities, more equal distribution could only be achieved by such direct redistributional policies as John Stuart Mill's inheritance tax proposal and Milton Friedman's and James Tobin's negative income tax. We will return to these and other policy issues later. Next, we explore the global linkages.

Chapter 11

THE GLOBAL LINKAGES

H. Peter Gray develops a paradigm for the analysis of international involvement (IEI) in his 1999 book.[1] He wants to avoid a formal construct, such as that characterizing the Heckscher–Ohlin–Samuelson theory (H–O–S) or even the intra-industry trade models based on economies of scale and product differentiation (Krugman). He shuns the later because their treatment of technology is too limited and they, at best explain trade only among the industrialized nations. Gray also dismisses the "technology gap" models of North–South trade for focusing exclusively on trade between innovating countries and follower countries while failing to explain differences among technology-intensive goods and other goods.

Gray is responding to the institutional change called globalization. A movement toward freer factor movements, sharp reductions in transportation costs, the integration of financial markets, and the growth of multinational corporations (MNCs) characterize globalization. More than trade is involved, however because technology and the factors of production have become increasingly mobile among nations. In Gray's perspective the most important institution in this involvement is the dominance of the MNC as a production unit. Inside the MNC, proprietary technology or what Dunning calls "created assets" is a critical factor of production. Therefore, in addition to H-0's natural resource goods and standardized

---

[1] H. Peter Gray, *Global Economic Involvement: A synthesis of Modern International Economics* (Copenhagen: Copenhagen Business School Press, 1999).

goods, the technology-reliant good or S-good is added to the global market basket.

Except for the new focus on MNCs Gray has tilled this global earth before. In his attempt to develop a "pragmatic theory" of international trade he included considerations related to specific human capital or "skill mix," Canterbery's vita theory, the Linder thesis, and the product cycle. These concerns reappear but with the focus on the MNC, S-goods are in the spotlight. Their production functions are more complex and they can generate quasi-rents. Imperfect competition requires markup pricing (as discussed in earlier chapters) rather than marginal cost pricing. In the world of the MNC both comparative and competitive advantage exist.

Canterbery attempted to provide a general theory of international trade based on the vita theory, innovations, and the product cycle but also on standardized technology.[2] With the expanded scope of the MNC, however, a gap exists between Gray's (and Dunning's) institutional analysis and Canterbery's formal representation. Herein I provide the missing links and suggest how they could be used to build a bridge to this century's formal model. In this regard it is useful to recall that the MNC is involved in the production of every kind of good, including the S-good. The United Fruit Company preceded Intel and the British East India Company preceded United Fruit. In the LDCs, of course, bananas preceded the United Fruit Company, crude oil reserves preceded OPEC, and so on.

The most obvious effects of the recent growth in MNCs are three-fold: (1) With all countries much more deeply integrated into the global economy, domestic markets are much more easily supplied from abroad. In turn, with more and more services (such as telephone, travel-tourism, distribution, education, motion picture production and distribution, healthcare, legal accounting, data processing, business consulting, advertising, architecture, golf course, engineering, transportation, and financial services) crossing borders, intra-firm trade has expanded. (2) Foreign direct investment (FDI), most MNC capital transfers, have been growing twice the rate of world trade, while world trade

---

[2] E. Ray Canterbery, "A General Theory of International Trade and Domestic Employment Adjustments," in Michael Landeck, ed., *International Trade: Regional and Global Issues* (London: The Macmillan Press, 1994), Chapter 16.

has been growing three times faster than world industrial production since the early 1980s. (3) Intra-industry trade in S-goods — reliant as they are on technology and other modes of differentiation — has greatly expanded. This expansion of MNC's could not have happened absent the blessing of the nation-states of the advanced or supra-surplus countries or even their active encouragement.

The Multinational Zone v. the Hot Zone

We are accustomed to thinking of trade as being between regions. Gray (1999, p. 1) identifies South–South, North–North, and North–South trade. However, he also denotes intra-firm and intra-industry trade. As to goods and services, he lists agricultural goods, natural-resource goods, S-goods/services, and H-O goods. Although MNCs produce and trade all types of goods and services, they specialize in S-goods-services that enter into intra-firm and intra-industry trade. At only the slightest hint of oversimplification, we can say that MNCs trade within their firms *and* industries. To the extent that their powers supersede or are an integral part of the powers of nation-states, the multinationals have established their own trading region, a zone virtually unconstrained by geography or politics.

Since intra-firm services include financial services, the giant multinational brokerage houses freely move portfolio and other capital around the world. Unlike the movement of goods and other services, however this movement of funds is not under the control of the non-financial MNCs. The quick movement of such funds can dramatically alter exchange rates (witness the 1997 East Asian currency crisis and its aftermath). The rapid and unpredictable movement of international finance can either speed or slow the growth rate of the non-financial MNCs. Thus, a potential constraint on the growth of MNCs is the behavior of their financial counterparts.

Defining the MNCs as comprising a new trading zone does not obliterate the usefulness of the old trading region pairings. Since MNCs generate the greatest value added in the world trading system, the value of their trade is mostly North–North. That part which is North–South or South–North is mostly in the emerging economies of East Asia, Eastern Europe, and Latin American. China, Taiwan, Singapore, Hong Kong, Republic of Korea, Poland, Thailand, Mexico, and Brazil come to mind. Still it might be more analytically useful to divide the trading world into the following categories: the MNC zone (MNC), emerging nations (EN), less-developed non-oil producing nations (LDC-NO), and less-developed oil producing nations (LDC-O). In turn, the MNC zone specializes in S-goods, the EN zone specializes in standardized manufactures and produce some S-goods based upon product differentiation rather than hi-tech specialization, the LDC-NO specializes in various natural-resource-intensive commodities, and the LDC-O zone produces, of course, crude oil. In the LDC trade zone, prices and proceeds mostly are determined in competitive world commodity markets, the exception being the OPEC nations whose cartel power waxes and wanes. The price of oil is rent-based, both a markup above unit costs and set in a world commodity market. Generally, however, the LDCs are price-takers.

Value added in the world trading system is the most important force driving trade growth and economic development. Except for the OPEC nations, the zone of underdevelopment relies on production whose value is decided in world commodity markets beyond its control. Wage rates and labor skills in such countries are low. Economies of scale and the use of marketing to differentiate products are the great advantages of standardized production in multinationals. Producers then have some control over their product markets and can stabilize their own prices. Such a process adds layers of value added in production and distribution and, by definition, grows the nations' GDPs.

Though the initial impetus for "importing" standardized technology is the presence of low wage rates, wage rates in manufacturing will exceed those in commodity production.

Toward a Formal Model

Can this simplified world trading system be expressed in a formal world trade model? In this regard we shift focus to Canterbery (1994). The original model was an input–output model of an open economy that was made dynamic by introducing a product cycle. The technical methods of production are given by a matrix of inter-industry coefficients in physical units denoted by A, and by a row vector of direct labor coefficients in physical units, denoted by a_n. These coefficients are decided by the optimal techniques of production, processes that are given initially for the period of production so that

$$[A, a_n],$$

where A is non-singular and the transpose of which can be written as

$$[A, a_n]'$$

Let us divide the world into those four major trading zones — the multinational MNC, EN, LDC_o, and LDC_{no}. The initial production systems are different for the countries in each region. The MNC zone would be a source of dynamic change in the world system, the EN would be attempting to capture some aspects of that change and the LDC_{no} mostly would be at the mercy of world commodity markets. The LDC oil-producing nations would benefit from OPEC's potential to control oil production and from the growing demand for oil in the MNC and EN zones.

In each zone, a country's inputs are physical quantities of raw materials, capital-type commodities and labor time. Necessary materials are treated the same as capital type goods since their functions are similar. All inputs except labor are treated as intermediate goods so that investment can only be identified as "capital-type durable goods and necessary materials," all of which is reproducible capital. The value added in each country equals the value of the commodities making up its net national income (or net product). This net national income is distributed as wages, rent, interest, and profits. In general wages are distributed in proportion to the contributed physical quantity of labor of a particular type and quality. However, a specific money wage rate is determined in the "labor market" for the labor type and quality required. Following the vita theory, labor is of different qualities and therefore the wage rates will vary by industry. Shadow wages are paid to managers and professionals. This, of course, does not foreclose the possibility that a great number of industries may be paying identical wage rates.

The MNC or Supra-surplus Zone

The production functions within the MNC zone are the most complex and therefore the most complete. The functions of the MNC zone are proto-typical for what is possible though perhaps not probably elsewhere. Put differently, production relations in the other zones are derivable from those of the MNC by attrition or attenuation. Skilled and managerial labor dominate the supra-surplus economies' labor markets even as hi-tech and otherwise differentiated goods dominate production. This analysis pro-ceeds at the industry level; alternatively, one could think of the production relations for each firm in an industry as decided by the best available technology and therefore either alike or comprising a monopoly.[3]

The general forms of production relations, labor markets, and price determination of each nation in any zone are identical. Only the specifics vary: the dominant industries may be somewhat different and so too the skill requirements of the labor force. Given $[A_{MNC,}\ a_{n,MNC}]'$ and the conditions regarding money wages and profit rates, money prices can be expressed as

$$P_{MNC} = P_{MNC}A_{MNC}\ (I + Z') + a_{n,MNC}W'_{MNC}\ (I + Z),$$

where P denotes the row vector of prices, Z' the column vector of markups (profit rates), and W' the column vector of wage rates. The first group of terms reflects the cost of using commodities or goods to produce com-modities and the second reflects the variable costs of labor in production. Since money prices are used, they are absolute rather than relative prices.

This system for each country (and for the world system) must be self-consistent in money prices. That is, a low price elasticity of demand in one commodity market raises the profit margin and thus prices of all com-modities that use the first commodity as an input beyond what their costs

---

[3] The origins of technology and its change are beyond the scope of this chapter. However, for an article on that subject that is consistent with the modeling herein, see E. Ray Canterbery, "An Evolutionary Model of Technical Change with Markup Pricing," in William Millberg, ed., *The Megacorp & Macrodynamics: Essays in Memory of Alfred Eichner* (Armonk & London: M. E. Sharpe, Inc.), pp. 87–100. The two models can be integrated.

would be if the input were priced at zero economic profit. This consistency is reflected in the solution of the price system for an MNC-zone nation, which is

$$P_{MNC} = a_{n,MNCWMN} C (I + Z') \{I - A_{MN} C(I + Z')\}^{-1}.$$

The inverted matrix in the above equation, $\{.\}^{-1}$, is non-negative and gives the total (direct and indirect) requirements of commodities for the production of final commodities (i.e., of consumption and new investment-type goods), taking into account their shares going to real profits in each industry. The equation also shows how money price changes are related to the interdependencies of complex techniques. Consider the price of good 1 in detail,

$$p_1 = a_{n2} w_1 (1 + b_1) a_{11} + a_{n2} w_2 (1 + b_{n1}) a_{21} + \cdots + a_{n,n-1} w_{n-1} (1 + b_{n1}) a_{ni-1,1}$$

in which the element a_{ij} $(i,j = 1,2,...,n-1)$ represents the physical quantity of the ith commodity needed in the economic system as a whole (including real profits allocations) to obtain eventually one physical unit of the jth commodity as a final good. The w's are wage rates related to the physical unit of each commodity as an input. (The element a_{ij} should not be confused with the identical notation usually used to denote direct and indirect input requirements unadjusted for physical products allocated to profits.) Since the form of the price equations for all goods in the world system are similar, the MNC identification sub-scripts are dropped for the above equation. The wage rates reflect quality differentials in human capital as well as demand conditions in particular labor markets (see Chapter 10). For the export market, both sides of the above equation would be multiplied by r, the trade-weighted foreign exchange rate for all other MNC-zone nations, the EN_S (the EN zone), and the LDCs. The exchange rate, however, is not independent of the value of exports and imports.

Total production of Industry 1 in a particular nation is

$$Q_1 = m_1 p_1 s_1 \{x_{11}, x_{12}...x_{1j} \cdots x_{1,n-1}\} \{y_1 + e_1\},$$

where m_1 is a cultural modifier or representation of a unique resource, p_1 represents proprietary knowledge, s_1 is a scale factor, y_1 is the level of real domestic demand, and $e_1 d_1$ represents the real value of exports or imports (imports being negative exports), though the value here is subsumed in e_1. Gray introduced the m, p, and s terms. In this production system the m and p equal either zero or one. If m is a cultural barrier, the industry will not exist. If m represents the presence of a unique natural resource such as oil or gold reserves, a product will not be produced in its absence. If the industry requires proprietary knowledge and p is required and exists, its value is one; if p is zero, the industry does not exist. If either m or p is zero, production of the good does not take place in a particular country. If either m or p is zero in every nation in a particular zone, the industry does not exist in that zone. Scale, of course, has no meaning in the absence of production; however, if production in Industry 1 takes place, $s \lesseqgtr 1$.

Gray's (1999) focus is upon S-goods in the MNC zone, goods that have positive values for p and s. Moreover, the more complex production functions in that zone require extensive arrays of direct and indirect requirements. Unique resources (m) also can be present such as crude oil reserves and a favorable soil–climate environment for agriculture, such as in the United States. For the production system of an entire MNC nation,

$$Q = [1 - A]^{-1} (y + e),$$

and aggregate output is the vector

$$Q = [Q_1\ Q_2\ ...\ Q_{n-1}].$$

In turn, the value added (V) for Industry 1 is

$$V_1 = a_n W_1 (1 + Z') (a_{11} a_{12} ... a_1, n-1) Q_1$$

or, for an entire economy,

$$V = a_n W' (I + Z') \{I - A(I + Z')\} Q.$$

This could represent the USA, the UK or other supra-surplus economy. As noted, the type of products and industries found in the MNC zone will have high levels of value added. Such values are major contributors to high levels of net national income in such an economy.

If labor requirements are expressed as numbers of workers, total employment under static conditions is

$$a_{n1}Q_1 + a_{n2}Q_2 + \ldots a_{n,n-1}Q_{n,n-1} = L,$$

where L equals total national employment at the levels of physical output. Different qualities of labor are used in different industries (or even in the same industry). More precisely, therefore, a_{nj} consists of several different types of labor. Represent each labor type by I, II, III, …,, D in which there are D labor types and

$$[a_I a_{II} a_{III} \ldots a_D].$$

The labor requirements for labor type 1, the highest quality type, become

$$L_1 = a_{11}Q_1 + a_{12}Q_2 + \ldots a_{1,n-1}Q_{n-1}.$$

This represents highly skilled labor such as that of a computer programmer. For an entire MNC zone economy,

$$L = [a_{jVIV}]_{n-1 \text{XD}} Q$$

where $[a_{jVIV}]_{n-1 \text{XD}}$ is the entire matrix of labor requirements by human capital type and Q is a column vector of output. These labor coefficients in the MNC zone change very slowly over time.[4] The net demand matrix

---

[4] The labor coefficients in the advanced economies change very slowly over time. For example, Milberg and Elmslie [William Milberg and Bruce Elmslie, "Technical Change in the Corporate Economy: A Vertically Integrated Approach," in William Milberg, ed., *The Megacorp & Macrodynamics: Essays in Memory of Alfred Eichner* (Armonk and London: M. E. Sharpe, Inc., 1992) pp. 101–130] find change in combined direct and indirect labor coefficients being less than 1 percent in a half decade across 20 industries in 8 advanced economies.

of labor markets for the MNC economy would include a strong dependence on senior executives, professionals, upper management, middle management, and highly skilled blue-collar workers.[5] They would be in the upper 1–10 percent of the income distribution. Such labor requirements mirror the production technology in hi-tech and differentiated S-goods.

A price solution comparable to an earlier equation but including labor by human capital type is

$$P = [a_{jVIV}]_{n-1XD} \; W'a(I + Z) \; \{I - A(I + Z')\}^{-1},$$

where $[a_{jVIV}]$ comprises the labor requirements matrix for all industries by labor type and W'_a is a column vector of "labor market" wage rates. Since the wage rates are from "labor markets," more than one wage now applies to each industry.

Wage rates for different human capital types and the size of the markup is critical to understanding the economies of the MNC or supra-surplus zone. Whereas Gray has "returns" to human capital and to proprietary knowledge as components of the unit costs of production, I assign higher wage rates to higher levels of human capital and view the return to proprietary knowledge as part of the markup. The initial costs of proprietary knowledge can be viewed as "sunk costs" that thereafter generate quasi-rents (that are included in the markup). Not only does the existence of extensive backward and forward linkages in the MNC zone contribute to value added, but so too do high wage rates and markups.

The bulk of trade within the MNC zone is intra-industry (or intra-firm). Different countries specialize in different hi-tech products whereas most produce otherwise standardized products differentiated by advertising and marketing. All produce pharmaceuticals but perhaps only three produce large commercial aircrafts. Most produce automobiles differentiated by styling, performance, and advertising but perhaps only one or two produce space shuttles. Still, the MNC largely supersedes the

---

[5] For a discussion of excess demands and supplies of labor by type based on the vita theory and their implications for protectionism, see H. Peter Gray, "Employment Arguments for Protection and the Vita Theory," *Eastern Economic Journal*, 10(1), 1–13.

nation-state. Irrespective of its "home" base, it has production and distribution branches in most other MNC-zone countries. If anything, most of the governments maintain the independence of the MNCs. Moreover, because of the high returns of human capital and high profit returns for quasi-rents, most of the world's financial capital originates in the MNC or supra-surplus zone.

To close the model, personal incomes must be generated and consumption take place. As profits are distributed in the MNC zone, the personal income of the kth individual is

$$y_k = hw_{kVIV} + c_1Z_1 + c_2Z_2 + \cdots + c_{n-1}Z_{n-1}$$

where w_{kVIV} is the wage of central tendency for individual k's HC type, h is the standard number of hours worked and the c's are k's share of the profits in the designated industries. For most workers of course, the c's are zero. The income distribution is a rank-order vector of all persons' nominal personal incomes. Total nominal personal income is y_k ($k = 1, 2, \ldots, v$).

An extended linear expenditure system can be used to estimate consumption. The value demanded by the kth individual for the ith commodity is

$$V_{ki} = p_i e_{ki} + B_{ki}(y_k - p_j e_{kj})$$

$$(i = 1, \ldots, n-1; k = 1, \ldots, v)$$

where the p's are given by the interdependencies of the production system with wage and profit rates. The e's are parameters representing basic needs, and B is the marginal propensity to consume out of income. The sum of the expenditures of all individuals for the MNC country is $v_{ki} = D$ for all i's and k's or aggregate demand while aggregate supply is given by the output vector.

The numbers of commodities that meet wants beyond basic needs as well as the amounts spent for such discretionary items are much greater in the MNC zone nations than elsewhere in the world system. Incomes in excess of those required to meet basic needs provide the motivation for advertising and marketing efforts to sell surpluses in the MNC zone.

In their respective forms, all the above equations that represent net production value added, labor markets, and demands in an MNC zone nation can be used to represent the entire region. That is, the MNC zone is comprised of sub-matrices of "national" economies and they are fully integrated.

The EN Zone, Technology Transfers and International Factor Mobility

An economy in the EN zone has the production characteristics of both an MNC country and an LDC. This amalgam is the consequence of the partial integration of the MNC zone with selected developing nations. Many of the EN countries have human capital types at least equal in quality to those in the MNC zone. Still, the EN countries are different in two important respects: wage rates, even those for comparable human capital types, are a fraction of the MNC wages; and home-based financial capital is severely limited. Thus, for human capital type I, $w_{zMNC} > P_{1EN}$, in domestic prices.

This relative status of the MC and the EN nations leads to the mobility of factors of production, as well as standardized technology. In mature industries, two gaps — the wage and financial capital gaps — enable the MNCs to infiltrate the EN zone. Managerial labor and financial capital mobility is combined with the exportation of standardized technology or proprietary knowledge to produce cheaper production in the EN zone. Indeed, this is the impetus for economic growth that defines the EN, such as Mexico or Brazil. The corporation is motivated to transfer standardized technology to the EN nations as product cycles in the MNC nations mature. Imitating the model of the MNC zone the EN nations eventually will begin to produce home grown multinationals that will begin to export their own brands of differentiated products to the MNC zone. Examples include Korean automobiles, Taiwanese personal computers, and Chinese cell phones. The critical proprietary knowledge in all three products is computer chip technology.

Free trade in finished goods becomes a moot issue in a world of multinationals. It is the freedom of movement of the multinational that defines the system. In turn, standardized technology freely moves and the changed pattern of trade depends upon its new location. Moreover, since the multinational generally produces differentiated products the prevailing imperfect competition makes theories based on perfect competition irrelevant.

The LDC Zones and the International Mobility of Materials

The production functions of the LDC zones are simplest, though most distinct. Production interdependencies are not complex so that few backward and forward linkages exist. Unskilled labor dominates its labor markets and capital-type intermediate goods are scarce. Low wage rates reflect the low skills of labor. The dominant good is the natural resources good which, in some instances can be a non-competitive good (bananas, sugar cane). For the non-competitive good, the importing nation is devoid of the required natural resource input (tropical climate and abundant agricultural land) and, therefore, has no production function for that commodity. Even though labor is abundant in the LDC, natural resources are the source of relatively higher returns, especially for non-competitive goods. Those higher returns are embedded in relatively high markups and thus profit rates. The markup includes then the "returns" paid to rent-earning inputs such as land. Still, for exports, the domestic prices of those goods in the vector of LDC prices are multiplied by the trade-weighted exchange rate of the MNC and EN zones, an exchange rate greatly favoring the MNC zone with its high value added and its financial capital dominance, the exception being when the LDC currency is tied to the MNC currency, such as the U.S. dollar or the euro.

In what is essentially a commodity-based economy, the total production in the key industry, say Industry 5, in the LDC-NO zone is

$$Q_{5e,LDC\text{-}NO} = m_{5,LDC\text{-}NO} S_{5,ldc\text{-}no} \{X_{11}X_{12}X_{13}X_{14}X_{15}\} \\ \{y_{5,lldc\text{-}no} + e_{5,ldc\text{-}no}\},$$

where proprietary knowledge is not required but a unique resource (m_5, LDC-NO) is. If the product is mined or produced by large-scale plantations, there will be economies of scale. Very few industries are linked to the production of a primary commodity; there may be only five as illustrated here. Thus, the value added in production is minimal, domestic demand weak, and the trade balance negative. The materials exported are used like factors of production in the MNC and EN zones. The negative trade balance is a by-product of importation of high value-added goods and the exportation of low value-added goods. Such production conditions and payments deficits generally define the less-developed economy.

The price of the commodity is determined in a world commodity market, making the LDC a price-taker, so that

$$P_{5,MNC} = P_{5,EN} = P_{5,ldc\text{-}no} = P_{5,LDC\text{-}O} = P_{5,world},$$

where at low costs of production, the unique resource will still generate rents for the LDC. The presence of large rents often is sufficient reason to discourage the LDC from diversifying into the production of other kinds of products. Cultural conditions generally lead to the concentration of such rents in a few hands or institutions. Perfect competition surely is not an optimal condition since a major purpose of economic development is to escape the pricing and rents consequences of competitive conditions.

The LDC-O Zone

All of which leads us to the LDC-O zone. In the LDC-O zone where the main export product is crude petroleum, only unskilled and managerial labor may be required and the main wage rates would be, say, $w_5 < w_{10}$. The main commodity inputs would be some portion of the crude oil reserves of the LDC zone plus complementary capital-type goods imported from the MNC or EN zones. The magnitude of the markup on oil exports (and rents) would depend on the effectiveness of OPEC in setting world crude oil prices. The total production in the key industry, crude petroleum (6), is

$$Q_{6,ldc\text{-}o} = m_{5,LDC\text{-}O} S_{6,ldc\text{-}o} \{Z_{13} Z_{14} Z_{15}\}$$
$$\{y_{6,lldc\text{-}o} + e_{6,ldc\text{-}o}\},$$

where, again, proprietary knowledge is not required but a unique commodity resource ($m_{6,ldc\text{-}o}$ = oil reserves) is. Economies of scale exist in the industry. Very few industries however are linked to the production of oil. The value added in production is minimal, but the trade balance will be positive. The positive trade balance derives from the mostly non-competitive characteristic of oil as an export plus the accrual of rents, especially when pricing is set by a cartel, so that

$$P_{6,ldc\text{-}o} = P_{6,en} = P_{6,ldc\text{-}no} = P_{6,O\text{-}OPEC} = P_{6,\text{world}} > \text{Competitive Price.}$$

The LDC-zone nations are otherwise most subject to the forces of traditional demand and supply forces because such forces determine world commodity prices whether they are for agricultural prices or for refined oil. Unlike the MNC zone nations, the LDC nations do not have sophisticated income support programs for agriculture. Thus, whatever the export, the value of both P and its fundamental r is determined in world markets for their commodity and for their currencies. Their vector of prices is set in world markets while their economic system has little capacity for adding value to those prices. Although rents can accrue in the LDC-O zone, the industries in the zone otherwise behave like perfectly competitive producers whose prices are taken off the world markets.

The zone's materials exports are critical and mobile "factors of production" for the MNC and EN zones. Again free trade is an obsolete term to describe such transfers. When an import is non-competitive, competition and counter-flows of goods become irrelevant.

Global Integration and Regional Trade Balances

To varying degrees every country in the world is integrated into the global economy. Even North Korea, the most isolated of nations, takes into account the improbable threat of an American invasion in its nuclear production plans. The MNC and the EN zones are tightly connected to the LDC-O zone by the necessity of importing oil. In turn, the LDC-O countries receive rents in the form of hard currencies. The EN zone is connected to the MNC zone by the need for financial capital inflows and the occasional threat of outflows. In return, the MNC zone can export its excess financial capital.

In this integrated global environment, it is difficult to identify fundamental values of exchange rates. Compounding the difficulty is the special role of the U.S. dollar which serves as the international currency; it is the key trading and reserve currency. If its fundamental value is determined by the trade balance and net financial capital flows, then

$$r_{US} = M_{US}/(X_{US} + \text{NET FINANCIAL CAPITAL OUTFLOWS}_{US}),$$

where r is the foreign exchange rate and trade values are in national currency units. Since the U.S. has been running a chronic trade deficit (mostly from consumer imports of differentiated or lower-cost goods plus oil imports priced in U.S. dollars) and is the major supplier of financial capital to the EN zone, the value of the U.S. dollar $(1/r)$ will be low relative to the value of other MNC-zone nations and even most EN zone nations. This condition can be sustained only as long as foreigners, including their central banks and treasuries, are willing to hold dollars and as long as OPEC desires to price oil in dollars.

Surplus trade balances in differentiated products characterize the low wage EN zone nations as well as many of the other MNC zone nations. As noted, the EN nations are net borrowers from MNC nations. The LDCs are running chronic trade deficits including even the oil-producing nations. This is a consequence of their being producers of low value-added products, including exports. Their main route to economic development is the importation of standardized technology from the MNCs, something prohibited only in orthodox trade theory.

The World System and Global Economic Growth

The world system is a super-matrix comprised of the interdependent matrices of the MNC, EN, LDC-O, and LDC-NO zones. The final outputs, value added, employment, and demand take the same forms represented in the above equations. The linkages of the MNC zone nations are though intra-firm and inter-industry trade, technology transfers by the MNCs to the EN zone and financial capital movements to (mostly) the EN zone. Obviously, the MNC zone is the most dynamic part of the world system.

U.K. Deals with Brexit

The U.K. is an MNC attempting to deal with its exit from the free trade area of the European Union. It faces competition from the emulating EN nations. U.K. treasury chief Philip Hammond pledged to boost investment in infrastructure as he warned that the British economy could face some turbulence as the country charts its exit from the European Union. He said that fiscal policy "will have a role to play" in cushioning the economy in the months and years ahead as Britain loosens its 40-year ties to the bloc. The new public spending includes 5 billion pounds ($5.49 billion) to help fund new housing, and prod the private sector to invest. The U.K. will give formal notice before the end of March that it intends to quit the EU, a move that will start the clock ticking on a negotiating process expected to last at least two years. The pound fell by as much as 1 percent against the U.S. dollar in response, reaching $1.284, its lowest point since August 15. The EU, consisting of mostly MNC nations is the U.K.'s biggest trading partner, and negotiating terms of the country's access to the bloc's vast single market once it leaves the EU will be among Prime Minister Theresa May's most critical tasks. While the British economy grew healthily in the third quarter, officials at the Bank of England and many economists still expect a slowdown late this year and in 2017. In August the Bank of England cut its benchmark interest rate to a new low as part of a package of stimulus measures. Mr. Hammond lamented the decades of underinvestment in U.K. roads, railways, and other infrastructure. He pledged "targeted public investment" to close the gap, and announced new funding for scientific research, with funds for developing drugs and medical devices and cutting-edge university research. He said that business is now uncertain about the future arrangements with the European Union, and uncertainty is unfavorable for investment.

Source: Excerpted from Jason Douglas and Nicholas Winning, "U.K. Vows Plan to Buffer Economy," *Wall Street Journal*, October 4, 2016, p. A10.

To have positive economic growth, technology must improve and advance, net savings and net investment occur, or both. The net product of the MNC zone, $Y_{MNC(t)}$, is no longer devoted entirely to using the commodities produced; some is set aside to provide for the expansion of output capacity. The net product not devoted to consumption is allocated to new investment. These investments are made in human capital as well as physical capital.

The simplest dynamic world model has consumer's preferences, technology, and the structure of prices constant through time. Thus, the composition of consumption does not change. Per capita consumption is constant so that the labor force and consumption grow at the same rate, g, so that

$$C(t) = cN(t) - cN()) [1 + g]t,$$

were $C(t)$ is the value of consumption and $N(t)$ is population. Let $J(t)$ equal new investment-type goods so that as at a fixed technology, A,

$$J(t) = gAQ(t)$$

and all physical quantities among the means of production $AQ(t)$ grow at the same rate. Therefore,

$$Q(t) - AQ(t) - AQ(t) = cN(t)$$

with the solution

$$Q(t) = [I - (1 + gA)]-1\ cN()\ [1 + g]t$$

and the total physical quantities in $Q(t)$ grow at the same rate, g, as do the physical quantities in $C(t)$. Put differently, at the exponential growth of consumption, $C(t)$, the above equation gives the total physical quantities, $q = Q(t)$, required, both directly and indirectly, including new investment, to keep the world system in dynamic equilibrium. Though this is what is necessary for dynamic world equilibrium, there is no assurance that all the necessary conditions will be met.

In line with the analysis of the MNC zone the labor required (and assumed to be demanded) in the world system is

$$L(t) = [a_{jVIV}]_n [1XD \; Q(t) = [a_{jVIVm-1XD}[1 - (1 + g)A] - 1 \; cN()) \; [1 + g]t$$

but full utilization of capacities and full employment further requires that

$$L(t) = L^*(t),$$

where $L^*(t)$ is the world's labor force and all labor quality types are growing at the same rate. Since the MNC zone countries contain the richest mix of labor qualities (including unskilled labor) the qualities in the world labor matrix is defined by that of the MNC or supra-surplus zone. Again, there are many reasons why full employment in the world system does not happen, not the least of which is inadequate incomes of the masses of unskilled labor and thus insufficient aggregate demand, though full employment may be achieved in one or more the supra-surplus nations, given sound fiscal and monetary policies (about which, more later).

Even in the static model the compositions of consumption and of labor requirements can change. Moreover, we know that in the long-run technology mutates (say, every 8 years), requiring an alternation in the composition of labor and capital requirements. New technology that produces new consumer goods (new industries) also changes the technology available to consumers for satisfying their needs and wants. The production coefficients in the A matrix of existing industries can change in the long run. Moreover, new industries give entirely new rows to the A matrix. With these new conditions the hypothesized wage rate and profit rate movements will cause different patterns of price variations.

Concluding Notes

The orthodoxy's general equilibrium theory usually proceeds from the particular to the aggregate. The input–output and initially linear approach used here shows how you can reverse this process and go from the aggregate to the particular. The central advantage from introducing realistic production, labor, and consumption relations is the ability to show how the multinational business corporation can be a dynamic force for global economic growth. At the same time, because the MNC or supra-surplus zone is the main source for financial capital, that zone introduces exchange rate instability into the world system even as it becomes a source of financial capital for the ENs.

The products and services produced and distributed by the multinational in the MNC zone cannot be explained by classical or Heckscher–Olin theories that require factor/technology immobility among nations and perfect competition in traded finished goods. The multinational freely moves its production, technology, and management wherever it finds profit opportunities. Proprietary knowledge has no national boundaries and floats freely, making the multinational nation-free. Even LDC commodity production and exports fail to conform to traditional models. There is little scope for factor-price equalization; or for prices based upon the marginal costs. Rather, production is demand-driven and prices are determined in world commodity markets, as producers become price-takers.

We next consider contemporary prospects for supra-surplus capitalism.

Chapter 12

STAGNATION AND INNOVATIONS

In the Beginning

Economic stagnation or economic immobilism, often called simply stagnation or secular stagnation, is a prolonged period of slow economic growth (usually measured by GNP growth rates), and usually accompanied by high unemployment. The term "secular stagnation" was originally coined by Alvin Hansen (1887–1975) of Harvard in 1938 to describe what he feared was the fate of the American economy following the Great Depression of the early 1930s: a check to economic progress as investment opportunities were stunted by the closing of the frontier and the collapse of immigration. It also refers to a condition of negligible or no economic growth in a market-based economy. Secular is in contrast to cyclical or short term, and suggests a change of fundamental dynamics which would play out only in its own time. Secular stagnation theory blamed the Great Depression on inadequate capital investment for hindering full deployment of labor and other economic resources. Hansen suggested that there may be innovations in the future comparable in their effect on investment to the railroad, the automobile, or electricity. It is highly unlikely, however that further technical change will be so much "more" capital using as to make up for the reduced rate of territorial expansion and population growth.

The general idea of secular stagnation runs through much of John Maynard Keynes *General Theory* which predated Hansen's work by a couple years and influenced him. Keynes. however, was focused on the

187

Great Depression and the deficiency of aggregate demand. While Hansen was often called "the American Keynes," his more definitive view of innovations went beyond Keynes into the long run. Keynes barely mentioned innovations, and then only "financial innovations". Clearly, to Hansen, and contrary to but not contradicting Keynes, the way out of secular stagnation was through innovations. Indeed, warnings of secular stagnation following deep recessions usually turned out to be wrong because they underestimated the potential of existing technologies, which in turn underestimated the problem of unemployment and underemployment created by new technologies.

Long before the United States became a supra-surplus nation, its economy was punctuated by episodes of stagnation. In looking at the causes, we will eventually come to consider whether this and other economies can emerge from such an affliction today. Since the way out of stagnation may be through innovations, we will consider the future possibilities for new technologies. At the same time, we need to examine the employment implications. First, we consider the history.

Historical Periods of Stagnation in the United States

The years following the financial Panic of 1873 known as the Long Depression were followed by periods of stagnation intermixed with surges of growth until steadier growth resumed around 1896. The period was interspersed with business bankruptcies, low interest rates, and deflation. The economic problems were probably the result of rapid changes in technology, such as railroads, steam-powered ocean ships, steel displacing iron, and the telegraph system. Since there was so much economic growth overall, how much of this era was stagnation remains controversial.

During the early 19th century the U.S. economy was primarily agricultural and suffered from labor shortages, which made slavery profitable. On the other hand, capital was so scarce before the Civil War that private investors supplied only a fraction of the money to build railroads, despite the large economic advantage offered by railroads. As new territories were opened and federal land sales conducted, land had to be cleared and new homesteads established. Hundreds of thousands of immigrants came to the United States every year and found jobs digging canals and building railroads. Because there was little mechanization almost all work was done by hand or with horses, mules and oxen until the last two decades of the century.

The celebrated decade of the 1880s, followed immediately by the Gay Nineties, witnessed great growth in railroads and the steel and machinery industries. Purchases of structures and equipment increased 500 percent from the previous decade. Labor productivity rose 25.5 percent and GDP nearly doubled. Labor did not share equally with the growth in productivity. The workweek during most of the 19th century was over 60 hours, and even higher during the first half of the century, with 12-hour work days common. As a result, there were numerous strikes and other labor movements for a 10-hour day. The tight labor market led to productivity gains allowing workers to maintain or increase their nominal wages during the secular deflation that caused real wages to rise in the late 19th century. There were temporary setbacks, such as when railroads cut wages during the Long Depression of the mid-1870s; however, the result was strikes throughout the nation.

In the next century came the Great Depression of the 1930s. It nonetheless was a period of high total factor productivity growth, primarily due to the building of roads and bridges, abandonment of unneeded railroad track and reduction in railroad employment, expansion of electric utilities and improvement in wholesale and retail distribution. World War II followed the Great Depression. Ironically, the building of infrastructure (financed by the government) during the great decline of the thirties and the rise in factor productivity enabled the United States to quickly convert back to peacetime production after the war.

During WWII factories that once produced automobiles and other machinery converted to the production of tanks, guns, military vehicles, and supplies. The government also built synthetic ammonia plants, synthetic rubber plants (tires), aluminum smelters, aviation fuel refineries, and aircraft engine factories during the war. Post-war, commercial aviation, plastics, and synthetic rubber would become major industries and synthetic ammonia was used for fertilizer. The end of armaments production freed up hundreds of thousands of machine tools which were made available for other industries. In particular, they were needed in the rapidly growing aircraft and automobile manufacturing industries. With the memory of war fresh in the minds of many, there was constant spending for defense programs creating what President Eisenhower called the military-industrial complex, which remains intact to this day.

The Great Depression which was for the most part global, was preceded by the high times of the Jazz Age. Some economists have argued that the seeds of the Great Depression were sown during the 1920s.

Just as the Great Depression followed the Jazz Age (as F. Scott Fitzgerald dubbed the 1920s), the case could be made that the recent stagnation in the United States is a continuation of the aftermath to the 2008-2009 financial crisis. While the Roaring Twenties and the more recent financial crisis were fueled by finance, in the aftermath of each, still more stimulus was required to achieve full employment. Take the more recent crisis as the more current concern. Since the Global Great Depression followed in the footsteps of the financial debacle, the specter of rising unemployment arose. Nobelist Paul Krugman has contended that fiscal policy stimulus and higher inflation to achieve a negative real rate of interest is necessary to achieve full employment. Larry Summers reached a similar conclusion in November 2013 when he said that even with artificial stimulus to demand there would be a lot of difficulty getting back to full employment.

Robert J. Gordon wrote in August 2012 that even *if* innovation were to continue into the future at the rate of the two decades before 2007, the U.S. faces six headwinds that are in the process of dragging long-term growth to half or less of the 1.9 percent annual rate experienced between 1850 and 2007. These headwinds include demography, education, inequality, globalization, energy/environment, and the overhang of consumer and government debt.[1] He suggests that future growth in consumption per capita for the bottom 99 percent of the income distribution could fall below 0.5 percent per year for decades.

Another hypothesis is that (high) levels of productivity greater than the economic growth rate are creating economic slack, in which fewer workers are required to meet the demand for goods and services. Firms have less incentive to invest and instead prefer to hold cash. If the expected return on real investment over the short term is presumed to be lower than the cost of holding cash then even pushing interest rates to zero will have little effect. That is, if you cannot push real interest rates below the

---

[1] Robert J. Gordon, "Is U.S. Economic Growth Over? Faltering Innovation Confronts the Six Headwinds," August 2012, Northwestern U., Economics Department.

so-called short-run natural rate (i.e., the rate of interest required to achieve the growth rate necessary to achieve full employment), you will struggle to bring forward future consumption, blunting the short-run effectiveness of monetary policy. Besides, if the policymakers fail to bring the short-term rate below the long-run natural rate there is a strong disincentive to increase fixed capital investment and a consequent preference to hold cash or cash-like instruments in an attempt to mitigate risk. This could cause longer-term problems and reduce an economy's potential output. This argument may explain why near-zero interest rates have had little effect except perhaps to encourage hoarding of money.

A prescient analysis of stagnation and what is now called financialization was provided in the 1980s by Harry Magdoff and Paul Sweezy, co-editors of the independent socialist journal *Monthly Review*. Magdoff was a former economic advisor to Vice President Henry A. Wallace in Roosevelt's New Deal administration, while Sweezy was a former Harvard Economics Professor. In their 1987 book, *Stagnation and the Financial Explosion*, they argued, based on Keynes, Hansen, Michal Kalecki, and Karl Marx, and marshaling extensive empirical data that, contrary to the conventional wisdom, stagnation or slow growth was the norm for mature, monopolistic (or oligopolistic) economies, while rapid growth was the exception.

Private accumulation had a strong tendency to weaken growth and elevate levels of excess capacity and unemployment/underemployment. This bad result could, however, be countered in part by such exogenous factors as state spending (military and civilian), epoch-making technological innovations (for example, the automobile in its expansionary period), and the growth of finance. In the 1980s and 1990s Magdoff and Sweezy argued that a financial expansion of long duration was lifting the economy, but this would eventually compound the contradictions of the system producing ever bigger speculative bubbles, and leading eventually to a resumption of overt stagnation. We will return to the Magdoff–Sweezy–Keynes–Hansen–Kalecki–Marx thesis in later chapters. The same argument might apply to Japan, next to be considered.

Thomas Piketty, in his landmark book, *Capital in the Twenty-First Century*, suggests that the high growth rates of the post-World War II era were, by and large, an aberration. While many people believe that growth ought to be at least 3 or 4 percent yearly, both history and logic dictate this to be illusory. Viewed in this light or darkness, the long-range projections from the Organisation for Economic Cooperation and Development (OECD), the Paris-based intergovernmental group for advanced economies, makes for sober reading. In a new report, "Policy Challenges for the Next 50 Years," the OECD warns that economic growth in the world's advanced industrial economies — including Europe, North America, and Japan — will likely slow even further from historic levels over the next half-century, while inequality will rocket to new heights and climate change will take an increasingly damaging toll on world GDP. Global GDP growth will steadily fall from 1.19 percent this decade to 0.54 percent between 2050 and 2060. Meanwhile inequality in these countries may rise as much as 30 percent or more.

If anything, these long-range projections are optimistic.[2] They assume that Europe and the United States each will absorb in the neighborhood of 50 million new immigrants over this period — an assumption that may run contrary to the restrictive politics of immigration playing out on both sides of the Atlantic.

Unfortunately, continuation of stagnation has profound implications. It would undermine the economic basis of traditional political hope of both left and right. It would mean ongoing high unemployment, ongoing deficits, ongoing struggles to fund public programs and, in all probability, ongoing and intensified political deadlock and wrangling as unemployment continues, deficits mount and a battle over narrowing economic possibilities for our grandchildren sets in.

Prospects for the largest economy appear grim. According to the Federal Reserve's FOMC, GDP growth rates fall from 2.2 percent in 2016 to 1.95 percent in 2018. This pattern is displayed in Figure 12.1.

Stagnation in Japan

With a GDP of $4.41 trillion, Japan has the third largest economy in the world. However, its GDP growth rate for the fourth quarter 2015 was

---

[2] For more concerns along these lines, see Gar Alperovitz, "Is Economic Stagnation the New Normal?" *Los Angeles Times*, September 4, 2014, op-ed page.

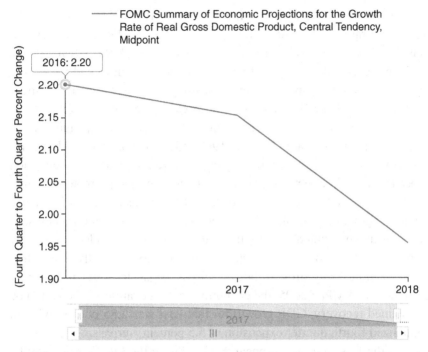

Figure 12.1 FOMC Summary of Economic Projections for the Growth Rate of Real Gross Domestic Product.

Source: US. Federal Open Market Committee, Federal Reserve Bank of St. Louis research.stlouisfed.org.

−1.4 percent, which has become typical since the early 1990s. With a per capita income of $34,870, some 16 percent of the population is below the poverty line. Japan is the third largest automobile manufacturing country, has the largest electronics goods industry, and is often ranked among the world's most innovative countries, leading in several measures of global patent filings. With increased competition from China and South Korea, manufacturing in Japan today now focuses primarily on high-tech and precision goods, such as optical instruments, hybrid vehicles, and robotics.

Growth in Japan throughout the 1990s was 1.5 percent and was slower than growth in other major developed economies, giving rise to the term Lost Decade. The decade experienced the collapse of the Japanese asset price bubble. As a consequence, Japan ran massive budget deficits (added trillions in Yen to the Japanese financial system) to finance large public works programs. Since, Abenomics, named after the Prime Minister, has thus far given the economy an unsteady growth. By 1998, Japan's public works projects still could not stimulate demand enough to end the economy's stagnation. In desperation, the Japanese government undertook "structural reform" policies intended to wring speculative excesses from the stock and real estate markets. As it turned out, these policies led Japan into deflation on numerous occasions between 1999 and 2004. Nobelist Paul Krugman argued that Japan was in a liquidity trap, requiring a plan to raise inflation expectations to, in effect cut long-term interest rates and promote spending.

Japan instead used a technique, somewhat based on Krugman's, called Quantitative Easing (QE). As opposed to flooding the money supply with newly printed money, the Bank of Japan expanded the money supply internally to raise expectations of inflation. Initially, the policy failed to induce any growth, but eventually began to affect inflationary expectations. By late 2005, the economy finally began what seemed to be a sustained recovery, GDP growth for that year was 2.85 percent with an annualized fourth quarter expansion of 5.5 percent, surpassing the growth rates of the U.S. and the European Union during the same period. Unlike previous recovery trends, domestic consumption has been the dominant driver of growth.

Despite interest rates hovering near zero for a long time, the QE strategy did not succeed in stopping price deflation. This led Krugman, some other economists, and some Japanese politicians to advocate the generation of higher inflation expectations. In July 2006, the zero-rate policy was ended. In 2008, the Japanese Central Bank still had the lowest interest rate in the developed world, but deflation had still not been eliminated and the Nikkei 225 had fallen over 50 percent (between June 2007 and December 2008). Then, on April 5, 2013, the Bank of Japan announced that it would be purchasing 60–70 trillion yen in bonds and securities in an attempt to eliminate deflation by doubling the money supply in Japan over the next 2 years. The Toyko Stock Exchange is the third largest in the world. Financial markets around the world responded positively to the government proactive policies, with the Nikkei 225 adding more than 42 percent since November 2012.

In what seems a paradox, secular stagnation is accompanied by massive innovations in Japan. It may be that the slowing growth in the working-age population in the last 20 years in Japan has led to persistent shortfalls of demand which can't be overcome even with near-zero interest rates. There remains the problem of building consumer demand at a time when people are less motivated to spend. The theory that internet and technological advancement in computers of the New Economy will have the same boost as the Great inventions of the past seems to hold little water. In fact, secular stagnation has been linked to the rise of the digital economy by some. Carl Benedikt Frey, for example, has suggested that digital technologies are much less capital-absorbing, creating only little new investment demand relative to other revolutionary technologies. Still another view is that the damage from the Great Recession was so long-lasting and permanent, that many workers will never get jobs again — that we really can't recover. The same argument could be made for the United States.

A third theory is related to the income distribution. So much of the recent gains have gone to the people at the top, who tend to save more of their money than ordinary working people who can't afford to do that. This has been a drag on consumption and by extension, on investment. Finally, a fourth theory is that advanced economies are paying the price for years of inadequate investment in infrastructure and education, the basic ingredients of growth. This could scarcely be said for Japan which has been investing heavily in infrastructure.

Figure 12.2 shows Japan's GDP growth rates since July 2013. The economy expanded 0.4 percent on quarter in the 3 months to March of 2015, boosted by private consumption, government spending, and exports. Figures came better than market expectations of a 0.1 percent growth and compare with an upwardly revised 0.4 percent contraction in the fourth quarter of 2015. GDP growth rates in Japan averaged 0.48 percent from 1980 until 2015, reaching an all-time high of 3.20 percent in the second quarter of 1990 and a record low of 0.4 percent in the first quarter of 2009, during the global financial crisis. Since July 2015, the average growth rate has been roughly zero. The stagnation continues.

BREAKING NEWS — Does U.S. Risk Japanese-Style Growth Slump?

In mid-June 2016 the Federal Reserve and the Bank of Japan left monetary policy unchanged. At the same time government bond yields reached fresh lows — they went negative in Germany, further negative in Japan and hit three-year lows in the U.S. There are many reasons for these declines. According to Greg Ip of the *Wall Street Journal*, three stand out. The first two are largely short term, but the third is more intractable and therefore more worrisome. It suggests that the U.S. and many other countries are coming to resemble Japan, which has been in a two-decades slump. The Fed has long assumed that it **would raise** short-term rates to some neutral level that is compatible with full employment and stable inflation. But that neutral level for short-term rates is elusive and keeps fallng; officials thought it was 4 percent in 2013, now think it's 3 percent, and Fed Chairwoman Janet Yellen said Wednesday it might be 2 percent. That day she cited "long-lasting or persistent" factors, such as aging societies and a global slump in productivity growth. A slower-growing workforce needs less equipment. Moreover, slow productivity growth also leads to slower growth in wages and profits, which discourage households from borrowing (because they will have less future income with which to repay). Worse, sluggish growth can be self-reinforcing. It is what Japan has been experiencing since 1990 wherein growth has averaged under 1 percent per year. Interest rates at zero and below have had limited effect at spurring business to invest more; they see their best growth prospects outside Japan. An aging population, slow productivity growth and a self-perpetuating pessimism depressing business investment are tough challenges to overcome. The verdict of the bond market is that they won't be overcome soon.

Source: This brief is based on a much longer article by Greg Ip, "U.S. Risks Japanese-Style Growth Slump," *Wall Street Journal*, June 17, 2016, p. A2.

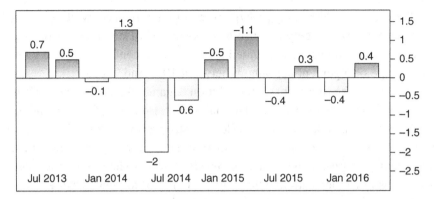

Figure 12.2   Japan GDP Growth Rate.

Source: www.tradingeconomics.com, Cabinet Office Japan.

Stagnation in the UK

The UK has a partially regulated capitalistic market-based economy. It is a supra-surplus economy. Today the UK is the fifth-largest economy in the world and the second-largest in Europe after Germany. HM Treasury, led by the Chancellor of the Exchequer, is responsible for developing and executing the British government's public finance policy and economic policy. The Bank of England, the Old Lady of Threadneedle Street, is the UK's central bank and is responsible for issuing notes and coins in the nation's currency, the pound sterling. The UK is a member of the European Union, but not the Euro zone. Pound sterling is the world's third-largest reserve currency (after the U.S. Dollar and the Euro). Since 1997 the Bank of England's Monetary Policy Committee headed by the Governor of the Bank of England, has been responsible for setting interest rates at the level necessary to achieve the overall inflation target for the economy that is set by the Chancellor each year.

The UK service sector makes up around 73 percent of GDP, led by a gigantic tourist industry. London is one of the three financial "command centers" of the global economy (alongside New York City and Tokyo). It is the world's largest financial center alongside New York, and it has the largest city GDP in Europe. Edinburgh is also one of the largest financial centers in Europe. London has the most international visitors of any city in the world. The U.K. plays a large role in global finance, well in excess of its overall size, largely because of its historical place in world finance. These creative industries accounted for about 7 percent of GDP and grew an average of 6 percent per annum between 1997 and 2005.[3]

Although the first industrial revolution began in the U.K., manufacturing now is only 16.7 percent of national output. Emerging from the industrial revolution, it led in the textile industry, followed by other heavy industries such as shipbuilding, coal mining, and steel making. British merchants, shippers, and bankers developed overwhelming advantage over those of other nations allowing the U.K. to dominate international trade in the 19th century. As other nations industrialized, coupled with economic decline after two devastating world wars, the United Kingdom began to lose its competitive advantage and heavy industry declined, by degrees, throughout the 20th century.

As in the U.S., the automobile industry is a significant part of the U.K. manufacturing sector, employing over 800,000 people. It is a major center for engine manufacturing and has a significant presence in auto racing. The aerospace industry is the second- to third-largest national aerospace industry in the world. Key names are the Airbus A3800, Eaton (fuel subsystem pumps), Messier–Bugatti–Dowty (the landing gear) and Rolls–Royce (the engines). Moreover, the U.K. space industry is growing very fast, while the pharmaceutical industry plays an important role in the U.K. economy and has the third-highest share of global pharmaceutical R&D expenditures (after the United States and Japan).

The U.K. did not escape the Great Recession, and like the U.S. has had difficulty recovering. Since July 2013 the GDP growth rate has never reached 1 percent. The British economy expanded a mere 0.4 percent on quarter in the first 3 months of 2016, slowing from a 0.6 percent growth in the previous period. Household spending continued to support growth while exports shrank and business investment contracted for the second straight quarter amid uncertain results for the European Union referendum. GDP growth rate in the U.K. averaged 0.51 percent from 1955 until 2016, reaching an all-time high of 5 percent in the first

---

[3] Carl Benedikt Frey, "The End of Economic Growth? How the Digital Economy Could Lead to Secular Stagnation," *Scientific American* 312(1), 2015.

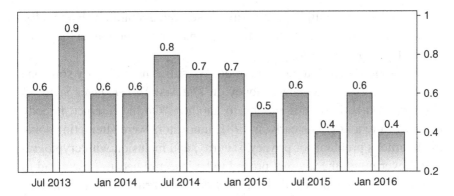

Figure 12.3   United Kingdom GDP Growth Rate.

Source: www.tradingeconomics.com, Office for National Statistics.

quarter of 1973 and a record low of –2.780 percent in the first quarter of 1974.

Given the condition of global stagnation, we naturally look for ways out. One remedy that is often mentioned is innovations. However, not all innovations are created equally; some, but not all, can lead to economic growth. In the past we can point to electricity, automobiles, steamships, and railways as innovations that led to rapid expansions. Can these be duplicated?

Innovations: The Blockchain Revolution

Once again, or so it appears, the technological genie has been unleashed from its bottle. As we learned from the 1960s TV show, *I Dream of Jennie*, once out of the bottle, she is very difficult to put back in.

A brief survey will show how we came to this point, a tipping point, as it were. The first four decades of the Internet brought with it e-mail, the World Wide Web, dot-coms, social media, the mobile Web, big data, cloud computing, and the early days of the Internet of Things. It has reduced the costs of searching, collaborating, and exchanging information. It also has lowered the barriers to entry for new media and entertainment, new forms of retailing, and various digital ventures. Through sensor technology, it has infused intelligence into our wallets or clothing, or automobiles, our buildings, our cities, and even our biology. Eventually, we will be so immersed in the technology that we will no longer "log on." We will already be online.

Some things the Internet cannot do. We still cannot identify someone or trust an entity to exchange money. In *The New Yorker*, Peter Steiner's 1993 cartoon had one dog talking to another, "On the Internet, nobody knows you're a dog." As early as 1981, innovators were attempting solve the Internet's problems of privacy, security, and inclusion with cryptography. Never mind, the Internet proved to be insecure because users had to divulge too much personal data. In 1993, the brilliant mathematician David Chaum invented eCash, a digital payment system that was "a technically perfect product which made it possible to safely and anonymously pay over the Internet." Then, however, users of the Internet were not concerned about security or privacy online and Chaum's Dutch company DigiCash went bankrupt in 1998.

About that time, Nick Szabo, a Chaum associate, wrote a short paper called "The God Protocol," a slight twist on Nobel laureate Leon Lederman's phrase "the God Particle," in reference to the Higgs boson in modern physics. God, according to Szabo, could be designated as the third party in transactions. Everyone would trust God. It's even engraved on our coins. All inputs would be sent to God who would return the outputs. Faith, however, can only reach so far. One "God Particle" that was missing in the puzzle was an acceptable currency.

Later, in 2008, when the global financial industry was crashing, a pseudonymous person or persons named Satoshi Nakamoto outlined a new protocol for a peer-to-peer electronic cash system using a cryptocurrency called bitcoin. Cryptocurrencies (digital currencies) are different from traditional fiat currencies because they are not created or controlled by governments or central banks. A set of rules — in the form of distributed computations — ensured the integrity of the data exchanged among billions of devices without going through a trusted third party such as God. Bitcoins have excited or otherwise captured the imagination of the computing world and has spread like wildfire to businesses, governments, privacy advocates, social development activists, media theorists, and journalists, to name more than a few, everywhere. Despite exclamations such as "My God, this is it!" God is held at a secular distance. No third party or middleman is required. Today thoughtful people are trying to understand the implications of a protocol that enables mere mortals to manufacture trust through clever code. This has never happened before.[4]

Of course, there is more to it than this. The protocol is the foundation of a growing number of global distribution ledgers called blockchains — of which the bitcoin blockchain is the largest. Blockchains enable us to send money directly and safely from me to you, without going through a bank or PayPal. It is the Internet of value or money. Big banks and some governments are implementing blockchains as distributed ledgers to revolutionize the way information is stored and transactions are made. The advantages — speed, lower cost, security, fewer errors, and the elimination of central points of attacks and failure.

How does the bitcoin blockchain work? The digital currency isn't saved in a computer file somewhere like the Internet. Rather, it is represented by transactions recorded in a blockchain — kind of like a global spreadsheet or ledger, which leverages the resources of a large peer-to-peer bitcoin network to verify and approve each bitcoin transaction. Each blockchain like the one that used bitcoin, is distributed; it runs on computers provided by volunteers around the world; there is no central database to hack. The blockchain is public; anyone can view it at any time because it resides on the network, not within a single institution charged with auditing transactions and keeping records. And the blockchain is encrypted.

Every 10 minutes, like a slow heartbeat of the bitcoin network, all the transactions conducted are verified, cleared, and stored in a block which is linked to the preceding block, thereby creating a chain. Each block must refer to the preceding block. This structure permanently timestamps and stores exchanges of value, preventing anyone from altering the ledger. If, say, you wanted to steal a bitcoin, you'd have to rewrite the coin's entire history on the blockchain in broad daylight, and that's practically impossible. Like the World Wide Web of information, it's the World Wide Ledger of value — a distributed ledger that everyone can download and

---

[4]Much of the following few paragraphs is based on Don Tapscott and Alex Tapscott, *Blockchain Revolution* (New York: Portfolio/Penguin, 2016).

run on their personal computer. This new platform enables conciliation of digital records regarding just about everything in real time.

The potential for blockchain goes beyond financial transactions. Blockchain mashes up cryptography and peer-to-peer networking to create what amounts to a shared database of transactions and other information — which can be open to all, but controlled by no one in particular. It's not simply for securely recording payments in crypto-coinage; a blockchain can manipulate complex transactions, even entire contracts. Collaborators will be able to work together as free agents instead of under the hierarchy of bosses. The poetic vision of a blockchain society is a flock of starlings at dusk; decentralized yet perfectly coordinated. In the starlings vision, blockchain could replace lots of bankers, accountants, and lawyers, as well as escrow accounts, insurance, and everything else that society invented pre-21st century to verify payments and contracts.

The design of blockchain prevents the owner of a currency token from committing fraud by spending it twice. The first time it is spent is recorded for all to see, so no one would ever accept it a second time. This "truth-telling" feature of blockchain makes it useful to banks, which have been among the first to start testing it. Last year Microsoft launched blockchain as a service. Nasdaq, an early adopter of blockchain, is using the technology to allow private companies to issue stock and stockholders of public companies to vote their shares. Everledger is using it to create a registry of diamonds to suppress trade in "blood diamonds" from zones of conflict.[5]

Some argue that it will never be possible to reduce the complex, fast-changing world of business to rules commanded by softwear. In practice, the system is elitist, controlled by those who build the new virtual machines and understand them. Machines are not God, but if we are to be the gods, we have to take control of the technology before it takes control of us. As we will see, it is a dilemma we face with robotic technology.

Innovations: The Driverless Car and Robots

While most people think that the driverless can won't be in their garages for another 5 years, guess again. In August, 2016 Uber Technologies will

---

[5] References to these applications are found in Peter Coy and Olga Kharif, "This Is Your Company On Blockchain," *Business Week*, August 24–September 4, 2016, pp. 8–9.

begin using self-driving taxis to ferry customers around, of all places, Pittsburg, PA. USA. Though Pittsburg was once part of the Rust Belt, it has since been the locale for high-tech industry. This is a first in an industry that is in a race to make driverless cars commercially viable. Uber's service uses Volvo XC90 sport-utility vehicles and Ford Focus. It may be a few months down the road before you can hail a cab with no one in the front seat. Two Uber employees will be sitting in the front seat, one in the driver's seat with hands on the steering wheel and the other simply observing from the "death seat." True, the one with hands on the steering wheel is an emergency backup; the vehicle is otherwise on its own, robot-like. Only a few self-driving taxis will be deployed at random, at first, but the Uber goal is for 100 in Pittsburgh and possibly elsewhere as 2016 rolls along. As one might expect from this new technology, there eventually will be a loss of jobs among Uber's 1.5 million live drivers worldwide.

With the downside for working stiffs, what is the motivation for using driverless taxis? Uber Chief Executive Travis Kalanick says "the technology is necessary to lower the cost of ride hailing and car ownership, even if it means the future loss of jobs."[6] It's all about competition. Uber wants to claim pole position in the race to implement technologies some think are years away from safe, widespread use. As ever, there are rivals. General Motors Co., Uber's chief rival, plans to test driverless Chevrolet Bolt taxis with its partner in 2017, Ford Motor Co. GM has set a goal a goal of producing fully self-driving fleet vehicles *with no steering or pedals* within in the next 5 years. Swedish Volvo Car Corp., which is owned by China's Zhejiang Geely Holding Group Co. is aggressively developing an automated car. Uber, a user of the vehicles, does not plan to produce any. But the company plans to move more than people with its automated vehicles.

Of course, the innovation behind these cars is robotics. Robots are not strangers in Pittsburg. The city is home to Carnegie Mellon University's robotics department, which has produced many of the biggest names robotics. Sebastian Thrun, the creator of Google's self-driving car, spent some 7 years researching autonomous robots at CMU. John Bares ran CMU's National Robotics Engineering Center for 13

---

[6] Greg Bensinger and Jack Nicas, "Uber Plans Self-Drive Taxis," *Wall Street Journal*, August 19, 2016, p. B1.

years before founding Carnegie Robotics, another Pittsburgh-based company that makes components for self-driving industrial robots used in mining, farming, and the military. How fast robots will populate all industry is an open question.

While Kalanick and other advocates envision a rosy future for driverless cars, there are dissenters. Initially, the Uber trips will be free, rather than the standard local rate of $1.30 per mile. In the long run, Kalanick predicts, prices will fall so low that the per-mile cost of travel, even for long trips, will be cheaper in a driverless car than in a private car.[7] This, of course, overlooks the 5-year time frame for driverless cars for private use. He downplays other issues. For example, robots are not necessarily good at navigating bridges, of which Pittsburg has about 500. For example, while crossing the Allegheny river in an Uber autonomous car, a chime sounded, a signal to the driver to take the wheel. (a second ding a few seconds later indicated that the car was back under computer control.) In July 2016 a driver using Tesla's Autopilot service died after colliding with a tractor trailer, which apparently neither the driver or the car's softwear saw. A tractor trailer is a large target. Also Google has seen a few accidents, which have been less severe, but it limits its cars to 25 miles per hour.

Will robots eventually outwit humans? Behind the robot is artificial intelligence (AI) and behind that are algorithms. To make AI knowledgeable on a grand scale the softwear must learn on its own. This requires learning the idiosyncrasies needed to translate every human language. That is a tall order. One camp thinks that if we correct algorithms when they make the wrong turns, they'll learn to avoid bad choices and choose only the right ones. Humans parent the AI until it reaches the ability to operate on its own. Another camp believes learning is also informed by self-awareness, which lets humans make decisions based on their limits. This camp says that algorithms could avoid bad decisions by understanding their limited abilities, as some have proved. Of course, we cannot avoid the obvious: algorithms are human-made. While humans are not going to be replaced by robots, robots are going to take on human jobs,

---

[7]For much more on Uber and driverless cars, see Max Chafkin, with Eric Newcomer, "Your Driverless Uber is Here," *Business Week*, August 22–28, 2016, pp. 22–26

which creates a huge problem in a slow-growing global economy. While robots can reproduce themselves only in a limited way, in the future they will create a surfeit of labor in the supra-surplus economies.

One of the most interesting applications of quantum mechanics is in computers — hence, in robotics. Quantum computers can take advantage of odd sub-atomic interactions to solve problems far faster than a conventional machine could. Such computers could speed advances in AI. Investment in the field from big business and the government, including intelligence agencies focused on breaking codes, is surging. The cryptographic tools commonly used to protect information online rely on very hard math problems, such as factoring large integers, that normal computers can't solve in a reasonable time frame. Quantum computers, though, could probably make quick work of such equations. Hence the possible application in robots.

Those Who Welcome Robots

Not everyone sees robots replacing human labor. Another point of view is that the robots are coming, let's welcome them. In this view technology always creates more jobs than its destroys. History is one place to look. Steam engines destroyed jobs for horse handlers, but enabled an explosion of manufactories, never imagined jobs and the Industrial Revolution. Autos did away with trolleys but enabled hundreds of millions of new jobs. Vacuums and washing machines destroyed jobs for domestic engineers but at the same time freed women to enter a much better paid workforce in factories. Computers replaced those who used rulers and exacto knives for laying out magazines or constructing spreadsheets. Media and Wall Street could not exist as we know them without Microsoft Office. In such cases technology aids humans, rather than replacing them.

The argument goes further. While some people are left behind, as society gets wealthier, we can help them catch up. In other words, it is a matter of getting our education system right. We have heard this argument before; that the fault lies within the education establishment. Doing more with less drives progress and robots are simply another way of increasing productivity. While we can teach computer science earlier, the teachers may well be robots. Even if societal wealth is improved, there is no assurance that it will be divided in an equitable way. Still, we can imagine salesmen with Google Maps, realtors with 3-D home views, carpenters with laser tape measures, and Doctors with robot-assisted minimally invasive surgery. We can imagine many things. Robots nonetheless comprise the only technology that directly replace the human. While robots may not be able to outthink people, they think faster with a horde of data.

Some Innovative Companies

We might expect innovations often to be made at the corporate level. We would be remiss not to mention a few of those changing the world, and making profits doing it. We are more interested in those that are taking on society's biggest problems. GlaxoSmithKline (GSK) is one such company: its roots go all the way back to a London apothecary called Plough Court Pharmacy, established in 1715. Along the way, it sold dried milk for infants (early 1900s), manufactured penicillin (WWII), and developed AZT, the first medicine approved for AIDS, in the early years of a global pandemic. Now, at the age of 300, the company is again reinventing itself, growing a pharmaceutical business whose aim is to serve not just patients in the wealthier nations but also consumers in less developed countries, the other 6 billion people in the world. The company has developed a vaccine for malaria, which has devastated huge areas of sub-Saharan Africa. Pilot vaccination programs in the hardest-hit areas may begin as early as 2018. GSK has partnered with the government of Botswana on an ambitious HIV treatment program, and is collaborating the National Institutes of Health on a vaccine for the Zika virus. What's more, the company bases it drug pricing on GNP per capita of each of the 150 countries where it does business. In dozens of the least developed nations, it reinvests 20 percent of its profits in local health care infrastructure and worker training.

A second company is IDE Technologies, an Israeli innovator. IDE is a leader in desalination technologies, turning salt water into freshwater. It supplies 70 percent of this Middle Eastern country's potable water. IDE builds and operates some of the biggest desalination plants in about 40 other countries, including Mexico, Chile, China, and the USA. In the USA, the company recently opened the largest such plant in the West, in

Carlsbad, California. The $1 billion undertaking makes seawater into potable water in just 45 minutes, and costs less than 0.5 cents per gallon. The company has developed a wide range of energy- and cost-efficient desalination processes, including the use of waste steam to generate electricity and a proprietary "pressure center" that allows large plants to perform maintenance via the Internet. With water shortages in some regions of the world, a situation aggravated by warming temperatures and climate change, these innovations are life-saving.

About a decade-ago, General Electric launched a massive sustainable-business strategy, Ecomagination, with a pledge to invest in clean technology. Through the end of 2015, the company invested $17 billion in clean R&D while generating $232 billion from Ecomagination products. These include the Evolution Series Tier 4 Locomotive, which claims 70 percent lower CO_2 emissions than GE's previous model, and the Digital Wind Farm, which can boost a wind farm's energy production by one-fifth.

A fourth company making a difference is Gilead, a force fighting HIV and hepatitis where money is scarce. While Gilead was attacked in the USA for the high price of its hepatitis-C cure Sovaldi, notorious as a "$1,000 pill;" in India, a 28-day supply of the drug costs just $100. Gilead has made arrangements with 11 Indian generic drug-makers to supply hep-C drugs to patients in 101 developing countries. It has been a decade since Gilead began licensing agreements in the developing world. It expects soon to treating 10 million people in poor countries. Perhaps patients in the rich USA cannot afford the hep-C drug, but Gilead is making it affordable in poor nations.

Nike is a familiar name, if only because Tiger Woods pitches its products. What is less known is its recycled shoe program that dates back to 1990, which has hit a steady sustainability stride ever since. Some 71 percent of its footwear and apparel used Nike Grind, which is made of recycled polyester and other materials. It has also been incorporated in more than 1 billion square feet of sports surfaces — including running tracks, playgrounds, and football fields — replacing materials like virgin rubber. Meanwhile, the popular shoe line is both innovative and eco-friendly. Engineers reduced waste by 60 percent on average for every Flyknit shoe v. what's used for traditional shoes, saving nearly 23 million pounds of fabric-scrap waste since 2012. New 2020 targets include sourcing 100 percent of cotton more sustainably and reducing landfill waste. This sportswear maker certainly is competitive in the race for sustainability.

Fortune has listed 50 companies changing the world and making profits doing it.[8] Among the others are Mastercard, First Solar, Coca-Cola, Intel, Scheider Electric (France), Olam (Singapore), Unilever (Netherlands), Compass Group (UK), Smart Communications (Philippines), Panasonic (Japan), Cipla (India), and Tesla. These companies, including many in the USA, are unique inasmuch as they are using a new profits paradigm. They are changing the face of supra-surplus capitalism by providing low-cost innovative products and services to impoverished nations.

Conclusion

What with blockchains, driverless cars and robots, one might suppose that the future for productivity is bright. True, most of us feel more productive than ever, with wi-fi and mobile data, smart phones and apps that let us do everything from hailing a ride to ordering groceries. We can get more done in more places, most of the time. Not so fast. The Bureau of Labor Statistics (BLS) tell us that's an illusion. Not only is productivity in America declining, it's been falling for over a decade. This is important since economic growth is the product of productivity and demographics. With birthrates falling and immigration down, productivity needs to grow — or we will be worse off than our parents. The U.S. is not alone: the number of other countries growing by less than 2 percent a year has been steadily rising. One of the reasons for the productivity slowdowns has been put forward in the aforementioned Robert Gordon's *The Rise and Fall of American Growth*. Gordon says that the digital-technology boom just is not all it's been cracked up to be — especially when compared with important shifts like indoor plumbing, electricity, and the combustion engine. In short, the Industrial Revolution at the turn of the 19th century had a much greater effect on economic growth than the personal computer revolution in the 20th. Indeed,

---

[8] See "Change the World," *Fortune*, September 1, 2016, pp. 59–74.

productivity growth began shrinking after the 1970s, when digital technology began to take off. Any productivity payoff from digital technology has already come and gone. While you may have some productivity growth from the use of smartphones and tablets, it is not nearly as much as from the PC boom. Meanwhile, at the company level, the profits paradigm has shifted, changing a major characteristic of supra-surplus capitalism. These companies are focused on matters beyond surplus product or simply productivity. Will the coming of robots and quantum mechanics make matters worse or better?

How far have the blockchains gone? The financial services industry has already rebranded and privatized blockchain technology, referring to it as distributed ledger technology, in an attempt to reconcile the best of bitcoin — security, speed, and cost — with an entirely closed system that requires a bank or financial institution's permission to use. Blockchains are considered more reliable databases than what they already have. Moreover, investing in blockchain start-ups is taking off, as did investing in dot-coms in the 1990s. The rate of investment recent doubled annually. Another dramatic development: the Bank of England's top economist, Andrew Haldane, has proposed a national digital currency for the United Kingdom. Despite all this interest or perhaps because of it, bitcoin's price has fluctuated drastically, and the ownership of bitcoins is still concentrated. The bitcoin price hit a 2-year high of $719 on June 14, 2016. In 2013 some 937 people owned half of all bitcoin, although that is changing daily. Huge institutions now control and own this new means of production and social interaction — its underlying infrastructure; massive and growing treasure troves of data; the algorithms that increasingly govern business and daily life; the world of apps; and extraordinary emerging capabilities, machine learning, and autonomous vehicles. Economic power has gotten spikier, more concentrated, and more entrenched. Rather than data being more widely and democratically distributed, it is being hoarded and exploited by fewer entities that often use it to control more and acquire more power. Worse, powerful digital conglomerates such as Amazon, Google, Apple, and Facebook — all Internet start-ups a one time — are capturing the treasure troves of data that citizens and institutions generate often in private data silos rather than on the Web.

Breaking News — Bitcoin Rallies

Bitcoin is a hot investment. Since September of 2015, monthly bitcoin prices have risen nonstop, with the rally accelerating in recent weeks. The virtual currency surged to $574.11 on Sunday, more than double its low in September of $326.61, according to digital-currency news service CoinDesk.

Never mind. It is no longer the hot topic it once was. The volume of media articles and blogs mentioning bitcoin worldwide tanked in 2014, and has failed to recover even as the value of the virtual currency started rising again toward the end of last year, according to Dow Jones & Co.

The media's faded interest reflects that most of the investment interest in bitcoin comes from China. There, interest has grown as bitcoin has appreciated. Two Chinese bitcoin exchanges, Huobi and OKCoin, now account for 92 percent of all global trading in this currency, according to data from blockchain,info. Fears of a sudden devaluation of the yuan have led Chinese investors to bitcoin.

By contrast, global interest in bitcoin's ledger technology, blockchain, continues to grow. Recently, J.P. Morgan Chase & Co. and Citigroup Inc successfully tested using the blockchain as a way to keep records on credit default-swap transactions. While bitcoin has lost its cool, blockchain has become hot.

Source: based on Jon Sindreu, "Bitcoin Rallies, but Lure Grows More Limited," *Wall Street Journal*, June 7, 2016, p. C4.

A New Look for the Global System's Second-oldest Profession

The current global system of finance is antiquated, built on decades-old technology that is at odds with our rapidly advancing digital world, making it oftentimes slow and unreliable. It is exclusive, leaving out billions of people with no access to basic financial tools. It is centralized, exposing it to data breaches, other attacks, or outright failure. Moreover, it is monopolistic, reinforcing the status quo and stifling innovation. Blockchain promises to solve these problems and many more as innovations and entrepreneurs devise new ways to create value on this powerful platform. According to Tapscott and Tapscott, there are six ways in which the global financial system will be transformed.[9]

1. Attestation: two parties who neither know nor trust each other can transact and do business. The blockchain technology can establish trust when trust is needed by verifying the identity and capacity of any counterparty through a combination of past transaction history (on the blockchain), reputation scores based on aggregate reviews, and other social and economic indicators. The blockchain network clears and settles peer-to-peer value transfers, and it does so continually so that its ledger is always up to date. Anyone, anywhere, with a smart phone and an Internet connection could tap into the vast arteries of global finance.

2. Speed: today remittances take three to seven days to settle. Stock trades take 2 or 3 days, whereas bank loan trades take an average of a staggering 23 days to settle. In contrast, the netcoin network takes an average of 10 minutes to clear and settle all transactions conducted during that period. Other blockchain networks are even faster, and new innovations, such as the Bitcoin Lightning Network, aim to dramatically scale the capacity of the bitcoin blockchain while dropping settlement and clearing times to a fraction of a second. The shift to instant and frictionless value transfers would free up capital otherwise trapped in transit, bad news for anyone profiting from the float.

3. Risk Management: blockchain technology can mitigate several forms of financial risks. The first is settlement risk, the risk that your trade will bounce back because of some glitch in the settlement process. The second is counterparty risk, the risk that your counterparty will default before settling a trade. Finally, and most significantly is systemic risk, the total sum of all outstanding counterparty risk in the system. For example, during the financial crisis, one of the risks was if I'm trading with somebody, how do I know they're going to settle on the other side? Instant settlement on the blockchain

---

[9]Tapscott and Tapscott, op. cit.

eliminates that risk completely. Irrevocability of a transaction and instant reconciliation of financial reporting would eliminate one aspect of agency risk — the risk that unscrupulous managers will exploit the cumbersome paper trail and significant time delay to conceal wrongdoing.

4. Value Innovation: the bitcoin blockchain was designed for moving bitcoins not for handling other financial assets. Since, however, the technology is open source, it invites experimentation. Some innovations are developing separate blockchains, known as altcoins, built for something other than bitcoin payments. Others are looking to leverage the bitcoin blockchain's size and liquidity to create "spin-off" coins on sidechains that can be "colored" to represent any asset or liability, physical or digital — a corporate stock or bond, a barrel of oil, a bar of gold, a car, a car payment, a receivable or a payable, or of course a currency. Sidechains interoperate with the blockchain though a two-way peg, a cryptographic means of transferring assets off the blockchain and back again without a third party exchange, so much the worse for God. Blockchain technology is already being used to record, exchange, and trade assets and liabilities, and could eventually replace traditional exchanges and centralized markets.

5. Open Source: being an open source technology means that blockchain can continue to innovate, repeat, and improve, as long as there is a consensus in the network. In contrast, conventional financial services cannot be changed easily. It stands "twenty miles high and on the verge of teetering over."

These benefits — attestation, dramatically lower costs lightning speed, lower risks, great innovation of value, adaptability — argue Tapscott and Tapscott, have the potential to transform payments, the securities industry, investment banking, accounting and auditing, venture capital, insurance, enterprise risk management, retail banking, and other aspects of the financial industry. This is a very strong statement and not everyone will agree; still blockchain technology is getting a lot of attention.

Moreover, there is much in conventional finance to criticize — to which we will return in the next chapter.

Certainly the financial services industry would change; it would change in many ways. There are eight core functions of finance that would be altered. First, there is authenticating identity and value. There would be verifiable and robust identities cryptographically secured. Second, it would be a way of moving value. The transfer of value can be in very large and very small increments. Since there is no middle man, these transfers can be made at dramatically lower costs and greater speeds. Retail banking, wholesale banking, payment car networks, money transfer services, and telecommunications would be affected. Third, value could be stored, whether it be currencies, commodities or financial assets. The payment mechanism combined with a reliable and safe store of value reduces the need for typical financial services. Bank savings and checking accounts would become obsolete. Retail banking, brokerages, investment banking, asset management, and telecommunications would be affected. Fourth, bitcoins have lending value — credit card debt, mortgages, corporate bonds, municipal bonds, government bonds, asset-backed securities and other forms of credit could be held on the blockchain ledger. Debt can be issued, traded, and settled on the blockchain. This would increase efficiency, reduce friction, and improve systemic risk. Wholesale, commercial and retail banking would be affected. Fifth, Value could be exchanged — speculating, hedging, and arbitraging would take place. Blockchain takes settlement times on all transactions from days and weeks to minutes and seconds. Investment, wholesale banking, foreign exchange traders, hedge funds, pension funds, retail brokerage, clearing houses, stock, futures, commodities exchanges, commodities brokerages, and central banks would be involved. Sixth, Funding and investing in an asset, company, start-up — capital appreciation, dividends, interest, rents, or some combination would take place. New models for peer-to-peer financing recording corporate actions such as dividends paid automatically through smart contracts would evolve. Investment banking, venture capital, legal audits, property management, stock exchanges, crowdfunding would all be affected. Seventh, Value and management of risk could take place, protecting assets, homes, lives, health, business property and business practices, and derivative products. Using reputational systems, insurers will better estimate actuarial risk, creating decentralized markets for insurance. Derivatives would be made more transparent. Insurance, risk management, wholesale banking, brokerage, and clearing houses would be affected. Eighth, the accounting for value would facilitate new corporate governance. Distributed ledger will make audit and financial reporting real time, responsive and transparent, and will dramatically improve the capacity of regulators to scrutinize financial actions within a corporation. As a mechanism for shared, decentralized, and replicated transaction records, blockchain is a golden resource.

There are some obstacles in the way of blockchain. For now, most people have only a vague understanding of bitcoin and cryptocurrency and very few have even heard of blockchain the technology. One would be hardpressed to locate a bitcoin exchange or a bitcoin ATM anywhere in New York City, much less in Athens. In other words, blockchain may not be ready for prime time. Hashing, the process of running pending transactions though the secure hash algorithm 256 (SHA-256) to validate them and solve a block, burns a lot of electricity. Estimates liken the bitcoin network's energy consumption to the power used by nearly seven hundred average American homes at the low end of the spectrum and to the energy consumed by the island of Cyprus at the high end. It would be greater than the aggregate output of the world's top five hundred supercomputers. This assumes that $3 billion worth of bitcoins is in circulation. Also, would bitcoins be regulated by government? To be able to persist, the blockchain network would have to hold its own against mighty central authorities. With the Internet, powerful corporations have captured much of the technology and are using it in their vast private empires to extract most of the value. Would they do the same with the blockchain technology? Will the blockchain be a job killer? It's difficult to know. The 2015 World Economic Forum annual meeting in Davos Switzerland discussed the impact of technology on jobs. All agreed that although technological innovations may disrupt labor markets temporarily, overall they generate new and incrementally more jobs. Would this time be different? The bitcoin community does not yet have formal oversight bodies such as the Internet Engineering Task Force, or the World Wide Web Consortium to anticipate development needs and guide their resolution. Moreover, the community prefers it this way; it eschews governance of any kind. Critics have also argued that, because the technology is decentralized, lightning quick, and peer to peer, criminals would exploit it. But there is nothing unique to bitcoin or blockchain technology that makes it more effective for criminals than other technologies. Anyway, all this is to say that the obstacles are formidable.

John Maynard Keynes once called for an international currency to replace the then dominant trading currency, the British pound, in international trade. Could the bitcoin be used as that international currency? It is doubtful since no international reserves are held in bitcoins; even the lowly Chinese yuan is held in modest reserves at the IMF. It would make more sense if the SDR were to become the international currency. It is already used as a unit of account and is held as international financial reserves. It would only need to be accepted as a trading currency. We will return to this issue later.

Part IV

CASINO CAPITALISM

Chapter 13

AT INCEPTION

Like the Roman God, Janus, supra-surplus capitalism has two faces. One is of industrial surplus and the other of financial excess which I chose to call "casino capitalism." Like all things, it has a beginning, but, like the movie "Casablanca," it could have any one of two endings. Or, like F. Scott Fitzgerald's *The Last Tycoon*, it may not have an ending. Present at inception was Ronald Wilson Reagan. It has reemerged every few years. It is instructive nonetheless to go back to the beginning and examine the residual.

A legacy of Reaganomics was the greatly enlarged importance of Wall Street in American society. The central message of Ronald Reagan was that not only were American corporations free to do whatever they wished, so could people with wealth. The perpetuation of these attitudes by the early Clinton Administration, often at the expense of those near the bottom, astonished and angered many Old Democrats, such as Harry S. Truman.[1]

Little distance separates wealth from Wall Street. Thus, Wall Street became the eye of a hurricane of financial vortices soon to engulf and shape a financially fragile American economy. During 1983–1989 the

---

[1] For the full story of Truman, see E. Ray Canterbery, *Harry S. Truman: The Economics of a Populist President* (Singapore/New Jersey/London: World Scientific, 2014).

United States imploded into Las Vegas — hence, the term "casino economy."[2] A similar kind of speculative bubble rose over Tokyo.

This unnerving transformation reached an apogee of financial speculation somewhere around the mid-1980s, conflated into a stagnation during the early 1990s, only to reignite into a speculative orgy during the last half of the 1990s. The latter was epitomized by the dot-com bubble in 2000–2001. Thereafter, financial speculation led to the 2008–2009 collapse, followed by what I have called "the Great Recession." In turn, since the economy here and in Japan never fully recovered, both countries have been experiencing a long era of stagnation, accompanied by zero and near-zero short-term interest rates. Many seemed to have rediscovered during these speculative episodes the Veblenesque pleasure in the making of money on money or financial assets rather than depending on profits from goods production alone. Others, out of greed, rediscovered the Gatsbyesque advantage of stepping beyond the bounds of propriety. The two societies began to resemble a giant money market fund in which the central function of households and businesses would be speculation. Speculative episodes punctuated by stagnation.

Debt epidemics in the public sector spread to the private sector. Business balance sheets shifted from equity financing (issuing new corporate stock) to debt financing (issuing corporate bonds, including junk bonds). Going back to the inception in the 1980s, we find that 1983 equity and debt issuance were $4.8 billion and $4.0 billion, respectively, a conservative businessperson's dream. In every year of the eighties thereafter, net equity issuance was negative while corporate net bond issues soared (to about $30 billion in 1989).

Although the post-recession 1980s has been Biblically called "the seven fat years," closer inspection makes it look more like simply a rebound from the ungodly recession of 1981–1982. By mid-1984 the USA economy had recovered only to its pre-recession level, much like the 1936–1937 recovery had reached the pre-Great Depression GNP level. Industrial production expanded by 67 percent during the robust 1960s, but

---

[2] I first introduced the term "casino economy" in E. Ray Canterbery, *The Making of Economics*, 3rd edition (Belmont, Calif.: Wadsworth, 1987), pp. 342–343.

only by 29 percent during the 1980s. The unemployment rate never rose above 6.7 percent (1961) during the 1960s; it never fell below 7 percent during 1980–1985, peaking at 9.6–10.7 percent in 1982–1983. Moreover, financial manipulation and speculation soared.

Since the ownership of interest-bearing debt is highly concentrated, rising interest rates shift the income and wealth distributions toward greater inequality.[3] When only a few have the bulk of the "bullion," they have to become wonderfully imaginative as to where to put it. As providence provided, increasingly deregulated financial institutions became remarkably innovative in creating new financial instruments, (CDs, jumbo CDs, junk bonds, options, derivative, and so on) in which wealth could be stored momentarily for quick appreciation. Put differently, if the rich are to speculate, they had to have an ample supply of chips. Initially, chips were supplied in the form of new Treasury bond issues; later, additional chips were provided by a new means of corporate acquisition, takeovers by leveraged debt.

Michael Milken: The Manipulator of the Junk Bond Market[4]

With the path to liberated markets being smoothed by Milton Friedman, the freeing of markets for moneymaking became a moral imperative for Reagan. The sole responsibility of business, wrote Friedman, was to increase its profits, a fifth echoes in Reagan's speeches. Word about the "magic of the market" spread quickly from the Reagan White House to the countryside. The key phrases on Wall Street were: (1) the Reagan Administration was against all government regulations affecting any market, including bond markets and (2) if money could be made doing

---

[3] By 1986 some 10 percent of families owned more than half of liquid assets, 86 percent of tax-exempt municipal bonds, and 70 percent of other bonds. The same 10 percent also owned 72 percent of corporate stock, with the top 2 percent alone owning half. Finally, the richest 10 percent held 57 percent of household net worth (value of assets minus value of liabilities) and 86 percent of net financial assets.

[4] Much of the following is taken from E. Ray Canterbery, The Making of Economics, 4th edition, Vol. III (New Jersey, London, Singapore: World Scientific, 2010), pp. 182–186.

something — anything — it was an immoral act not to just do it. Michael Milken was a natural by-product of this free market revival.

Milken, an intense business student at the University of California at Berkeley during the mid-1960s, was reading about low-grade and unrated corporate bonds while other students were mellowing out on marijuana. Later, as a securities salesman at Drexel, Milken preached a new gospel. To Milken, the higher yield on low grade bonds simply reflected a risk well worth taking at such high expected returns. He was convinced that the *only* problem with low-grade debt was its lack of liquidity or quick convertibility into money.

Eventually, Milken dispelled customers' initial aversion to high-risk bonds. Milken's sales ability solved the "lack of liquidity" problem; he attracted financiers who saw no stigma attached to low-grade securities. As their returns met or exceeded their expectations, the early buyers became enthusiastic backers of Milken.

By early 1977 Milken already controlled a quarter of the national market in high-yield securities. He had become a *market-maker*. Milken could assure the holder of bonds that he would buy their bonds whenever the holder wanted to cash out or go liquid. In turn, Milken could resell the securities, keeping any difference between the unpublished "buy" and "sell" prices he amassed. Only Milken and a few colleagues knew of the widening spreads between the buy and sell prices, a source of rising richness for Milken.

The Securities and Exchange Commission (SEC), the main regulatory agency for the securities markets, did not register the offerings and the Milken Market went unregulated, just as Friedman, Reagan and the supply-siders fancied. Milken always operated with more knowledge than any buyer or seller because he *was* the low-grade bond market.[5] Those buyers and sellers on the other side of the market might as well have been smoking something; they were no match for Milken's secret information. Thus, much of the "magic" of this market came from Milken's concealment of the key to it.

---

[5] Many more details about Michel Milken and many other Wall Street characters can be gleaned from a book by Pulitzer Prize-winning reporter James B. Stewart's *Den of Thieves* (New York: Simon & Schuster, 1991.)

A half century trend favoring risk aversion and opposing excessive debt ended during the 1980s.

The LBO Mania

Despite the slippery slope on which the junk bond market was built, it led to a new era of leverage buyouts (LBOs) during the 1980s and 1990s, and, ultimately, to downsizing the working class. Though *being* the junk bond market was highly lucrative, Michael Milken saw still bigger money in mergers and acquisitions. A corporation, a public company, would be bought out by a group of financiers with money generated by selling junk bonds to insurance companies, banks, brokers, and S&Ls. In this wonderful arrangement the financiers did not have to use any of their *own* money. Moreover, all those handling the transactions, including the CEOs selling their own companies and Milken, made tens of millions of dollars.

Some new forces would sustain Milken at a time when his business otherwise would have been slowing. During the Reagan years a conglomerate rush, the merger of unrelated enterprises, was encouraged by both tax policy and by an antitrust policy most notable for its aggressive laxity. By 1983 the arrangement of mergers had become a growth industry led by a legendary Texas tycoon by the misnomer of T. Boone "Slim" Pickens, who returned to the Texas oil fields in 2008. Fortuitously, by 1985 Michael Milken and his Drexel colleagues had more client money than they could place. To increase the supply of junk bonds, they began to finance corporate raiders such as Pickens, Carl Icahn, Ronald Perelman, and, notably, Kohlberg Kravis Roberts & Co. (KKR).

The KKR executives from 1984 to 1989 borrowed more money through Drexel than any other client of the junk-bond firm: KKR became the dominant takeover artist.[6] Insurance companies, banks, and S&Ls virtually stopped financing the buying of capital goods, drilling for oil, or building houses; they instead lent billions to KKR in their purchases of junk bonds from Milken. KKR completed nearly $60 billion in acquisitions during the 1980s, culminating in the purchase of RJR Nabisco for

---

[6]The complete story of KKR is told by George Anders, *Merchants of Debt: KKR and Mortgaging of American Business* (New York: Basic Books, 1992).

$26.4 billion in late 1988, then the largest takeover in history and sufficiently notorious to become not only a book but a TV movie. These takeovers of large corporations generated billions of dollars worth of junk bonds, for even the use of leverage diminishes the value of outstanding bonds of former blue-chip corporations to junk. Milken's salary and bonus continued to climb — exceeding $440 million in 1986 alone.

So, we now know what Casino Capitalism was at inception. In the next few chapters, we will consider the consequences, including the effect on the wealth distribution, the Casino Effect of T, the Minsky Moment, and Inequalities in general.

Chapter 14

A NET WORTH PERSPECTIVE

Most economists do not like to look at net worth or wealth, except perhaps their own. If we are to understand the effects of the shift of supra-surplus capitalism to Casino Capitalism, however, we will find the answers in balance sheets. Balance sheets were once for nerds, but accounting firms could not flourish without them, nor could the Federal Reserve keep track of wealth changes.

Where the Money Initially Went

Inflation in the prices of ordinary goods and services during the 1980s and 1990s declined, while the prices of financial assets boomed. Moreover, the values of tangible asset values were declining or stagnant, even as debt burdens soared. When we consider the distribution of assets by type — financial or tangible — we can further understand why wealth inequalities widened so rapidly.

The super-rich (top 0.5 percent of families) held 46.5 percent of corporate stock and 43.6 percent of outstanding bonds in 1983, whereas the lower 90 percent of American families held only 10.7 and 9.7 percent, respectively. For real estate, the source of a typical family's net worth, the shares are nearly flipped, about half of all real estate being held by the lower 90 percent.

The great disparity between financial asset inflation and tangible asset deflation or stagnation had adverse effects on the lower 90 percent during the 1980s. In the 1983–1989 period the average wealth of the top 1 percent, the super-rich, rose from $7.1 million per household to $9.0 million. This is the average, while half the households had more than $9.0 million. Meanwhile, wealth fell for the bottom fifth (from –$3,200 to –$18,100 per household and for the next fifth (from $12,300 to $10,100). Michael Milken had made $3 billion in his junk-bond deals during a few years ending in 1989, and was one of the ten richest persons in the United States. It would be easy to conclude that — since the rich were getting richer — business firms must be too. This would be easy, but like so many easy things, would be wrong. Drexel Burnham Lambert Inc., Milken's own firm, filed for bankruptcy protection on February 13, 1990.

As to other firms, if the change in net worth of businesses is combined with that of households, the annual growth of net worth per adult is a flatliner during the 1980s. Moreover, from 1982 to 1992 the net worth of the non-financial business sector grew at the feeble pace of 0.62 percent yearly. The growth of net worth in the economy apparently had switched from business firms to selected families. The United States was getting poorer even as its elite were getting richer.

This switch from firms to super-rich families failed to stimulate the overall economy. By the time of the presidential elections of 1992, the country seemed to be mired in a dark, foreboding malaise. A troublesome recession, beginning July 1990, ending officially in 1991, and followed by several years of snail-paced growth gave character to the stagnation even as the greatest American bull market in stocks began to roar. Everything was looking up on Wall Street. To understand what happened requires a new approach.

A Business and Household Net Worth Approach[1]

To understand casino capitalism, this special phase of supra-surplus capitalism, we need to go beyond conventional economics. In this way we can know the connection between Wall Street and wealth inequalities. The

---

[1] The balance-sheet equations used in this section can be found in their original form in E. Ray Canterbery, "Reaganomics, Saving, and the Casino Effect," in J. Gapinski, ed. *The Economics of Saving* (Boston/Dordrecht/London: Kluwer Academic Publishers, 1993),

method is universal and can be applied to other economies. While it does require some patience, anyone who has taken Accounting 101 will find the modest equations easy to follow. What's more, this chapter is mercifully short. With shortness, we blithely go on to consider the economy as a series of balance sheets. In this respect, often one household's or organization's asset is another's liability. Thus, when we speak of changes in assets, we often speak as well of co-movements in liabilities. Sometimes the co-movements occur within the same balance sheet. Banks and S&Ls that used high-interest-rate CDs and junk bonds (their liabilities) during the early 1980s to finance mortgages that began to depreciate by 1988 (their assets) learned dearly this latter connection. There are at least three sources of change in assets. First, value appreciation or depreciation occurs as the prices of the items go up or down. The price of a machine tool can quickly change. Second, physical depreciation can happen as machines and buildings wear out or become obsolete. A particular machine tool can suffer middle-age stress. Third, exchange (which presumes a change in ownership of the asset) can increase or decrease holdings. Exchange possibilities characterize "free" market economies.

Bear with me for a few moments while I indulge is some simple mathematics. The aggregate net worth of the private business sector (G_b) is equal to its money and money market asset holdings (M_b), plus its value of goods holdings that include inventories of finished goods, goods in process, raw materials, buildings and equipment, and land (Q_b), plus the net household indebtedness to business ($K_h - k'_h$), where K_h is total debts (such as installment credit) due to businesses from households and k'_h is the total debts due from businesses to households plus government bond holdings (B_b). The k'_h consists mostly of corporate bonds held by households. Business firms hold debt of other business firms but, in the aggregate, business-to-business debt cancels. New issues of equities increase the money and market asset holdings of the firm. Change in aggregate business net worth during any accounting period is

$$dG_b = dM_b + dQ_b + dK_h - dk'_h + dB_b = S_b. \tag{14.1}$$

---

pp. 164–169. The full chapter is reprinted in E. Ray Canterbery, *Beyond Conventional Economics* (New Jersey/London/Singapore: World Scientific, 2016) Chapter 38.

Because the quantity dG_b is that part of profits not distributed in dividends, it comprises business saving or dissaving ($Bb = Sb$).

In words, which are most welcome at this juncture, the change in the aggregate net worth of business equals the changes in its moneyed asset holdings, plus the changes in physical holdings (including physical capital), plus the change in net household indebtedness to business, plus the change in bond holdings. It is that simple. In turn, the change in aggregate net worth is the same thing as total savings by business.

Net worth (savings) increases through the revaluation of assets above costs, normally at the moment of sale through Kaleckian markup increases. Despite ritualistic chanting against inflation by business, inflation in goods prices through higher markups is a reliable, even preferable, route to greater increases in net worth (and business saving). Money and money market assets ideally provide firms only with liquidity. Physical depreciation or value depreciation decrease total savings. Of course, an increase in debts due from the household increases business savings even as it decreases household savings.

In a Keynesian–Kaleckian style model, the amplified retained earnings of businesses are not only a source of investment funds but an incentive for *more* investment. A price markup is used to increase the value of the goods that businesses sell, adding to the funds flowing from household spending. Retained earnings from sales revenue becomes corporate savings, some of which will be invested, depending on expectations. In turn, rising sales revenue nudging full capacity is itself an impetus to expand. These internal funds so generated by the firm can be levered by debt to finance still more capital assets. The more that is invested, the greater will be the sales of capital goods and the profits' share in the national income. In this regard it is the hope of firms that households will not be spendthrifts. Because of low transactions costs, retained earnings are a preferred source of funds to new issues of preferred or common stock or, in a tax-neutral world, to increased corporate debt (dK_h). Indeed, increases in corporate debt to households reduce business saving. In the *aggregate*, nonetheless, investment requires *external* funds and reliance on the bond and stock markets or, in a pinch, private commercial banks.

And so, equation (14.1) illustrates how easily one can slip into the awkward supply-side error whereby saving "causes" investment. Household savings *are* a source of corporate debt, an indebtedness no doubt incurred solely for *real* business investment purposes. However, these household savings only enter the firm when *new* corporate bonds are issued. Otherwise, households are merely exchanging ownership of corporate (and no doubt government) bonds with each other, which is cozy and comfortable but not very productive. In that process nonetheless the value of financial assets may be bid up and the wealth and income distribution may be altered. A redistribution toward those of highest marginal and average propensities to save will diminish corporate sales revenue and the impetus for *real* investment. Moreover, there is no guarantee that any particular corporation will use retained earnings to enhance real investment. The decision to invest is a most uncertain venture.

Because real investment, when it does finally happen, raises the retained earnings of the capital goods industry, its employment, and the incomes of those it employs, the more believable parable is that investment "causes" saving. This view too, as we can see from the equation, is an oversimplification, but at least the *direction* of causality is clear. Moreover, for the 1980s and other eras, it is a relationship whose pattern is found in the data.

A little noted component of declining saving is the slump in *business* savings. Business savings are conventionally measured in the national accounts by retained earnings of corporations. As a percentage of GNP, they fell from around 4.5 percent in the mid-1960s to 2.75 percent in the late 1970s, and to 1 percent during the late 1980s. Alternatively, the Federal Reserve balance sheet measure of corporate savings (which includes stock dividends and non-dividend cash payments) suggests that corporate saving actually turned *negative* during the late 1980s. This striking consequence is connected to the outbreak of leveraged buyouts and stock repurchases to fight them.

Now we turn to the ledger sheets of the household. Surely it is so that household savings equals household income less household consumption properly measured. It is equally so that household savings comprise the change in household net worth. By simply substituting the subscript h for the subscript b, the household equation for savings comparable in every other respect to that for the corporation is

$$dG_h = dM_h + dQ_h + dK'_h - dK'_h + dB_h + dE_h = S_h, \qquad (14.2)$$

where dB_h is the increase in the value of government bond holdings of households and dE_h is the increase in the value of equities. Any increase in goods holdings would be in durables and would include the increase (or decrease) in the value of housing. A reminder to the unwary reader: as long as these items are expressed in nominal terms, they can rise and fall from changes in either units or prices. In fact, a positive dQ_b in a business firm's balance sheet can be seen as a price increase *only,* given that firms attempt to sell products above cost. Even though the act of exchange is merely a change in asset ownership, those holding assets rising in price enjoy increased net worth. Now you may quibble, because you may not know of a household that holds bonds. And, there is no reason why you should, but you need only look up at the mansion on the hill. In the aggregate households do hold bonds, though they are closely held by the upper income classes.

We now move to the national income and its distribution. We will try to keep in mind our earlier discussion of the national income accounts. We will also be mindful of Kalecki's trade-off of profits and wages. Aggregate profits of business (V) is the gross increase in net worth (i.e., gross business savings), out of which interest and dividends are paid (D), or

$$V = S_b + D. \qquad (14.3)$$

Substituting the components of business saving from equation (14.1),

$$V = dQ_b + (dM_b + dK_h - dk'_h + D) + dB_b. \qquad (14.4)$$

Since household income is comprised of wages (W) and dividends and interest paid (D), we can write

$$S_h = (W + D) - C_h, \qquad (14.5)$$

where C_h is household consumption. Simply put, household savings equal household income minus consumption, something we already knew. Substitute the values from equation (14.2) for S_h and

$$W = Ch + dQh - (-dMh + dKh - dk'_h - dB_h - dE_h + D). \quad (14.6)$$

If we ignore the direct transfers to and from governments and assume the inventory of government bonds to be constant for the period, there are transfer items that flow between the business and the household sectors comprised of changes in money holdings (the M's), changes in debt (the K's), changes in government bond holdings (the B's), increases in equity holdings (the E), and dividend and interest payments (D). The transfer item (T) defined in equation (14.4) is

$$T = dM_b + dK_h - dk'_h + dB_b + D, \quad (14.7)$$

has the lightness of being highly liquid assets and liabilities. Without denoting exact ownership shares, dropping the subscripts h and b, T can be written as

$$T = dM + dK - dk' + dB + D. \quad (14.7a)$$

The "T" for the household differs from the "T" for the business firm by the value dE_h, or the change in equity holdings. This complication requires some elaboration. An increase in household equity holdings can come from new stock issues, existing stock in the secondary market, or a rise in stock market prices. *Only* when a positive dE_h comes from *new* issues (about 1 percent of the value of all such transactions) does the corporation experience an increase in money offsetting the decrease in household money holdings (i.e., $dM_b = -dM_h$). Otherwise, the change in equity holdings merely shifts the ownership of equity and liquidity among households. The implications of this complication can begin to be understood by redefining the household "T" as XT from equation (14.6) or

$$XT = -dM_h + dK_h - dk'_h - dB_h - dE_h + D. \quad (14.8)$$

Now, we can simplify equations (14.4) and (14.6) to read

$$V = dQ_h + T \quad \text{and} \quad W = C + dQ_h - XT.$$

Aggregate wages and profits exhaust the value of aggregate output so that national income is

$$Y = W + V = C + dQ_h + dQ_b - (XT - T). \tag{14.9a}$$

The left-hand expression is reminiscent of Kalecki's equation for national income, in which there is a trade-off *between* wages and profits. *Only* when $T = X T$ would nominal saving be $dQ_h + dQ_b$ and national income be

$$Y = C + dQ_h + dQ_b. \tag{14.9b}$$

The value "T" then would simply disappear as transfers between firms and households cancel. Anyone who has struggled to understand T and who by now associates T with "torture" no doubt must be disappointed greatly to see it disappear! The nature of equation (14.9b) and, to a lesser extent, equation (14.9a) as identities tends to hide everything that went on in the economy in the determination of national income and its division, including the strategic role of T. In particular, we note that a net positive value of T transfers financial resources from households to businesses. However, these transfers can go in the reverse direction.

If net savings are decided independently from dividends, then business dividends are a "widow's cruse and Danaid jar:" The more business distributes in interest and dividends, the more will return in profits to be distributed.[2] The corporation, if no one else is pleased. There is a potential downside. The more business *pays* in interest, the lower its profits will go.

---

[2] The formidable Kenneth Boulding correctly disclosed this relationship even though he made some missteps along the way in *A Reconstruction of Economics* (New York: John Wiley, 1950), pp. 255–258. In Boulding's update of his theory of distribution, he corrects his 1950 effort. See Kenneth Boulding, "Puzzles Over Distribution," *Challenge* (November/ December 1985), 4–10. I express values in money terms whereas Boulding uses the traditional definitions of real saving and investment. When expressed in money terms, the effects of speculation become visible.

Anyone who has held a balance sheet in their hands will understand the logic of this. Whereas the corporation can increase its cash from equities only with *new issues* (which were rare during the 1980s and rare during many periods since), the household, which may well consist of business executives, can enjoy secondary-market appreciation in its equities holdings (via *XT*) without sharing such benefits with business.

Because *XT* and *T* differ only by dE_h or the change in household equity holdings in equation (14.9a), the nominal national income is

$$Y = C + dQ_h + dQ_b + dE_h. \qquad (14.10a)$$

National savings then are bolstered by an increase in household equity holdings, even by a rising stock market. Nominal national income would rise without a matching increment of *real* investment. This helps to explain why, since 2008, the U.S. and other supra-surplus countries have experienced a bull market in stocks but flat real investment and slow real GNP growth. In this environment a cut in corporate taxes would only add to nominal national income without altering real investment and real GNP.

Thus far, we have abstracted from the creation of new money by the central bank and private banks, nor is the federal government issuing new debt (new bonds). These conditions are easily relaxed, so that equation (4.10a) becomes

$$Y = C + dQ_h + dQ_b + (dM_h + dM_b + dB_h + dE_h). \qquad (14.10b)$$

Now the national income can swell (inflate) as a direct result of credit and money creation. An increase in real national income is by no means guaranteed because real investment may not increase. The consequences of financialization can be seen in these equations, particularly as we return to those for *T* and *XT*.

Upon examination, it can be seen that the various components of *T* and *XT* swirl about their own axes without necessarily intersecting with *real* investment and saving. But the wary reader can ignore the equations and consider the following. Financial transactions in existing assets are not real output and not included in *real* national income. Still, not only do they exist, they have dominated the supra-surplus economies for quite some time. Banking, savings and loan, and brokerage firms are unique among businesses in holding demand deposit liabilities that are assets of other businesses and of households (M_b and M_h). During the 1980s, a period when new financial instruments such as junk bonds streamed out of Wall Street, the behavior of such accounts was the basis for what I call the "Casino Effect," the subject of the next chapter.

Chapter 15

THE CASINO EFFECT OF *T*

The idea of a casino and speculation at its tables is not new. Casino Baden–Baden in Germany has been operating since 1809. It is one of the most exclusive and elegant in all of Europe and features 14 table games, for American roulette, Baccarat, French roulette, and poker. Despite this attraction, most people come to Baden–Baden for its therapeutic mineral springs. Still, no visit would be complete without a visit to the Casino's tables. Perhaps most famous is the Casino de Monte Carlo, which has been attracting visitors, including royalty, movie stars, and the world's filthy rich since 1863. It is the top tourist attraction in tiny Monaco. Macao, China is known as "the Monte Carlo of the Orient," in part because of the Venetian Macao, which has over 800 table games. The Venetian is also the largest hotel in Asia. It's enough to make Donald Trump envious. There are dozens of casinos in Moscow but the most elegant is the Casino Metropol, located just a few minutes from Red Square and the Kremlin.

As one might suspect, these worldly casinos attract mostly wealthy patrons. The movies have enhanced the romance and intrigue of the casino. *To Catch a Thief* (1955) starring Cary Grant and Grace Kelly was filmed in and around the Casino de Monte Carlo. Ironically, Grace Kelly, now Princess of Monaco, was killed in a car accident on the same road as a famous chase scene in the movie. The elegance of the two stars added to the mystique of the Casino. Later, a James Bond film, *Casino Royale*

(2006) was filmed in a fictional Casino in Czechoslovakia. A famous scene has James Bond playing poker at the gaming tables.

Despite the attraction of wealth to casinos, some are built with the average family in mind. The middle class can emulate the rich, though it is usually found around the slots rather than the gaming tables. This is only fitting because the middle class does not have the chips to play in the Casino Economy. So, there is more to some casinos than just gambling. The American Gaming Society, for example, estimates that roughly one quarter of the U.S. population over 21 visit casinos. While black jack or roulette might be the main revenue stream, other amenities are offered such as floor shows, free drinks, all-you-can-eat buffets, and plush accommodations. Las Vegas now bills itself as a family destination as well as a gambling mecca. The Bellagio in Las Vegas pampers its customers with a branch of New York's swank Le Cirque restaurant as well as Hermes and Chanel boutiques. While it would be ennobling to rub elbows with royalty at London's exclusive casino, Clermont Club, only the rich can afford it. Las Vegas remains a viable option.

Having tasted the often elegant substitutes, we now return to our main course of how the greater Casino Economy arose from the ashes of Reaganomics. By the mid-1980s interest payments as a share of net national income had risen from only 1 percent to 10 percent. A major shift toward debt finance occurred in the aforementioned business balance sheets. Whereas in 1983 equity and debt issuance were $4.8 billion and $4.0 billion, respectively, every year of the 80s thereafter, net new equity issuance was negative while corporate net bond issues soared (to about $30 billion in 1989). The irresistible combination of a fast-rising U.S. private and public debt and soaring U.S. interest rates was responsible for skyrocketing net monetary interest. By 1991 federal government interest payments to bondholders were exhausting half of all personal income tax revenue. Along with nostalgia, there is today in a negative interest rate world a feeling of quaintness about the world of Ronald Reagan.

The 1980s was supposed to be the Golden Age of Entrepreneurship. The tax cuts aimed at corporate coffers and the super-rich combined with deregulation by government certainly tilted the economy in that direction. For various reasons, the Golden Age did not materialize. Contrariwise, during the Reagan years the entrepreneur's share of national income declined drastically even as the rentier's (unearned) income share soared. All of the increase in disposable income during the 1980s is more than accounted for by the rise in the share of interest income, while the shares of labor and other income sources declined. Surely this is not the way the script was written. Sometimes even movies have unhappy endings.

Of course, an economy can never reach a state in which 100 percent of its national income is net interest, because the sum of employee compensation, proprietor's income, and corporate profits would be zero! This is so, irrespective of the dreams of the 1980s bondholders. Even so, the interest part of interest and dividends was eating away at manufacturers' net worth. It was an early warning sign of how finance can displace manufacturing. We can begin to picture an economy whose main industries would be printing (for credit instruments and money), financial firms, and retail outlets and in which all manufactured goods and services would be imported. The central function of businesspeople in such an environment would be speculation.

The society would be a giant money market fund in which households and businesses would spend each day shifting financial assets about in their gigantic portfolios. The United States would implode into Las Vegas or a Casino Royale — hence, what I have called the "Casino Economy." During economic expansion such an economy can operate almost independently of real production, but its downward spiral during a recession such as the Great Recession is dangerous. Worse, the ownership of most interest-bearing assets is highly concentrated. In 1983, when Reaganomics was climaxing, the top 1 percent held 33.8 percent of total net worth, the next 19 percent, 47.5 percent, leaving 18.7 percent for the bottom 80 percent. Since, the concentration has actually increased. By 2010, the top 1 percent held 35.4 percent of total net worth, the next 19 percent 53.5 percent, leaving only 11.1 percent for the bottom 80 percent. The picture gets darker when we look at particular financial assets. Take, for example, financial securities, most of which earn interest, the top 1 percent held 64.4 percent, the next 9 percent 29.5 percent, leaving only 6.1 percent for the bottom 90 percent. The bottom dwellers do slightly better with stocks, thanks to mutual funds. In 2010, the top 1 percent held 35 percent, the next 9 percent, 45.8 percent, and the bottom 90 percent holding a respectable 19.2 percent. In 2010, the *average* household financial wealth of the top 1 percent was $15.2 million and for the bottom 40 percent –$14,800.[1] Updates through 2013 show that the wealth concentration increased further.[2]

Although the monetary system is at the core of the debt creation and repayment process, its stability depends on profit flows to borrowers sufficient to service their loans. The central problems of present-day capitalism are connected to the ownership, creation, and financing of capital assets whose distribution, in turn, has contributed to speculation in financial assets. Credit has become notoriously unstable.

What comprises net worth (or worthlessness) in the casino economy? In the financial system, we are interested in the value of net worth because such institutions are intermediaries for the savings in the economy. Consider the simplest possible balance sheet for the financial industry in which net worth (G_t) is, for the accounting period

$$G_t = dCR_t + dK_{fh} + dK_{fb} - dDD_f - dCD_f, \qquad (15.1)$$

where dCR_f is the change in cash reserves, dK_{h}, and dK_{fb} are the changes in the values of loans to households and businesses, respectively, dDD_f is the change in demand deposit liabilities, and dCD_f is the change in value of long-term certificates of deposit. We will assume that most of the loans to the household sector are to keep it housed and most to the business sector are for commercial real estate, whereas long-term CDs are used as the primary source of funds for such mortgages. (Of course, such institutions also play a role in the creation of money to finance stock market purchases.) The link between this financial industry and the real economy is the value of real estate. During 1983–1988 the appreciation of houses (as well as the building of more luxurious houses) was a major source of household personal savings. (The *increase* in the value of housing had nearly doubled in 5 years — from $158.3 billion in 1983 to $313.1 billion

---

[1] G. William Domhoff, "Wealth, Income, and Power," Retrieved September 11, 2016 from http://www2.ucsc.edu/whorulesamerica/power/wealth.html. Domhoff's data is based on the net worth balance sheets of the Federal Reserve System.

[2] See "The Concentration of U.S. Wealth," Federal Reserve Bank of St. Louis, Retrieved December 31, 2015 from https://www.stlouisfed.org/on-the-economy/2015/december/wealth-becoming-more-concentrated-richest-families.

in 1988. The value of new corporate bond issues during this time pales alongside this huge figure.) Apparently expecting real estate to appreciate forever, the financial industry scurried to provide high-cost mortgage money financed from high-yielding CDs. (The S&Ls, of course, also placed heavy reliance on junk bonds.) The increased concentration of wealth or savings during this era is linked to the demand for real estate and the supply of funds for CDs. Let RE be the value of real estate, K_r be the value of total mortgages held by the financial industry at any point in time (that change at the rate $aKr_f\,dt$), and W be the real value of wealth ("real" = deflated by goods prices) of the upper quintile of the distribution. This wealth is created by the dynamics of T and XT. These values are connected in a circular way even though the circle can expand or contract in space. In the simplest model the circles do not intersect, so that a system of curves or circles whose position depends

$$[RE(t) - W(t)]^2 + [K_r(t) - W(t)]^2 = [W(t)]^2, \qquad (15.2)$$

on the value of real wealth (W) at any point in time. The center of the circle is (W, W) and its radius is W. The following constraints define the curves: $0 \leq RE \leq W$, $0 \leq K_f \leq W$, and $RE + K_f \leq W$. As W gets larger, the center of the circle moves away from the origin along a line bisecting the angle between the axes (45° line), and the radius of the circle increases. Imagine tossing different-sized units of gold bullion (W) into a smooth-surfaced lake; the larger the volume of bullion, the greater the circle made from the ripples. (Hopefully, I will not be accused of making a circular argument.) This simple model says that an increase in real wealth in the upper reaches will increase the potential values of RE and K_f. Because the values of mortgages as financial assets are also colinear with the value of real estate, RE and K_f most likely will follow the 45° line. If the real wealth of the top quintile declines, so too will the value of real estate and mortgages. If much of the real wealth is tied to real estate and the prices of real estate drop, this event can shrink the circle. This happens if real estate prices drop faster than goods prices in the economy. The supply-siders are correct about the importance of relative prices; but it is the relative price of real estate and goods rather than the relative price of leisure that is critical in the Casino Economy. Now we arrive at the Casino

Effect. Although *RE* and K_f may move together with respect to real wealth, their time path need not be (and has not been) linear. Rather, with respect to time the pattern would be exponential or

$$RE(t) = a_1 e^{k_1 w(t)} \qquad K_f(t) = a_2 e^{k_2 w(t)},$$

where the *a*'s are positive integers and the *k*'s are positive fractions. The *k*'s, provisionally constant, are velocities at which wealth is trundled into its real estate and mortgage incarnations. The velocities, combined with the exponential nature of the function, give the Casino Effect.[3]

Of course, as real estate values fall, the exponents will become negative. There is not a satisfactory way to model this sudden shift from asset appreciation to asset depreciation except to say that the initial state and conditions have changed. Indeed, the exponential pattern — up or down — did not characterize the era before the late 1960s. Events changed the initial state and conditions beginning at that time. First, income and wealth distributions became much more concentrated during the 1980s. Second, the Carter and Reagan administrations turned dramatically toward the deregulation of the financial industry. Third, the deposit insurance systems and the lender of last resort stance of the Fed — which had provided needed confidence to depositors after the Great Depression — now seemed to take the risk out of overexpansion by the financial industry. Historically, speculative episodes have been preceded by rapid shifts of wealth toward smaller and smaller numbers. Why does this movement cause speculative bubbles? Why does *T* spin out of control and create

---

[3] There are other candidate equations, the most promising of which relate to the wave equation. Simeon Poisson developed a formula for the propagation of a wave with specified initial conditions that satisfied a second-order partial differential equation. A quite different method was used by Riemann in the course of his work on the propagation of sound waves of finite amplitude. Bernhard Riemann considers a second-order linear differential equation that defines a curve and space. His method depends on finding a Riemann or characteristic function that satisfies an adjoint equation. The Reimann method is useful only for hyperbolic equations in two independent variables. Later the Helmholtz equation was used to represent all harmonic, acoustic, elastic, and electromagnetic waves. The work of Hermann von Helmholtz was used by Gustav Kirchhoff to obtain another solution of the initial-value problem for the wave equation. These equations have since been generalized.

larger and larger circles? One reason relates to ability to pay; the household needs wealth in excess of basic needs in order to "afford" to speculate. Moreover, such high-risk finance pays off during economic expansions, especially when there is a wealthier "greater fool" to bid assets still higher. Even generally cautious persons tend to jump onto the bandwagan. (No less a cynic than Thorstein Veblen took an uncharacteristic dive into the stock market during the 1920s but mercifully died a few months before the Great Crash.) Finally, in an environment of cutthroat competition in the financial industry, firms offer higher and higher interest rates to attract funds that in turn must be lent at still higher rates, requiring higher-risk loans. The compounding of the values of these assets and liabilities gives the exponential path.

We call such financial episodes "speculative bubbles" for their tendency to burst. Real estate values on a cost basis have slumped about 20 percent since their peaks in 1988. By historical standards this decline is huge. This slump has nonetheless been punctuated by speculative bubbles. Still, just as sharp rises in real estate values relative to goods prices led the parade of high-yielding mortgages, CDs, and junk bonds, the decline in real estate values relative to modest inflation in goods prices has produced non-performing loans nearly to the point of extinction of the S&L industry and to the point of grave threat to the banking industry. Even the insurance industry is threatened with a possible run, as it has about twice the share of junk-bond assets than was originally reported. Meanwhile, the prolonged recession beginning in July 1990 has led to sharp increases in bankruptcies throughout other industries as sales revenue growth has been insufficient to service heavy, existing debt. (Business failures per week have risen from 900 at the beginning of 1990 to more than 1700 by April 1991 and continue to rise periodically.) This contagion has spread to households, which also are filing record numbers of bankruptcies. The values of assets and liabilities in *T* indeed are connected in a nearly unbroken circle. The widening of the circle has now been reversed.

Conclusions

Every 40–50 years the policies of free enterprise's most devoted disciples bring American capitalism to its knees. The ideology renews itself as soon as the wounded generation has died or slid into a forgetful senility. Capitalism's survival — in newly directed and regulated form — speaks well of its strength. Each time it has survived the best efforts of its friends.

Properly measured, personal money *and* personal real savings soared during the 1980s. The main effect of supply-side "incentives" was to increase the disposable income of the highest-income families and in this way bolster personal savings. The other main source of personal savings is found in the speculative bubbles in real estate. The explanation, however, is not Reaganometric but Keynesian.

We arrive at a dichotomy inexplicable in conventional thought: Real business saving and investment slumped. The dichotomy is explained by the Kaleckian–Keynesian tendencies within the economy. It takes rising sales from households having high average and marginal propensities to consume in order to motivate more investment, even as they provide internal funds to leverage debt that becomes *real* investment. During the 1980s retained earnings were damaged by income and wealth redistributions that shunted luxury spending toward foreign nations, by skyrocketing debt service costs, and by real investment's displacement by massive federal borrowing. Only when business is making real investments does personal saving become real saving.

With the slowdown in real net business investment, high levels of personal savings were diverted into the Casino Economy, creating speculative bubbles that have been exploding with an eerie regularity since October 1987. The American economy has shifted its focus from using money to produce goods to using money for speculative profits. Shifting tax policy to favor highest-income savers is part of the problem, not the solution. In fact, the use of public policy to encourage personal saving is based on mistaken notions regarding the true incentives for business investment.

For the first time since the Great Depression, the economic decline called "The Great Global Recession" had financial causes. Financial fragility has led to failing S&Ls, banks, and insurance companies. Thus far, the government has decided that it must rescue those financial institutions "too large to fail." However, the public is increasingly aware of their contingent liabilities in these bailouts. We know that the loans made by the U.S. Treasury will someday have to be paid. This awareness is coming at a time when state and local governments (having inherited the social welfare role diminished by the Reagan administration) are raising taxes for mandated budget balancing. If taxpayers revolt against these continued bailouts, the failing institutions will become "too big to save."

The growing tax burden for the average household is coming at the worst of times. The 1990 recession was not an ordinary downturn, nor was The Great Recession. There is a danger that a rising tax burden and shrinking liquidity in an increasingly risky business environment could keep our economy in a troubled state for many years. That would be the most tragic legacy of Reaganomics and, now, Trumpanomics. It is making the rich so much richer that their speculative excesses have led to demands for their rescue. If we have so little compassion for the working poor, how can we find it in our hearts to bail out the bondholders?

Chapter 16

A MINSKY MOMENT

Hyman Minsky (1919–1996), a laconic but persistent American Post Keynesian with Italian connections, connected the dots between Kalecki's markup, retained earnings, and inside money to financial fragility.[1] Minsky's theory of investment focuses on how Keynesian uncertainty, speculation, and an increasingly complex financial system lead to business cycles. Minsky has extended Post Keynesian monetary theory to include not only credit, but the special problems of financial speculation. The system's stability depends on profit flows to borrowers sufficient to service the loans. Charles P. Kindleberger (1910–2003) extended Minsky's theory to the global economy.

Minsky emphasized how the retained earnings from the markup levered by debt could finance the acquisition of additional capital assets. The capital assets acquired by the non-financial firm may be purchased out of the existing plant and equipment (corporate takeovers, mergers, etc.) or through the production of new investment goods. Only in the latter case will new increments and industrial capacity be added to the economy's productive potential.

---

[1] I had the pleasure of knowing Hyman Minsky. Among other things, he served on my doctorial committee, including the oral exam. He seemed to be sleeping during my oral presentation, but at some point, he looked up, gave a brilliant summation of my paper in a few sentences, then once again closed his eyes. He was a giant of a man, with unruly hair, and a casual manner. He always spoke without notes, including lectures in the classroom.

Minsky's theory of investment focuses on how Keynesian uncertainty, speculation, and an increasingly complex financial system lead to business cycles. Any sustained "good times" stagger off into a speculative, inflationary binge and a fragility of financial institutions. Minsky's ideas are no longer orphans; events have overtaken his explanation.

Since business debt has to be serviced (scheduled payments on principal and interest made), Minsky suggests that such cash flows (and debt-servicing commitments) determine the course of investment and thus of output and employment. In this manner, Minsky has extended Post Keynesian monetary theory to include not only credit, but the special problems connected with financial speculation in a capitalistic system.

The monetary system still is at the core of the debt creation and repayment process. Money is created as banks make loans, mostly to business, in response to profits expectations. Minsky emphasizes, however, that this "inside money" is destroyed as profits are realized and loans are repaid to the banks. The monetary system's stability depends on profit flows to borrowers sufficient to service the loans. Thus, the central problems of capitalism are connected to the ownership, creation, and financing of capital assets that, in turn, contribute to business cycles.[2]

Tilting Toward a Minsky Moment

The prelude to a financial crisis is some "outside" shock to the system, such as war (Vietnam), crop failure, OPEC, a Schumpeterian basic innovation such as the driverless vehicle, or some massive debt disturbance. Whatever the origin of the shock, it significantly changes profit opportunities in at least one important branch of industry. If new profit opportunities arise, increased investment and production generate a boom — a boom fueled by the expansion of banks and other forms of credit.

Since profit opportunities create lending opportunities, booms ordinarily *are* financed at some interest rate. Moreover, financial innovations

---

[2]All economists should have in their library the following books by Hyman P. Minsky: *John Maynard Keynes* (New York: Columbia University Press, 1975); *Can "It" Happen Again?* (Armonk, NY: M.E. Sharpe, 1982); *Stabilizing an Unstable Economy* (New Haven, CT: Yale University Press, 1986). Much of what follows is based on these works.

emerge in the form of new financial institutions and new credit instruments such as CDs, junk bonds, and even financial derivatives, instruments based upon existing credit instruments. This evolution of credit explains why financial institutions are among the first to be regulated.

Rising wage costs during an economic expansion at a constant markup elevate production costs. Since the amount of markup is not unlimited (price elasticity of demand for products is not zero, and neither is the elasticity of the markup), only a generalized inflation can ensure full employment. In this process a rising share of investment is financed by debt. Bankers and business people go along with the rising ratio of debt to internal financing so long as they are reasonably convinced of the continuance of inflation.

Speculation in financial assets eventually spills over into enhanced Keynesian effective demand for goods. Pressure on the capacity for goods production elevates prices still more. Rising prices of both goods and financial assets provide still more profit opportunities. Thus, a round robin of new investment increases ready income, motivating still more investment, still more income. The prices of goods or financial assets now include a speculative "markup" or what I have called a "casino effect." Many market participants will become pure speculators who buy goods for resale rather than for use. In the United States pure speculation characterized much of the housing and commercial real estate markets during the 1970s, early 1980s, and the early 2000s. A similar kind of speculation was happening in the commercial real estate market in 2017.

Eventually, the number of firms and households buying strictly for resale rather than for further production begin to dominate the economic environment. What normally characterizes the bond and stock markets, where only about 1 percent of all transactions directly lead to real investment, becomes more and more characteristic of goods markets. A large share of the economic actors are now placing bets rather than making real investments. A continuation of the boom means higher prices, interest rates, and velocity of money. Policy issues emerge when knowledgeable people begin to talk about the need to control the explosion in credit.

The boom may end because of price resistance by consumers. After all, it is because the price elasticity of demand for products is non-zero (and so too the elasticity of the markup) that the amount of markup is limited. The boom may end because the central bank begins to contract credit. Eventually wages and thus costs and inflation will slow.

Any slowdown in wage rates, however, does not alter contractual debt commitments so that the burden of debt rises during disinflation\or deflation. Debt-financed investment decreases, and purchases of investment goods financed by money supply increments decline. Business firms will begin to pay off debt instead of buying new plant and equipment. As in Keynes, employment falls with the decline in use of the existing capital stock. Once again business conditions are at the mercy of uncertainty and financial market behavior.

The leveling-off of prices brings financial distress for certain participants and industries. Firms, including farms, have counted on a particular inflation rate for their products in order to service their mounting debt. (The same could be said for middle-class homeowners, who since World War II have counted on appreciation of houses as a source of net worth.) Yet, those most in the know in the financial markets, the insiders, take their profits and run. This is the start of a race toward liquidity as financial assets are cashed in.

As Keynes had it, the holding of money "lulls their disquietude." Outright financial panic can be avoided only if (1) prices fall so low that people move back into real assets; (2) the government sets limits to price declines (e.g., agricultural price supports), closes banks (e.g., the "bank holiday" of 1933, and shuts the exchanges; or (3) a lender of last resort steps in, as the Federal Reserve did in the financial turbulence following the Penn Central collapse (1959–1970), the Franklin National Bank bankruptcy (1974–1975), the Hunt–Bache silver speculation (1980), and the stock market crash of 1987, and as the Federal Deposit Insurance Fund (FDIC) did in nationalizing Illinois Continental Bank (1984) or banks since. Such interventions prevent the complete collapse of the value of assets.

The Federal Reserve did not function as lender of last resort during the Great Depression and massive unemployment followed. As Minsky tells the story, however, what the government and the Federal Reserve (as its agent) do to shore up values to avoid depressions sets the stage for still higher inflation. Since debt inflation also means profits deflation in the casino economy, the otherwise stabilizing effect of government deficits and last-resort lending has its dark side.

Liabilities such as junk bonds and other financial innovations of the boom are validated as the central bank refinances the holdings of financial institutions. This propping up of capitalism creates the base for still further expansion of credit during the economic recovery, a process that helps to explain the inflation following the financial crises of 1969–1970, 1974–1975, and 1980. Goods inflation, but not financial speculation, was tamed by the near-depression of 1981–1982 and the Great Recession of 2007–2010.

Preceding and contributing to the Great Recession was the global financial crisis of 2008–2009. Many have called it a "Minsky moment," as well they should. His financial instability hypothesis that described the transformation of an economy from a "robust" financial structure to a "fragile" one explains what happened. Of course, there were the precursors to the main event described above, including the stock market crash of 1987. Each of these crises led to U.S. government intervention that prevented a downward spiral of financial markets or of the economy (although in some cases, recession followed the crisis). After the dot-com crisis of 2000–2001, the belief was that a new and great moderation had taken hold in the United States, making serious downturns impossible. This false notion encouraged more risk, more financial layering, and more leveraging (debt issued against debt, with little net worth backing it up). All of this dangerous financial structure fits Minsky's arguments about a growing financial instability.

The Evolution of the Financial System

While Minsky had his "moment," his later writing during the late 1980s and through the 1990s focused on the long-term transformation of the financial system since the late 19th century.[3] He began with a "commercial capitalism" stage that coincides with the dominance of commercial banking. Banks were important them for financing the production process itself — lending to firms so that they could hire labor and purchase the

---

[3]What follows is based on L. Randall Wray, *Why Minsky Matters* (Princeton, NJ and Oxford: Princeton University Press, 2016), pp. 138–156. Wray gives Minsky his due in a book that should be read from cover to cover.

materials need for production. Investment goods, however, were mostly purchased with internal funds, provided by the firms' owners. As investment goods became increasingly expensive, owners had to look for external funds. This new problem led to a demand for the services of the investment bank. The investment bank would either provide long-term funding directly, or it would float the debts or equity of the investing firms.

Minsky's second stage is finance capitalism, dominated by investment banks that provided the finance for corporations. This made possible external finance for the expensive projects undertaken by the steel and energy firms and railroads owned by the "robber barons." Such finance became globalized as shares and bonds were sold in international markets. By the late 1920s, toward the end of the Jazz Age, investment banks were largely devoting their efforts to financing speculation on financial assets, particularly in equities issued by the subsidiary trusts of the investment banks. These were pyramid schemes — speculating in essentially worthless shares, much like the infamous schemes of Charles Ponzi or the modern-day Bernie Madoff.

The third stage is managerial-welfare state capitalism. The Great Depression and the New Deal reforms of the financial sector and a much bigger role of the federal government in managing the economy bred the managerial-welfare state capitalism. Therein, the Federal Reserve and the Treasury promoted stable economic growth, high employment, and rising wages with falling inequality. This "golden age" lasted from the end of World War II through the early 1970s. Minsky saw the problem thereafter as being one where stability is destabilizing. That is, the absence of deep recession and severe financial crises encourage innovations that increased financial instability. Moreover, conservatives were slowly chipping away at the New Deal reforms that promoted growth and equality. After 1974, median male earnings stopped growing and began to fall as workers lost effective representation by unions, the social welfare net was frayed, and unemployment came to be seen as a desirable outcome — a tool used by policymakers to keep inflation in check. Financial institutions were deregulated and desupervised, and their power grew in a self-serving way. They were able to capture a greater share of profits, while their political power subverted or eliminated regulations so that they could gain an even larger wshar3 of profits. Business was being replaced by pure finance. This is what I have called "casino capitalism." Under casino capitalism, incentives and rewards were changed such that risky bets, high leverage ratios, and short-term profits were promoted over long-term firm survival and returns to investors. This served no broader social purpose as top management of financial institutions became incredibly rich. Among the richly rewarded were the top executives at Goldman Sachs.

Minsky called this fourth stage of evolution, money manager capitalism. In it huge pools of funds were put under management by professionals — pension funds, sovereign wealth funds, hedge funds, university endowments, corporate treasuries, and so on. The economy had become a giant money market fund. Power shifted from commercial banks to the very lightly regulated money managers at shadow banks. To compete, banks had to subvert regulations through innovations and then have them legislatively eliminated. This allowed banks to increase leverage ratios, and thus risk, to keep pace with shadow banking practice. Those institutions that could reduce capital ratios and loss reserves the most quickly were able to increase net earnings and thus rewards to management and investors. This encouraged short-term focus on performance in equity markets through market manipulation (both legal and illegal). In short, to keep returns high and rising, money managers and bankers had to turn increasingly to esoteric financial speculation — in areas that not only did not serve the public purpose but actively subverted it.

One example was the rise of index speculation in commodities markets that drives up global prices of energy and food, leading to hunger and even starvation around the globe. Another example is the dot-com bubble wherein speculators drove up the prices of stocks of Internet companies with no business model or prospective profits. The inevitable crash wiped out hundreds of billions of dollars of wealth. Finally, there was the speculation in U.S. real estate that began before 2000 and finally collapsed in 2007, triggering the global financial collapse of 2008–2009. This was the greatest speculative orgy in U.S. history and was driven by money managers who created complex securities and derivatives for speculative bets — with many of those bets actually paying off if the homeowners defaulted and lost their homes.

Beyond Dodd–Frank

Almost as soon as the financial crisis struck in late 2007, policymakers began working to prevent another one. The roots of the crisis lay in reckless lending and excess debt; banks had made massive loans to "subprime" borrowers who had little ability to repay them and the banks funded these investments with borrowed money. When the U.S. housing bubble burst, millions of American defaulted on their mortgages, and the overleveraged banks collapsed, one by one The government had to bail them out, and the U.S. taxpayers picked up the bill.[4]

In July 2010, President Barack Obama signed the Dodd–Frank Wall Street Reform and Consumer Protection Act. Reformers hope that the act would make another financial crisis less likely. To some extent, Dodd–Frank has succeeded. Thanks in part to the act, banks have to fund themselves with more capital and less debt, which equips them to absorb more losses in a future downturn. Nonetheless, during the 2016 presidential campaign, Dodd–Frank came under attack from both sides of the aisle. Senator Bernie Sanders argued that its reforms did not go far enough. He called for the government to break up the largest U.S. banks and reinstate Glass–Steagall, the 1933 act that separated commercial from investment banking until Congress repealed it in 1999. Republicans, including presidential candidate Donald Trump, believes Dodd–Frank went too far, arguing that its regulations are crippling U.S. banks and stifling growth.

These criticisms detract from the real problem; in dealing with reckless lending and excess leverage, the act misses one of the most important causes of the crisis — "runnable liabilities," or short-term debt that the government does not insure. The U.S. financial sector holds trillions of dollars of such debt. During a crisis, short-term lenders, unlike long-term lenders, can demand their money back immediately, leaving borrowers unable to pay all their creditors quickly. The financial sector stops lending money, credit dries up for consumers and businesses, and the economy

---

[4] Much of what follows is based on Robert Litan, "America's Brewing Debt Crisis," *Foreign Affairs*, September–October, 2016, pp. 111–120.

grinds to a halt. This is what happened during the Minsky moment of 2007 and 2008, when massive runs on short-term debt spread panic throughout the financial sector and helped trigger the Great Recession. Dodd–Frank has done little to mitigate this fundamental problem.

Dodd–Frank was supposed to solve the problem that some banks, such as Citigroup and J.P. Morgan, were "too big to fail." When these banks were faced with collapse the government had to come to the rescue, or else risk allowing the whole economy to go down with them. Dodd–Frank was supposed to solve this problem in two ways. First, the act raised the minimum capital requirements for all banks and imposed especially strict requirements for those with $50 billion or more in assets — the "systemically important financial institutions" (*SIFIS*). Dodd–Frank also requires banks to hold more liquid assets, money they can use to pay back depositors during a sudden panic. The act gives a new body, the Financial Stability Oversight Council (FSOC), the authority to designate certain large financial institutions as SIFIC, which the Fed can then regulate more stringently. Second, Dodd–Frank gave Washington new powers to preemptively shut down large, complex banks and other financial institutions, making bailouts unnecessary. The act gave the (FDIC) powers to close SIFIS without taxpayers bearing the cost; instead shareholders, creditors, and mangers would lose out without causing wider damage to the financial system. Banks must now prepare "living will," plans that detail how regulators shut them down in case of emergency.

The act also took aim at financial derivatives. One particular type of derivative, credit default swaps which allow buyers to insure against the failure of a company to pay back its loans has been especially controversial. The insurance giant AIG issued far too many of these contracts without insisting on enough collateral, and when the mortgage market collapsed, AIG collapsed as well prompting a massive rescue by the Federal Reserve. Dodd–Frank requires many derivatives to be settled through central clearing-houses, where regulators can more easily monitor them. All this has no doubt strengthened the U.S. financial system.

Dodd–Frank does not cover all financial institutions. "Shadow banks" are financial institutions that are similar to banks, in that they also issue very short-term liabilities, but are not regulated as such. They include investment banks, money-market mutual funds, and various other financial firms. These shadow banks and other issuers of short-term debt collectively account for roughly $16 trillion in short-term debt (dwarfing the $6 trillion of insured bank deposits), and no equivalent of the FDIC exists to prevent the holders of these instruments from running on the institutions that carry this debt. It is almost as large as the nation's GDP. Meanwhile, even in banks, deposits above $250,000 are still at risk of a run, as are Eurodollar deposits (dollar-denominated accounts in foreign banks), which the FDIC does not protect.

Does the problem of runnable debt have solutions? Morgan Ricks argues in his new book, *The Money Problem*, that the government should drop the pretense that its insurance extends only to $250,000 worth of deposits. The government implicitly insures more than that, but only if the deposits are in the big banks which the government will preserve so as not to risk the entire economy. If the FDIC formally promises to insure all accounts, regardless of size, it would eliminate the risk of runs on banks. Ricks has proposed further banning any financial institution that isn't a bank from issuing runnable liabilities — in short, he calls for the end of shadow banking, bringing banking back out into the sunshine. He also suggests eliminating Dodd–Frank. If shadow banking persists, another Minsky moment is just around the corner.

The Global Spectra

Charles P. Kindleberger (1910–2003), once a long-time Professor of Economics at MIT and a leading architect of the Marshall Plan, extends Minsky's theory to the global economy. Kindleberger sees pure speculation spilling over national borders. International links are provided by exports, imports, and foreign securities. Indeed, interest rates in the United States in 1983 and 1984 would have been much higher in the absence of massive purchases of U.S. Treasury securities by foreigners.

At the same time, however, these foreign purchases add to the credit pyramid that will again tumble should such speculators again lose confidence. Kindleberger points a finger at the enormous external debt of the developing countries, accelerated by rising oil prices (up to at least 1979), "as multinational banks swollen with dollars tumbled over one another in trying to uncover new foreign borrowers and practically forced money on the less-developed countries (LDCs)."[5]

We next turn to a concern which also worried Hyman Minsky, namely inequality.[6]

---

[5] Charles P. Kindleberger, *Manias, Panics, and Crashes: A History of Financial* Crises (New York: Basic Books, 1978), pp. 23–24.
[6] See Hyman P. Minsky, *Ending Poverty: Jobs, Not Welfare* (Annandale-on-Hudson, NY: Levy Economics Institute, 2013).

Chapter 17

INEQUALITIES

The darkest side of supra-surplus capitalism is inequality, which has been growing since the 2008 financial crisis, that has left the American and global social fabric fraying at the edges, the rich getting richer, while the rest face hardships is inconsonant with many dreams. While inequalities prevailed before, they have worsened since the Great Recession following 2008. This is the case not only in the USA but in many other countries. The growth in the financial sector, the rise of Casino Capitalism, has contributed to increased inequalities, at home and abroad. Jamie Galbraith has shown that countries with larger financial sectors have more inequalities and it is it not accidental.[1] Inequalities are driven by CEO pay that varies by industry and by state. Deregulation and hidden and open government subsidies have distorted the economies, not only leading to larger financial sectors but also enhancing the ability to move money from the bottom to the top. The persistence of monopoly pricing and power has contributed to the problem. As a result, there are even inequalities among those in the top 1 percent.

The Extraordinary Costs of Inequality

Not everyone agrees that inequality is a bad thing. Some say it is the drive wheel of economic growth in a capitalistic society. The argument goes:

---

[1] James K. Galbraith, *Inequality and Instability: A Study of the World Economy before the Great Crisis* (New York: Oxford University Press, 2012).

since the rich save the most and since savings determine investment, economic growth depends on concentration of income in the upper 1–10 percent. The poor need not worry, because like the crumbs from the dinner table of the wealthy that feed the servants, there is a "trickle-down" of income from the top to the bottom. The argument has been used to keep taxes low for the rich. The argument is easily dispensed with for it belongs in the trash bin of rubbish fiction.

Even the giant bank, Morgan Stanley, has contended that inequality is a bad thing for the economy.[2] The central thesis of the bank bears repeating. Amid stagnant wages, and little to access to credit, lower-to middle-income U.S. households have limited spending for bare necessities; food, housing health care and education. Discretionary spending is a luxury. These segments make up 50 percent of total households and account for 40 percent of consumer spending. Working class households, which rely more on salary income, have taken the biggest hit. No wonder the recovery from the Great Recession has been so anemic. There is more to it than only economic costs.

Three broad categories comprise the arguments against inequality. First, there are those economic costs. Economic performance can suffer from the economic costs. With great income comes great power, and as noted, great power can corrupt. Democracy itself may be a risk because of power concentrations. And, there are social costs. Social problems arise and individual relationships tend to suffer when inequality becomes too great.

Let us consider the economic costs. Economic growth will slow if inequality reduces spending or if inequality interrupts productivity growth. We produce less because of insufficient aggregate demand or because of lost economic efficiency, the former being the concern of Morgan Stanley. Nobel Prize winner Joseph Stiglitz has written a book about this particular cost.[3] John Maynard Keynes has provided the necessary lexicon. He noted that the rich have a lower propensity to consume and a higher propensity to save than everyone else; so if more income goes to the very rich, aggregate spending levels will fall. The national

[2] Morgan Stanley, "The Economic Cost of Inequality," Retrieved January 23, 2015. From http://www.morganstanley.com/ideas/the-economic-cost-of-inequality.
[3] Joseph E. Stiglitz, *The Cost of Inequality* (New York, London: W.W. Norton, 2013).

spending rate is a weighted average of everyone's propensity to spend. where the weights are the income received by each household. As more income goes to those with a greater tendency to save, spending falls to the detriment of economic growth. Larry Summers and other Keynesians have warned of the possibility of secular stagnation due to such problems of insufficient demand. Trickle-down fiction has one thing right: the rich have a greater tendency to save than the poor. Charles Dicken's Thomas Gradgrind serves society well in this regard while Stephen Blackpool, a worker, does not.

Thomas Piketty has slapped some numbers on this for the USA. He finds that the percentage of income received by the top 10 percent has risen from less than 35 percent in 1980 to 50 percent in 2012. Most of this income has gone to the top 0.1 percent, those making more than $1.9 million.[4] With US GNP at around $17 trillion, this income transfer for 2014 works out to nearly $3 trillion. If the top 0.1 percent saves 15–20 percent more of its income than average (which includes the top earners), there will be $500 billion less in aggregate spending as a result of rising income inequality. With a multiplier of 2, output will be lower by $1 trillion, a little more than 5 percent of U.S. GDP. Put differently, average income levels in the U.S. would be around 5 percent greater this year if income were distributed more equally and if this led to more spending and greater economic growth. This gain is in addition to the income gains for a large majority of the population from having a more equal distribution of income.

A related problem is the slowdown in productivity growth. Productivity is measured as the output per worker. More than anything, productivity growth decides living standards. Productivity tends to rise with upswings in the economy and fall during downswings. Productivity is said to be pro-cyclical. With economies of scale, a rise in output will assure productivity increases. The productivity of the sales force in Macy's, the productivity of Century One real estate agents, and the productivity of the *New York Times* reporters, all depend on the value of sales. When people are not spending, the productivity of the sales force declines. It can mean the death of a salesman.

---

[4]Thomas Pikerty, *Capital in the Twenty-first Century* (Cambridge, Mass., London: Harvard University Press, 2014), p. 24.

There is an unmistakable connection between productivity growth and inequality. Take the U.S. as an example. Two dramatic pictures tell the story — Figures 17.1 and 17.2. Productivity growth was greatest during the 1950s and 1960s, the two decades when income equality had reached

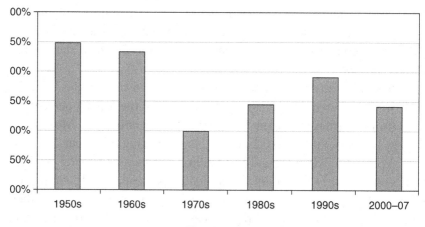

Figure 17.1

Source: Bureau of Labor Statistics, Except for the 1950s which comes from the Groningen Database.

The top decile share in U.S. national income dropped from 45–50% in the 1910s-1920s to less than 35% in the 1950s (this is the fall documented by Kuznets); it then rose from less than 35% in the 1970s to 45–50% in the 2000s-2010s. Sources and series: see piketty pse.ens.fr/capital21c and the book (see next footnote) by Steven Pressman.

Figure 17.2   Income Inequality in the United States, 1910–2010

a high plateau after the great inequality during the twenties and thirties. Since then as inequality has sharply risen, productivity growth has declined.[5] This is at the macro level: one might expect that rising productivity would add to workers' incomes, but this is so only if profits are reduced. There is another, not exactly contrary, view. Harvey Leibenstein coined the term "x-efficiency" to indicate that much worker effort is discretionary. Workers who feel that too much income goes to the top executives may work more slowly, diminishing plant productivity.[6]

As noted in Chapters 15 and 16, rising inequality can lead to financial instability. Casino capitalism is the mirror image of secular stagnation. The dot com bubble of the late 1990s and the housing bubble of the 2000s, not to mention the 2008–2009 financial collapse, became the only way to sustain economic growth when spending falls. Slow growth leads central bankers, in the absence of fiscal policy stimulus, to push down interest rates. Those seeking higher returns on their wealth will then have to take on more risk. This added risk generates financial bubbles as greater demand pushes up the prices of risky financial assets. The casino effect becomes stronger as the financial sector expands relative to the non-financial sector. Debt levels rise leading to a Minsky moment.

The Political Costs of Inequality

There is a long history of the political effects of inequality. The Greek philosopher Aristotle questioned whether democracy and great inequality were compatible. Alexis de Tocqueville in the 19th century wrote about how economic equality sustained political democracy in America. During the Gilded Age Justice Louis Brandeis suggested that we can have a democratic society or we can have great concentration of wealth in a few hands, but be cannot have both. An important study of 71 countries in 1996 found that between 1950 and 1985 rising inequality tends

---

[5] The figures are from Steven Pressman, *Understanding Piketty's* Capital in the Twenty-first Century (London and New York: Routledge, 2016), pp. 40–41.

[6] H. Leibenstein, "Allocative Efficiency vs. X-Efficiency," *American Economic Review*, 56, 392–415.

to result in constitutional changes or unconstitutional changes such as *coups d'ettat*.[7]

Perhaps most important is the political access that wealth provides. Moreover, Congress tends to represent the views of their high-income constituents more than the view of their low-income constituents.[8] Enormous wealth can also subvert the legal system and it enables a select people to influence government regulators, including the IRS.

Globalization, if managed for the 1 percent, provides a mechanism that simultaneously facilitates tax avoidance and imposes pressures that give the 1 percent the upper hand not just in bargaining with a firm but also in politics. The trend is not limited to the USA; it is a global phenomenon, and in some countries matters are far worse than in the United States.

The most vivid examples have arisen in nations that have become over-indebted. The debtor countries have to turn over power to creditors. It was one thing for these events to occur in poor developing countries; it's another for them to occur in advanced industrial economies. But that is what has been happening recently, as first Greece and then Italy allowed the International Monetary Fund (IMF), together with the European Central Bank (ECB) and the European Commission to dictate parameters of policy and then appoint technocratic governments to oversee the implementation of the program. When Greece proposed to submit the tough austerity program that had been prepared for a public referendum there arose a shout of horror from European officials and the bankers. Greek citizens might reject the proposal, and that might mean that the creditors would not be repaid.[9]

Twice in the 1990s Lluiz Ina'cio Lula da Silva was on the verge of being elected President of Brazil and twice Wall Street objected, exercising what amounted to a veto. It signaled that if he were elected it would

---

[7] A. Alesina & A. Perotti, "Income Distribution, Political Instability and Investment," *European Economic Review*, 40, 1203–1228.

[8] See R. Bartels, *Unequal Democracy: The Political Economy of the New Gilded Age* (Princeton: Princeton University Press, 2008).

[9] For much more on Greece, and more of the same on Ireland, Portugal, Spain, and Italy, see E. Ray Canterbery, *The Rise and Fall of Global Austerity* (New Jersey, London, Singapore: World Scientific, 2015), pp. 139–160.

pull money out of the country, interest rates that the country would have to pay would soar, the country would be shunned by investors, and its growth would collapse. The third time, in 2002, the Brazilians, said, in effect, that they would not be dictated to by the international financiers. Prsident Luila turned out to be an excellent president, maintaining economic stability, promoting growth, and attacking his country's extreme inequality. After 8 years he still enjoyed the popular support that he had in the beginning.[10]

The Social Costs of Inequality

In addition to bad economic and political outcomes, inequality has significant social costs. It tears at the social fabric. Great inequality contributed to two World Wars in Europe during the first half of the 20th century. It continues to contribute to wars in the Middle East.

A considerable literature points to the negative impact of inequality on health, including life expectancy. Studies show that greater inequality is not only associated with lower life expectancy, higher infant mortality rates, and greater health problems.[11] G.B. Rodgers was the first to show that life expectancy was related to both average income and income distribution using international data.[12] Later, Wilkinson showed that in the developed world income inequality was a more important factor than average income.[13] Income inequality also contributed to death rates U.S. states and cities. This relationship has been duplicated in other studies. Additionally, inequality has had negative effects on crime rates, family formation, and social mobility. In the latter case,

---

[10] See Joseph E. Stiglitz, *The Price of Inequality* (New York & London: W.W. Norton, 2013), pp.173–175 for this example and others.

[11] See S. Babones, "Income Inequality and Population Health: Correlations and Causality," *Social Science and Health*, 55, pp. 1614–1526 and S. Subramanian and I. Kawachi, "Income Inequality and Health: What Have We Learned So Far?," *Epidemiological Review*, 25, pp.78–91.

[12] G. B. Rodgers, "Income and Inequality as Determinants of Mortality: An International Cross-Section Analysis," *Population Studies*, 33, pp. 343–351.

[13] R. Wilkinson, *Unhealthy Societies: The Afflictions of Inequality* (London & New York: Routledge, 1996).

social mobility or intergenerational mobility is a good indicator of equality of opportunity.[14]

A large literature shows how inequality imposes enormous economic, political, and social costs on the afflicted nations. This justifies the study of inequalities across the globe.

Income Inequality in the USA

The upswing in inequality in the USA, which began in the late 1970s, continues in the post-Great Recession era. This is a story that goes beyond Wall Street and the financial sector. This despite the outsized rewards from speculation in financial markets in the greater New York City metro-politan area. Every state is affected, and so too are the nation's metro areas and counties, many of which are more unequal than the country as a whole. The unequal income growth since the late 1970s has pushed the top 1 percent's share of all income above 24 percent (the national peak scaled during the Jazz Age) in five states, 22 metro areas, and 75 counties. It is a problem when the CEOs and financial-sector executives appropriate more than their fair share of the nation's (slowly) expanding economic pie. Hence comprises a summary of the findings of the Economic Policy Institute (EPI) in 2016.[15] This important report by one of the most respected institutions on the planet cannot be ignored. The report uses the same methodology employed by an earlier study by Thomas Piketty and Emmanuel Saez to generate their widely cited findings on the incomes of the top 1 percent in the USA as a whole.[16]

We will now focus on the rising inequality since the Great Recession. While incomes at all levels declined during the Great Recession, income growth has been lopsided since the recovery began in 2009. The top 1 percent captured an alarming share of economic growth while enjoying

---

[14] For much more on social costs of inequality, see Steven Pressman, *Understanding Piketty's Capital in the Twenty-First Century, op. cit.*, pp. 48–52.

[15] Estelle Sommeiller, Mark Price, and Ellis Wazeter "Income Inequality in the U.S. by State, Metropolitan Area, and County" (Washington, DC: Economic Policy Institute, June 16, 2016).

[16] Thomas Piketty, Thomas and Emmanuel Saez, "Income Inequality in the United States, 1913–1998," *Quarterly Journal of Economics*, 118(1), 2003.

relatively high income growth. Specifically, between 2009 and 2013, the top 1 percent captured 85.1 percent of total income growth in the USA. The average income of the top 1 percent grew about 25 times as much as the average income of the bottom 99 percent, which grew only 0.7 percent. In 24 states the top 1 percent captured at least half of all income growth between 2009 and 2013. In 15 of those states the top 1 percent captured *all* income growth between 2009 and 2013. These states were Connecticut, New York, New Jersey, Florida, Georgia, Louisiana, Maryland, Mississippi, Missouri, Nevada, North Carolina, South Carolina, Virginia, Washington, and Wyoming. These were the Golden States for the Golden Age of 2009–2013 for the super-income-earners. Notably, the financial industry is concentrated in Connecticut, New York, and New Jersey, while South Florida, Nevada, and Wyoming are the playgrounds for the rich. In 10 states, top 1 percent incomes grew in the double digits, while the bottom 99 percent incomes fell. Among these states were Connecticut, New York and New Jersey.

The good times really did roll for top USA executives during the 1980s, 1990s, and 2000s, particularly relative to other wage earners or even high wage earners. The growth of CEO and executive compensation was a major factor driving the doubling of the income shares of the top 1.0 percent and top 0.1 percent of U.S. households from 1979 to 2007. Income growth since 2007 has also been very unbalanced as profits have reached record highs and, correspondingly, the stock market has boomed while wages of most workers (and their families' incomes) have declined over the recovery. The inverse relation between profits and wages can be predicted from Kalecki's theory of the income distribution. The stock market was related to a Minsky moment. Looking at longer-term trends, from 1978 to 2013, CEO compensation, inflation adjusted, increased 937 percent, while the typical worker's compensation gained only 10.2 percent. The average CEO compensation was $15.2 million in 2013 (from a sample of the top 350 USA firms). The CEO-to-worker compensation ratio has not always been this extreme. It was 20-to-1 in 1954, 29.9-to-1 in 1978, growing to 122.6-to-1 in 1995, peaking during the dot-com bubble at 383.4-to-1 in 2000, and dipping modestly to 295.9-to-1 in 2013.[17] If it had been a

---

[17] See Alyssa Davis and Lawrence Mishel, "CEO Pay Continues to Rise as Typical Workers Are Paid Less," Economic Policy Institute, pp. 1–2. Retrieved September 19, 2016. From https://www.epi.org/publication/ceo-pay-continues-to-rise/

horse race, the winning (average) CEO would have lapped the losing wage earner at least 100 times. Everyone would say that such a horserace was rigged.

The AFL–CIO has been keeping track of the CEO race to the finish line in its Paywatch.[18] Among the 100 highest paid CEOs in 2015 were 5 in the financial industry. They were Laurence D. Fink of BlackRock ($25.8 million), Lloyd C. Blankfein of Goldman Sachs Group ($22.6 million), James P. Gorman of Morgan Stanley ($22.1 million), James M. Cracchiolo of Ameriprise Financial Services ($20.7 million), and John G. Stumpf of Wells Fargo & Company ($19.3 million). They received above average compensation. Lloyd Blankfein is a familiar face. He assumed the CEO position when Henry Paulson was nominated to be U.S. Treasury Secretary in May 2006. Blankfein's net worth is $1.1 billion, placing him among the Forbes 400. In an Interview in 2010, he declared that as a banker, "I'm doing God's work."[19] While doing this work, he visited the White House at least 13 times. According to the Bible, Jesus Christ did some heavy lifting for God for very little compensation.

Goldman Sachs Group is also familiar to us. Its executives have a revolving door to various high level government positions. Robert Rubin and Henry Paulson were U.S. Treasury Secretaries, Mario Draghi heads the ECB, and Mark Carney is Governor of the Bank of England. Goldman Sachs is a virtual farm club for government finance players.

Geography turns out to be important. New York state hosts 41 financial firms with the dominant ones being in New York City. Among the highest paid CEOs are the aforementioned Laurence Fink (BlackRock Inc.), James P. Gorman (Morgan Stanley), and Lloyd Blankfein (Goldman Sachs). Additionally, there is the familiar James Dimon at JPMorgan Chase & co. ($20 million), Michael Corbat of Citigroup Inc. ($14.5 million), Peter D. Hancock of American International Group Inc. (AIG) ($12.1 million), Gerald L. Hassell of Bank of New York Mellon Corp. ($11.7 million), and Joseph R. Ficalora of New York Community Bancorp Inc. ($11.2 million). The average CEO pay in New York state is $7, 308,331, while the average worker's pay is $49,330. James Dimon is

---

[18] http://ftp.workingamerica.org/Corporate-Watch/Paywatch-2015.

[19] Interview of Lloyd Blankfein, *Sunday Times*, January 6, 2013.

worthy of special mention, as head of the largest of the Big 4 banks. He has served on the Board of Directors of the Federal Reserve Bank of New York. He has repeatedly been named among *Time* magazine's 100 most influential people. He was a character in the HBO movie *Too Big to Fail* (2011) and was a character in the BBC TV film, *The Last Days of Lehman Brothers*. He was often seen around the Obama White House, though he disagreed with the President's plan to rein in the big banks. He was investigated by the U.S. Senate in the "London Whale" scandal in which some $6 billion was lost on JPMorgan Chase accounts.

Let us come up to date on the one percenters. Between 1979 and 2013, the top 1 percent's share of income doubled nationally, to 20.1 percent. The same 10 states that had the biggest jumps in the top 1 percent from 1979 to 2007 had the biggest increases (at least 9.5 percentage points) from 1979 to 2013. Once again, these included four states with large financial services sectors (New York, Connecticut, New Jersey, and Illinois). Similar results are found in Piketty and Saez's updated (2015) findings.[20] They find the share of income captured by the top 1 percent climbed from 9.95 percent in 1979 to 23.50 percent in 2007. Tax planning helped reduce the top 1 percent's take of all income to 20.08 percent in 2013, returning to 21.24 percent in 2014. A comparison of the Piketty and Saez's results with Sommeiller, Price and Wizeter is provided in Table 17.1. Since they used similar methods and definitions, it is not surprising that the two results track well.

The 2015 Hedge Fund Rich List

Within the top 1 percent there is considerable inequality, not the kind of inequality that keeps the wage earner awake at night. At the tip of the top we find the incomes of hedge fund managers. As it happens, 2014 was the worst year for this elite group of financial investors since the stock market meltdown of 2008. The *average* earnings were a mere $467 million in 2014, down from $846 million the previous year. But consider those at the top of the list. Kenneth Griffin, CEO of Chicago-based Citadel garnered $1.3 *billion* in fees and gains on his own financial capital. James Simons

---

[20]Thomas Piketty and Emmanuel Saez. 2015. Downloadable Excel files with 2014 data updates to tables and figures in Piketty and Saez (2003).

Table 17.1   Inequality of Labor Income Across Time and Space

Share of different groups in total labor income	Low inequality (≈ Scandinavia, 1970s–80s)	Medium inequality (≈ Europe 2010)	High inequality (≈ U.S. 2010)	Very high inequality (≈ U.S. 2030?)
The top 10% "Upper class"	20%	25%	35%	45%
including: the top 1% ("dominant class")	*5%*	*7%*	*12%*	*17%*
including: the next 9% ("well-to-do class")	*15%*	*18%*	*23%*	*28%*
The middle 40% "Middle class"	45%	45%	40%	35%
The bottom 50% "Lower class"	35%	30%	25%	20%
Corresponding Gini coefficient (synthetic inequality index)	0.19	0.26	0.36	0.46

Note: In societies where labor income inequality is relatively low (such as in Scandinavian countries in the 1970s–1980s), the top 10% most well paid receive about 20% of total labor income, the bottom 50% least well paid about 35%, the middle 40% about 45%. The corresponding Gini index (a synthetic inequality index going from 0 to 1) is equal to 0.19.

of New-York-based Renaissance Technologies was No. 2 with 1.2 billion. He now spends a good chunk of his time on his 226-foot yacht *Archimedes*. Raymond Dalio, founder of Bridgewater Associates earned $1.1 billion in 2014. After this, we run into the impoverished making less than a billion. David Shaw, founder of eponymous D.E. Shaw Group earned only $530 million, while David Harding, founder and CEO of London-based Winton Capital Management is tied for No. 22 with only $188 million in income. Now, we are in the below-average pikers. Still, the legendary David Tepper of Appaloosa managed to tie for No. 11 with $400 million, thanks to a huge stockpile of his own cash in Appaloosa's funds. You almost have to admire someone who risks his own money.[21]

---

[21] See Stephen Taub, "The 2015 Rich List: The Highest Earning Hedge Fund Managers of the Past Year," *Institutional Investor's Alpha*. Retrieved May 5, 2015. The curious can find

The hedge-fund manager will be the first to tell you that the risks are high. "SAC Capital Advisors Steven Cohen, No. 2 in 2013 with $2.4 billion, is no longer in the hedge fund business. He shut down his Stamford, Connecticut-based firm and returned all client money as part of SAC's settlement of insider trading charges with government prosecutors." [22] He was never personally accused of a crime. In the past there have been hedge fund managers who have served time. The foregoing goes a long way toward explaining the sources of some of the greatest inequalities.

Piketty and Pressman: The Big Picture on Income Inequalities

In what follows we rely on two major sources — Thomas Piketty and Steven Pressman.[23] We begin with Piketty's Chapter 7 which discusses the relationship between the functional and personal distribution of income. His key point is that wealth yields returns, or provides its owner with income every year. As such, wealth inequality generates income inequality. In the decades following World War II, inherited wealth lost much of its importance, and for the first time in history, perhaps, work and study became the surest routes to the top.[24] Chapter 7 goes on to explain how the decline in inequality stemmed from the destruction of wealth due to the two world wars and from the high taxes there were necessary to fight them. During the several decades following World War II income inequality remained stable as tax rates remained high. Once these rates began to fall, beginning in the 1970s and 1980s (dates vary with the country), inequality began to rise again, like the Phoenix from its ashes.

---

the top 25 list at http://www.institutionalinvestorsalpha.com/Article/3450284/Th-2015-Rich-List-The-Highest-Earning-Hedge-Fund-Managers-of-the-Past-Year.html.

[22] *Ibid.*, p. 3.

[23] Thomas Piketty, *Capital in the Twenty-First Century* (Cambridge, Mass., London: Harvard University Press, 2014) and Steven Pressman, *Understanding Piketty's Capital in the Twenty-First Century* (London and New York: Routledge, 2016). While much of the original data comes from Piketty, we lean on Pressman for his excellent interpretation of the data.

[24] Piketty, *op. cit.*, p. 241.

Table 17.1 displays the inequality of labor income across time and space. Distribution figures are quite similar around the globe for labor income. For the USA, during the year 2010, the top 10 percent received 17 percent of labor income and the top 1 percent received 12 percent of labor income. For Europe, the figures were 25 percent and 7 percent, respectively. Even for egalitarian Scandinavia in the 1970s and 1980s, the top 10 percent of earners received 20 percent of all income and the top 1 percent received 5 percent of all labor income.

As ever, wealth inequality is much greater than income inequality. In the U.S. in 2010 the richest 10 percent of households own 70 percent of all wealth and the richest 1 percent own 25 percent of all wealth. For Europe, the shares are 50 percent and 25 percent, respectively. For egalitarian Scandinavia, the figures are 50 percent and 20 percent. Piketty's wealth estimates are fairly consistent with other estimates of wealth distribution relying on different data sources. Edward Wolff uses the Survey of Consumer Finances as his primary source but expands his sample by using data from the IRS. According to Wolff, mean net worth in 2010 (the very bottom of the top 50 percent) was a mere $57,000, after having fallen by half due to the Great Recession. This is explained by the fact that two-thirds of their net worth consists of home equity. According to the Survey of Consumer Finances, the top 10 percent in the USA owns over 70 percent of aggregate wealth, a figure similar to that of Piketty. The U.S. median net worth in 2010 was a mere $77,300. Those in the bottom quintile had a median net worth of only $6,200.[25]

Much of what we have said about executive pay explains inequality of incomes in the Anglo-Saxon world. The salaries of top managers in the Anglo-Saxon nations are hundreds of times average salaries, but in other countries like France the divergence is not nearly as large. Figures 17.3 and 17.4 compare four Anglo-Saxon nations with three European countries and Japan. This makes clear that inequality of labor income started rising in the former nations beginning in the 1980s; but in the latter set of countries the wage shares received by the top 1 percent have remained relatively stable since 1980. In Europe and Japan the top 1 percent gained another 2–3 percent of total wage income over the past 30 years; in the

---

[25] See Pressman, *op. cit.,* p. 100.

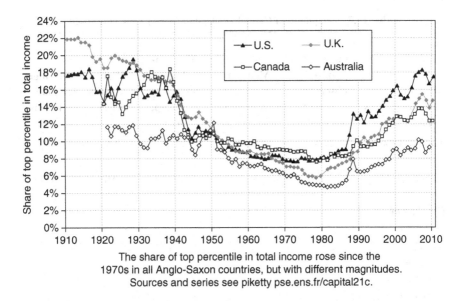

The share of top percentile in total income rose since the
1970s in all Anglo-Saxon countries, but with different magnitudes.
Sources and series see piketty pse.ens.fr/capital21c.

Figure 17.3   Income Inequality in Anglo-Saxon Countries, 1910–2010

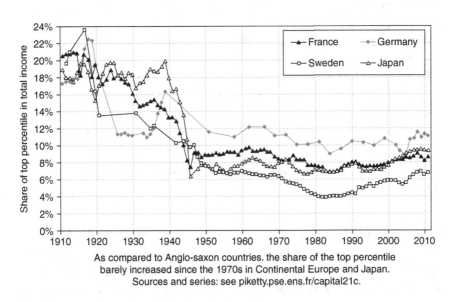

As compared to Anglo-saxon countries. the share of the top percentile
barely increased since the 1970s in Continental Europe and Japan.
Sources and series: see piketty.pse.ens.fr/capital21c.

Figure 17.4   Income Inequality: Continental Europe and Japan, 1910–2010

Table 17.2 Inequality of Capital Ownership Across Time and Space

Share of different groups in total capital	Low inequality (never observed; ideal society?)	Medium inequality (≈ Scandinavia, 1970s–80s)	Medium-high inequality (≈ Europe 2010)	High inequality (≈ U.S. 2010)	Very high inequality (≈ Europe 1910)
The top 10% "Upper class"	30%	50%	60%	70%	90%
including: the top 1% ("dominant class")	10%	20%	25%	35%	50%
including: the next 9% ("well-to-do class")	20%	30%	35%	35%	40%
The middle 40% "Middle class"	45%	40%	35%	25%	5%
The bottom 50% "Lower class"	25%	10%	5%	5%	5%
Corresponding Gini coefficient (synthetic inequality index)	0.33	0.58	0.67	0.73	0.85

Note: In societies with "medium" inequality of capital ownership (such as Scandinavian countries in the 1970s–1980s), the top 10% richest in wealth own about 50% of aggregate wealth, the bottom 50% poorest about 10% and the middle 40% about 40%. The corresponding Gini coefficient is equal to 0.58.

USA the top 1 percent garnered another 10–15 percent of total wage income. Conventional theory explains such diverges with marginal productivity theory. But, if such a theory were correct, and wages were rising because of globalization and/or technical changes were increasing the productivity of CEOs, we should see the same changes in all countries portrayed in these two figures. As noted, we earlier explained CEO pay in

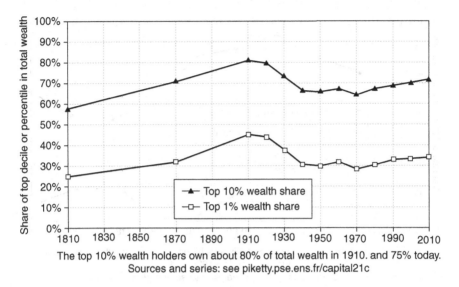

The top 10% wealth holders own about 80% of total wealth in 1910. and 75% today.
Sources and series: see piketty.pse.ens.fr/capital21c

Figure 17.5 Wealth Inequality in the U.S., 1810–2010

the United States, where CEO compensation is similar to that in other Anglo-Saxon nations.

A longer-run view is provided by Figure 17.5. In it, the U.S. looks like a less extreme version of Europe. The wealth holdings of the top 1 percent rose from around 25 percent to around 45 percent from 1810 to 1910, the gilded age. They then fell to 30 percent by 1940 and have since crept back up to around 35 percent.

Piketty looks to the return on financial capital as the basis for inequality in France over time, with that return declining in recent decades (Figure 17.6). Wealth tends to grow at around 5 percent per year. Piketty estimates that growth rates for wealth averaged around 5 percent in France during the nineteenth and early 20th centuries — sometimes a bit higher (nearly 6 percent in the middle of the nineteenth century) and sometimes a bit lower (4 percent at the end of the century), but the fluctuations are small and are centered around 5 percent.[26] At this rate, as income from

---

[26] Figure 17.6 runs from the years 1820 to 1910. Textual references to other years are based on Piketty's text, not on the Figure.

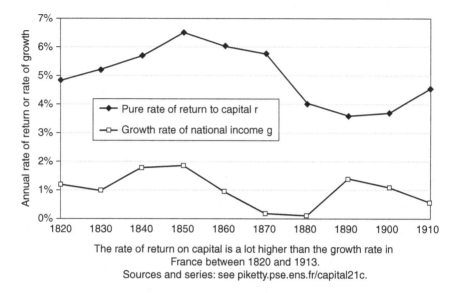

The rate of return on capital is a lot higher than the growth rate in
France between 1820 and 1913.
Sources and series: see piketty.pse.ens.fr/capital21c.

Figure 17.6   Return to Capital and Growth: France 1820–1913

capital grows, it becomes easier to save and accumulate even more capital.
This is especially the case when tax rates on income from capital are low.
However, there was one important exception to $r = 5$ percent — the early
and *middle* parts of the 20th century, where due to a variety of factors the
return to capital was only 2.5 percent, a bit less than the growth rate of
3 percent. These circumstances, according to Piketty, cannot continue.
Economic growth is slowing due to a slowdown in population growth and
productivity growth, and the returns to wealth have returned to 5 percent.
With $g = 1$ percent and $r = 5$ percent, wealth holders must save only a bit
more than 20 percent of their gains to ensure that their wealth grows faster
than average income. Taxation could reduce the rate at which wealth
accumulates.

USA Wealth Holdings: A Closer Look

Upon closer inspection, we find great inequalities among the wealthiest
individuals. The bulk of this wealth comes from different — and more
lucrative — assets sources than ordinary Americans. American's top

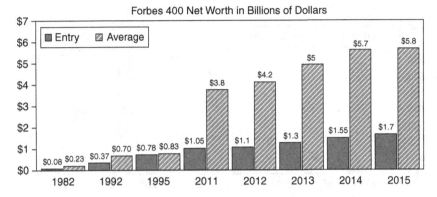

Figure 17.7

Source: Combined Net Worth. Forbes 400. 1982–2015.

1 percent, for instance, hold nearly half the national wealth invested in stocks and mutual funds. Most of the wealth of Americans in the bottom 90 percent comes from their principal residences, the asset that took the biggest hit during the Great Recession. These same Americans also hold almost three-quarters of America's debt.

The most visible indicator of wealth inequality in the USA today may be the *Forbes* magazine list of the nation's 400 richest. In 1982, the "poorest" American listed in the first annual *Forbes* magazine's list of America's richest 400 had a net worth of $80 million. The average member of that first list had a net worth of $230 million. In 2015, rich Americans needed net worth of $1.7 billion to enter the Forbes 400, and the average member held a net $5.8 billion, over 10 times the 1982 average after adjusting for inflation. Figure 17.7 shows how the threshold level of wealth and the averages have climbed over the years.

Even within the Forbes 400, inequality is sky rocketing. The net worth of the richest member of the Forbes 400 has soared from $2 billion in 1982 to $76 billion in 2015, far outpacing the gains at either the Forbes 400 entry point or average. The dramatic differences are illustrated in Figure 17.8.

Next, consider the black–white and Latino households in 2015. The stark differences are seen in Figures 17.9 and 17.10. Obviously, the Forbes 400 is comprised of only 400 individuals. Compare their total net worth with that of 15 million black Americans and 15 million Latinos. As you

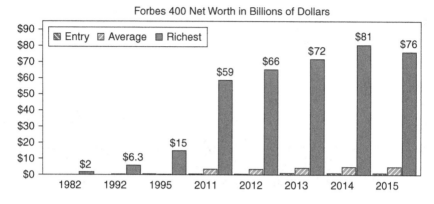

Figure 17.8

Source: Combined Net Worth, Forbes 400, 1982–2015.

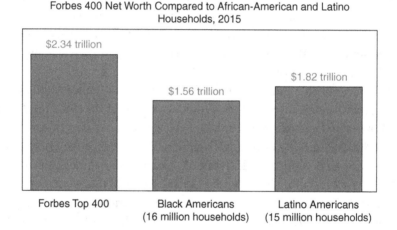

Figure 17.9

Source: Institute for Policy Studies, Billionaire Bonanza: The Forbes 400 and the Rest of Us, December 2015.

can see, the 400 minority group outclasses the millions of blacks and Latinos by a wide margin. When it comes to median household wealth comparisons, the ratio of white-to-black had risen to 13:1 by 2013 (see Figure 17.10).

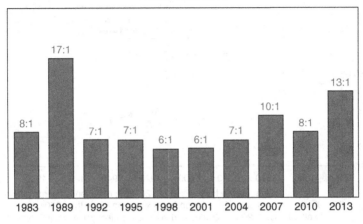

Ratio of Median U.S. White Household Wealth to Black Household Wealth, 1983–2013

Figure 17.10

Source: Pew Research Center analysis of Federal Reserve Survey of Consumer Finances data, December 2014.

Inheritance and Wealth Inequality

Wealth originating in the past grows more rapidly, even without labor, than wealth stemming from work. It has long been recognized that great fortunes can be inherited. This is a consequence of $r > g$. Figure 17.11 illustrates this for France. The figure shows the ratio of inheritances to national income. While remaining steady at around 20 percent for most of the 19th century, it rises to 24 percent by 1880 and then falls precipitously to 4 percent by the end of World War II. Essentially, the two world wars sent the growth rate of National Income back to near zero. The great inequality that existed at the beginning of the 20th century disappears and wealth becomes a less important determinate of income inequality. This gave hope that one downside of capitalism had been eliminated. Not so fast — at the end of the 20th century wealth inequality again began to rear its ugly head. Inheritances and gifts rose to over 12 percent of National Income. While still less than in the 19th century and early 20th century, it points to a return of the rentiers.

Similar patterns are found for Germany and the U.K. As Figure 17.12 shows, inheritances as a share of National Income fell in these two nations

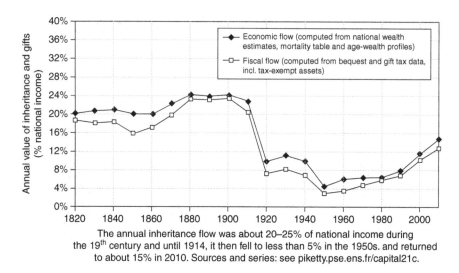

The annual inheritance flow was about 20–25% of national income during the 19th century and until 1914, it then fell to less than 5% in the 1950s. and returned to about 15% in 2010. Sources and series: see piketty.pse.ens.fr/capital21c.

Figure 17.11   The Annual Inheritance as a Fraction of National Income, France 1820–2010

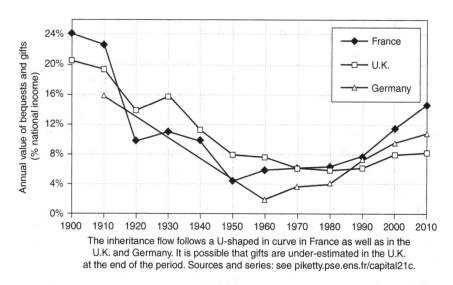

The inheritance flow follows a U-shaped in curve in France as well as in the U.K. and Germany. It is possible that gifts are under-estimated in the U.K. at the end of the period. Sources and series: see piketty.pse.ens.fr/capital21c.

Figure 17.12   The inheritance flow in Europe 1900–2010

during most of the 20th century. But, starting in 1980, we see a resurgence of inheritances relative to the size of the economy. Worse, $r > g$ implies that the entrepreneur always tends to turn into a rentier. The children of Bill Gates do not have to work; they can live off the wealth that Bill Gates has accumulated (unless he gives it all away). After just a few generations a little bit of wealth can grow and render the income from labor irrelevant to one's current standard of living. This process can deprive society of a great deal of creative talent.

There is more at stake than simply money. The top 1 percent of wealth owners are an elite that plays a central role in shaping the economic, political, and symbolic structure of society. This was the case of the aristocracy in 19th-century France; it is the case today for who have inherited a great deal of wealth. For those born between 1910 and 1950 this was not the case, for much wealth had been destroyed. We see the control by wealthy individuals everywhere, in the media, Rupert Murdoch controlling Fox News and the *Wall Street Journal*. We see it in lobbying efforts in Congress to support the well-to-do.

The Global Growth Rate of Wealth

Is the growth in wealth exponential? While the average return on financial capital is 5 percent, there are those earning less and those earning more. Those with more wealth tend to earn higher returns than average and those with less wealth tend to earn smaller returns. That makes the inequality problem even worse than what follows from $r > g$. Because the wealthiest 0.1 percent or 0.01 percent earn more than average they pull away faster from the merely wealthy (others in the top 1 percent) and from the milling crowd. For one thing, those owning a great deal of wealth can hire better financial consultants and advisors, who will get them above average returns. Secondly, if you risk more, you will earn (on average) higher returns on your wealth. Those with more wealth can afford to be more patient and to take more risks.

Some evidence for this outcome is found in *Forbes* magazine. Since 1987 Forbes has compiled a list of the world's billionaires and the net worth of these billionaires. Table 17.3 shows that the very wealthy have done much better than average. The top 1/(100 million) highest wealth holders gained 5.8 percent per year over the Forbes era. The top

Table 17.3   The Growth Rate of Top Global Wealth, 1987–2013

Average real growth rate per year (after deduction of inflation)	1987–2013
The top 1/(100 million) highest wealth holders (about 30 adults out of 3 billions in 1980s, and 45 adults out of 4,5 billions in 2010s)	6.8%
The top 1/(20 million) highest wealth holders (about 150 adults out of 3 billions in 1980s, and 225 adults out of 4,5 billions in 2010s)	6.4%
Average world wealth per adult	2.1%
Average world income per adult	1.4%
World adult population	1.9%
World GDP	3.3%

Source: see piketty.pse.ens.fr/capital21c.
Note: Between 1987 and 2013, the highest global wealth fractiles have grown at 6%–7% per year, vs. 2.1% for average world wealth and 1,4% for average world income. All growth rates are net of inflation (2.3% per year between 1987 and 2013).

1/(20 million) highest wealth holders gained slightly less at 5.4 percent This included about 150 adults of 3 billions in the 1980s, and 225 adults out of 4.5 billion in the 2010s) The average world wealth per adult grew only 2.1 percent per year.

The net result of $r > g$, in conjunction with the fact that higher returns go to those with great wealth, is that large fortunes get concentrated in relatively few hands. Enormous wealth can then perpetuate itself and grow rapidly while everyone else struggles to survive.

Some Conclusions

The inequality $r > g$ generates income and wealth distributions skewed toward the top 1 percent and top 0.1 percent. Worse, wealth and income inequalities are mutually reinforcing. Greater income inequality means a greater ability to save and accumulate wealth, moreover greater wealth inequality means that those with great wealth receive larger annual returns to their wealth (which is more income). It is a vicious circle. As inequality rises, entrepreneurs will become extremely wealthy and not work any more, nor will their children, grandchildren, or great-grandchildren have to work. They become rentiers, collecting interest and dividends, while producing nada.

Part V

POLICIES

Chapter 18

THE NEGATIVE-INTEREST-RATE GLOBAL SOCIETY

While it is customary to think of interest rates belonging to individual nations, a handful of economists have referred to a global real interest rate. By "real," they simply mean that the nominal rate has been deflated by a price index. One such economist is Olivier Blanchard. He was chief economist at the International Monetary Fund during 2008–2015, a most interesting period. He is a handsome, mature Frenchman who is now a Senior Fellow at the Peterson Institute and Robert Solow Professor of Economics at MIT. He is arguably the most cited economist in the world today. According to Blanchard, the global real interest rate fell from a peak of about 5 percent in 1986 to about 2 percent before the Global Crisis of 2008, and to about 0 percent in 2012. At low inflation rates, it has gone negative since. This may be the legacy, among others, of the Crisis. He considers this "bad news" for monetary policy but good news for fiscal policy. Given his credentials, we cannot ignore Blanchard, though there are some who disagree with him.

Figure 18.1 shows the evolution of the global real interest rate over the past 30 years. To be specific, it is the evolution of the GDP-weighted average of 10-year real interest rates on sovereign bonds across 19 advanced economies since 1987. The sample includes the United States, United Kingdom, France, Germany, and Japan plus 14 other countries. The figure has two striking features. The first is the decline in the rate from a peak of

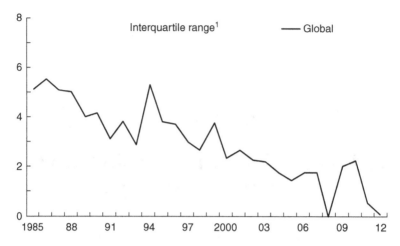

Figure 18.1   Short- and Long-term Global Real Interest Rates (% per year)

Source: IMF (2014).

[1]The sample consists of: United States, United Kingdom, Austria, Belgium, France, Germany, Italy, Netherlands, Norway, Sweden, Switzerland, Cananda, Japan, Finland, Greece, Portugal, Spain, Australia, and New Zealand. Global is based on the GDP-weighted average.

about 5 percent in 1985 to 2 percent before the Crisis and to about ground zero in 2012. This evolution had led to the possibility that the rate needed to maintain output at potential may remain very low in the future, perhaps even negative. Such a negative rate is plausible if the global stagnation continues and inflation remains low. This suggests that one can, and according to Blanchard, must, think of a global interest rate decided in a global market.

We can think of the global real rate as being decided by four elements. The first three of which determine the "natural" or "Wicksellian" rate, the real interest rate consistent with potential output and stable inflation. The third element is monetary policy, which can cause temporary deviations from the natural rate. "Wicksellian" rate is a nod to Knut Wicksell (1851–1926) of the Stockholm school of economics.[1] The first of the three elements that decide the natural rate is the supply of loanable funds or global

---

[1]Wicksell invented the term natural rate of interest which he defined as the interest rate compatible with stable prices. Blanchard is taking liberties with the idea since Wicksell did not know of the idea of potential output.

saving at full potential output. Shifts in saving can by related to many factors, including changes in current and expected income, changes in uncertainty that alter precautionary saving, demographic changes, financial innovations, and shifts in public spending. What Blanchard calls "saving," I prefer to call "savings" because saving can only happen as it is caused by business investment. Savings is what happens in-between and refers to changes in net worth or weatlth.

Still, we will continue with the Blanchard story.[2] The second of the three elements that decide the natural rate is the demand for loanable funds, or global investment, with output at its potential. We are going to take the Keynesian train to the final destination by presuming that investment determines saving. Shifts in investment can be caused by many things, such as changes in expected investment profitability (expectations), changes in the relative price of capital goods, as well as changes in the financial environment. The third element is the relative demand for safe v. risky assets. A shift in investors' preferences towards safe assets — be it due to increases in risk, to increases in market risk aversion, or to changes in financial regulation — will lead, other things being the same, to a lower rate on safe assets and a higher rate on risky assets. By "investors" Blanchard apparently means investors in private capital goods and services. All of which raises the question of which of these elements can explain the decline in global real interest rates.

In the pre-crisis era, Blanchard believes that all three elements played a major role. During the crisis, many factors combined to sharply increase the natural interest rate. Among these, the collapse of financial intermediation, the increase in uncertainty and its effects on precautionary saving and on investment, increased risk, together with rising market risk aversion, decreased the safe rate relative to the rate on risky assets. Monetary policy played an involuntary role, while the zero lower bound on nominal rates and low inflation prevented the actual rate from declining as much as the natural rate. Having worried through these effects, Blanchard suggests that they have since either disappeared or at least receded. What

---

[2] See especially, Olivier Blanchard, Davide Furceri, Andrea Pescatori, "A Prolonged Period of Low Real Interest Rates?" VOX CEPR's policy Portal, pp. 1–2. From http://voxeu.org/article/prolonged-period-low-real-interest-rates.

matters, in his mind, is what legacies the crisis will leave, and for how long.

With the complexity of what decides the natural rate of interest, any forecasts of the future global rate are precarious. This being said, Blanchard ventures that the global real interest rate is likely to remain low.[3] Most of the elements that led to low rates are still present. If anything, the rate will be lower than before the crisis. If rates do turn out to be low, this, according to Blanchard, is bad news for monetary policy. It makes it more likely that countries will bounce along the lower bound. Of course, the effectiveness of expansionary monetary policy is diminished when all the reserve bullets have been fired. Lower rates may be good news for fiscal policy because it is easier for Treasuries to sustain or decrease debt. In fact, increases in federal spending may not lead to increases in public debt. Because fiscal policy was taken off the table, easy monetary policy was the only tool left, or so it was thought. We will return to issues related to fiscal policy in the next chapter.

Negative Rates in Ordinary Life

Negative interest rates for the person on the street where you might or might not live has different implications than a negative interest rate policy at a nation's central bank. Negative interest rates were proposed in the distant past, and the past is a good entre to the present. In the late 19th century the notable Silvio Gesell proposed a negative interest rate as the free money component of his free economy system. Gesell described a negative interest rate as a "tax on holding money." To prevent people from holding cash (and thus earning 0 percent), Gesell suggested issuing money for a limited duration, after which it had to be exchanged for new bills. Attempts to hold money would result in it expiring and becoming worthless. The legendary John Maynard Keynes once approved of the idea of a carrying tax on money, but dismissed it due to administrative difficulties. In 1999, a carry tax on currency was proposed by Marvin Goodfriend, a Federal Reserve employee, to be implemented via magnetic strips on bills, deducting the carry tax upon deposit, the tax varying with the time period

---

[3] *Ibid.*, p. 3.

the bill had been held. A student of Greg Mankiw, who shall remain anonymous, proposed a negative interest rate that would be levied on paper currency via a serial number lottery, such as a randomly chosen number 0 through 9 and declaring that notes whose serial number ends in that digit be worthless. This, he estimated, would yield an average 10 percent loss of paper currency holdings of hoarders, whereas currency with a two-digit number could match the last two digits on the note for a 1 percent loss. All these schemes are aimed at reducing the hoarding of money, holding on to cash for its own sake. This had some appeal to Keynes during the Great Depression when people were burying cash in tin cans.

How do negative interest rates affect private bankers? Quite simply, a bank offering a negative deposit rate would find few takers. The money holder would have to pay the banks to hold their money. Bankers already have low self-esteem. Profit-seeking lenders, such as banks and S&Ls, will not lend money at 0 percent, much less below 0 percent. Still, we should note that in the USA interest on savings deposits are around 1 percent. Loans on new cars hover just below 3 percent per annum. Banks, unhappy with these profit prospects, have begun to move into derivatives. Moreover, both the European Central Bank (ECB) and the Bank of Japan (BOJ) pursued negative interest rate policies in 2014 and 2016, respectively. In 2016 Sweden, Denmark, and Switzerland had negative interest rates in play. Janet Yellen at the Federal Reserve has not ruled out the use of negative interest rates under some circumstances. The Riksbank, Sweden's central bank, has reported no disruptions in financial markets.

Negative Rates at the Central Bank

Contrary to the common view that central banks are "out of ammunition" when policy rates fall to zero, they still can provide stimulus. They can do so by pushing rates negative and though aggressive forms of quantitative easing (QE). If there seems to be a danger in the lower bound, a modest increase in the central bank's inflation target can ease the problem. Still, the lower bound on interest rates has constrained monetary policy since 2008. For example, in the U.S. a pre-crisis Taylor rule dictates a federal funds rate of −5 percent or −6 percent. The Taylor rule stipulates that for each one-percent increase in inflation, the central bank should raise the nominal interest rate by more than one percentage point.[4] The actual rate never fell below zero. According to a 2016 Geneva Report on the World Economy, the U.S. unemployment rates from 2009 through 2015 averaged more than a percentage point higher than they would have if there were no lower bound on interest rates.[5] Unemployment would have been higher still if not for the Federal Reserve's policy of QE.

In truth, even modest economic downturns are likely to push interest rates to zero in the current environment. This is because (1) central banks have chosen low inflation targets, often close to 2 percent and (2) because of the fall in the natural real interest rate over the last two decades, with current estimates at 1 percent or lower. Together, these figures say that the steady state nominal interest rate is 3 percent. Beginning from this level, a central bank can reduce its policy rate only 300 basis points[6] before hitting zero, which is not enough stimulus to offset a moderate-size shock to the economy.

Zero is not an absolute lower bound on interest rates. After all, zero is just a number; well, it is more than that. Around the world, several central banks have explored sub-zero rates. Switzerland's rate was the lowest in fall 2016 at –0.75 percent. These negative rates have influenced domestic asset prices and exchange rates in much the same way as cuts in policy rates have done when still positive. Moreover, negative policy rates have not adversely affected financial systems thus far. Perhaps rates .can be pushed even lower without unduly adverse side effects.

Besides, there is always QE, not unrelated to sub-zero rates. In the U.S., for example. QE purchases of long-term bonds between 2008 and 2015 had macroeconomic effects equivalent to those of a sustained

---

[4] The Federal Reserve does not explicitly follow the Taylor rule. Despite this aversion by the U.S. central bank, many economists have said that the rule provided a fairly accurate summary of U.S. monetary policy under Paul Volcker and Alan Greenspan. Similar observations have been made about central banks in other countries like Canada and New Zealand that have officially adopted inflation targeting rules. According to Taylor, the rule was not followed in part of the 2000s, possibly leading to the housing bubble.

[5] See Laurence Ball, Joseph Gagnon, Patrick Honohan, and Signe Krogstrup, "What Else Can Central Banks Do?" September 2, 2016. Retrieved from p. 1. http://voxeu.org/article/what-else-can-central-banks-do.

[6] A basis point is one hundredths of one percent.

reduction of about 200 to 250 basis points in the Fed funds rate. The effects would be even greater with a greater volume of purchases. There are nonetheless bounds to QE expansionism. There is the "tantrum" fear when yields on bonds jump sharply. Only weak growth and low inflation can prevent this. Otherwise, the bondholding class can throw a tantrum in the bond market. The stock market usually follows with a fit of its own. At the least, we can expect more volatility in financial markets.

Central bankers have been very innovative in doing more, just when you except them to don casual jackets and retire to the cigar room for a glass of whisky. QE can be expanded by including risky assets such as corporate debt and equities, though this can make some already nervous business executives twitchy. Those who believe that supra-surplus capitalism is strictly for the corporate boardroom consider this to be intrusive. Still, with substantial quantities of purchases, this broader version of QE, no matter how reprehensible to the boardroom boys, would have stronger effects on asset prices and costs of funds. The effects are very direct. From asset effects, the impact on economic activity can be stronger than purchases of government bonds.

Besides the fissures in capitalism, unwanted side effects of such an expansionary monetary policy include the risk of overdoing it and causing a surge of inflation, ever-present risks of asset bubbles, disintermediation of the banking system (the hoarding of cash), challenges to the profitability of private commercial banks, and the possible loss of monetary policy independence through political backlash. However, "surges of inflation" seems laughable in the 2016–2017 global environment. As noted, there are ways of ending the hoarding of cash, though not without risks too. Some economists think that banks already are suffering in the pocketbook, but financial markets are gradually displacing private banks. As to the independence of central banks, broader issues are involved.

At the risk of creating a global congested highway system, there is still another route that can be taken. This route opens up if all monetary stimulus policies fail, and it requires that historical pride be swallowed by the central bankers. The greatest fear of central bankers historically has been inflation. Yet an alternative policy would be a modest increase in central banks' inflation targets. The current global target is 2 percent per annum. Raising the target would elevate the nominal interest rate, giving central banks more room to ease policy in response to recessionary threats. The story of the Great Recession might have been rewritten if the Federal Reserve had gone into the debacle with a 4 percent rather than a 2 percent inflation target. The real Fed funds rate still would have moved quickly to zero, but with greater inflationary expectations, the real rate would have been more deeply negative, thus giving a bigger boost to the economy.

Challenging the Independence of the Central Bank

The original purposes of the Federal Reserve System, as stated by Congress, were "to give the country an elastic currency, to provide facilities for discounting commercial paper, and to improve the supervision of banking." More recently, the Board of Governors of the Federal Reserve has recognized broader responsibilities to "counteract inflationary movements and to share in creating conditions favorable to sustained high employment, stable value, growth of the country, and a rising level of consumption." While the Fed, as it is affectionately called, has obviously governmental functions, it is a quasi-public agency, partially owned by the private commercial banks it regulates and virtually independent of the rest of government. Members of the Board of Governors of the Federal Reserve are appointed by the President, with the consent of Congress, to a 14-year term of office. The theory was that since no president could expect to appoint more than two or three members, he would keep his hands off monetary policy. Unwashed politicos, it was thought, would be more responsive to the demands of debtors for a greater supply of "cheap" money and might seek monetary plentitude to cover the costs of large government programs.

The basic premise behind independence is so obvious — or so embarrassing — that it is seldom mentioned: the general public is either too ignorant or too immoral to be trusted with money management. It is an argument once made by Kings and Queens. Having risen above the murky depths of politics, the "Supreme Court of Finance" is regally beyond the influence of the carping citizen. Fed officials can exert their power over the economy with no need to take account of the various special interest groups — or, if the truth be known, the general public.

Yet, clearly the attitudes and interests of the private financial community have often dominated the Fed. Although the Fed was created to supervise the American banking system, sometimes one might suppose that the relationship was just the reverse, given the solicitude with which Fed officials consider the views of bankers and other financial players on Wall Street. It can always be said that monetary policymakers should pay attention to financial experts. As Joseph Stiglitz has written,

> "…an independent central bank, captured by the financial sector, is going to make decisions that represent the beliefs and interests of the financial sector. Even if it were desirable to have a central bank that was independent from the democratic political process, the board should at least be representative and not dominated by members of the financial sector. Several countries do not allow those from the financial sector to serve on their central bank board — they see it as an obvious conflict of interest. There exists a wealth of expertise outside the financial sector.[7]

As critical of the cozy relationship of the Fed and finance that he is, Stiglitz, an economics Nobel Prize winner, is even more harsh with the European Central Bank (ECB). The ECB, which rules over the seventeen-country Eurozone, is supposed to focus only on inflation. "It also reflects the mindset of the banks and financial community even more than the Fed does."[8]

Stiglitz is not alone with his criticism. Randall Wray wants to end the regional Federal Reserve banks, as they have such terrible conflicts of interest, strip out all regulatory power from the Fed (since it doesn't believe in regulation, anyway), and implement monetary policy with a very small staff. Congressman Dennis Kucinich introduced a bill to nationalize the Fed, to end the "casino capitalism" gambles of commercial banks that are bound to fail.

Some years ago I recommended that Congress be given more control of the Fed. At the time the proposal was considered "radical." Today, in light of the alternatives that have been proposed, it appears quite

---

[7] Joseph E. Stiglitz, *The Price of Inequality* (New York/London: W.W. Norton & Company, 2013), pp. 317–318.

[8] *Ibid.*, p. 319.

modest.[9] First, the Joint Economic Committee would be given authority to set up a watchdog committee, the Congressional Monetary Committee (CMC), comprised of academic and technical experts who would evaluate monetary policy on a continuous basis within the framework of the Employment Act of 1946. The responsibilities of the CMC would be comparable to the federal budget analysis now provided by the Congressional Budget Committees. The findings of this subcommittee, which could include dissident former Federal Reserve economists, would be published monthly, with a lengthier year-end report issued.

In order to add force to the recommendations of the CMC, the Joint Economic Committee itself should be given authority to introduce legislation embodying reforms based on the reports of its committee of experts. The new power of Congress could be somewhat balanced by allowing the President to appoint a Board Chairman with a term that corresponds to his own. (Parts of the above reform measures have since been adopted by Congress.)

Another reform would be to change the internal workings of the Federal Open Market Committee (FOMC). The practice of placing five regional Reserve Bank presidents on the FOMC, four of whom are on a rotating basis, would be discontinued. These persons are generally career Fed employees and are, in any event, subservient to the Board. This would of course remove from the FOMC the President of the New York Fed, currently a permanent member of the committee, who, next to the Chairman, generally has had the most to say about the course of monetary policy. This reform would also weaken the close ties of the Fed to its financial constituency, especially the New York banking community. It is a more modest version of the Wray proposal.

The effect of these reforms would be to exhume the Federal Reserve from solitary confinement and to make it a political institution, subject to appropriate pressures from the public at large, rather than permitting it to cater to the policy preferences of a small coterie. The high-handed inference that only an exclusive club of inbred alumni can understand monetary policy is at best a self-fulfilling myth that stems from the Fed's own cultivation of a cult of obscurity. And as the Fed becomes less of a

---

[9] The original proposal, which has aged gracefully, appears in E. Ray Canterbery "The Awkward Independence of the Federal Reserve," *Challenge, The Magazine of Economic Affairs.* 18(4), 1975, p. 48. Reprinted in E. Ray Canterbery, (Ed.), *Beyond Conventional Economics* (New Jersey/London/Singapore: World Scientific, 2016), Chapter 43.

Breaking News: Is Independence Overrated?

In their battle against inflation, sometimes imaginary, governments granted significant independence to central banks over recent decades. Now, some economists say that same independence could be hampering their ability to fombat the current era's problem: inflation that's too low. To safeguard their independence, major central banks may have deployed "second-best" policies that distort financial markets and face diminishing returns, such as negative interest rates and large-scale bond purchases, and shunned potentially more effective tools such as "helicopter money." Helicopter money could involve an increase in public spending or tax cuts financed by the central bank, which takes central banks beyond their realm of influencing the price and volume of credit to determine how public money is spent — traditionally the domain of politicians. Bank of Japan Governor Haruhiko Kuroda warns that helicopter money would be an unacceptable intermingling of fiscal and monetary policy. He says this in a moribund economy. Former Fed Chairman Ben Bernanke proposed in April that the Fed could credit a special Treasury account with funds if it assessed such a stimulus was needed to achieve its employment and inflation goals. The U.S. government would then determine how to spend the funds, or could leave them unspent.

Source: Summary from Tom Fairless, "Is Central Bank Independence Overrated?" *Wall Street Journal*, September 12, 2016, p. A2.

mystery, its standards of economic policy — and its sense of public responsibility — will inevitably be raised.

Alice Rivlin: In Defense of Independence

On July 14, 2015 a Congressional hearing on "Fed Oversight: Lack of Transparency and Accountability" was held.[10] Alice Rivlin, who served as

---

[10] "Fed Oversight: Lack of Transparency and Accountability," Subcommittee on Oversight and Investigations Committee on Financial Service, U.S. House of Representatives, July 14, 2015.

Director of the Office of Management and Budget (OMB) (1993–1995) and as Vice Chair of the Federal Reserve Board (1996–1999) was the Founding Director of the Congressional Budget Office (1975–1985), does not agree with the premises of the Subcommittee.[11] She is also the daughter of the physicist Allen C. G. Mitchell and the granddaughter of astronomer Samuel Alfred Mitchell, and has received many honors.

She makes three basic points. First, current monetary policy alternatives are controversial, but they are not mysterious or opaque, while Federal Reserve officials are making extraordinary efforts to explain to Congress and the public the dilemmas they face.

> When the economy plunged into deep recession after the financial crisis of 2008 the Federal Reserve engaged in aggressively accommodative monetary policy aimed at arresting the steep decline of economic activity and accelerating recovery. It brought short-term interest rates close to zero and engaged in several rounds of bond-buying to put downward pressure on long-term rates and flood banks with reserves. As the economy recovered, the Fed phased out its bond purchase programs.[12]

Now, she continued, the Fed must decide when to begin raising short-term interest rates and how fast to bring those rates back to a more normal range, requiring a judgment call. Different people weigh the factors differently, but there is nothing obscure or inscrutable about this dilemma, for the FOMC minutes lay out the arguments. Chairman Janet Yellen and other Fed officials explain their views frequently and lucidly in speeches. Moreover, the Chairman testifies and answers endless questions both in hearings and in press conferences.

Second, Rivlin argues, nothing terrible or irreversible is likely to happen if the Fed acts too slowly or too fast. Rather, threats to our future prosperity are more likely to come from fiscal gridlock. Here her target is the Congress. It has long been contended that monetary policy is much more flexible than a fiscal policy that is in the unwieldly hands of a divided Congress. While some argue for higher rates on the grounds that

---

[11] Alice Rivlin, "Preserving the Independence of the Federal Reserve," *Ibid.*
[12] *Ibid.*, p.1.

inflationary dangers are lurking out there in the darkness, but this, it seems to most, is far-fetched. Still, fiscal policy has a great opportunity to improve our future prosperity by modernizing our decaying infrastructure, bolstering scientific research, and investing effectively in the skills of the labor force. The problem there remains political gridlock.

Third, the creators of the Federal Reserve were wise to insulate its decisions from political pressures. Having a second group to second guess monetary policy decisions would undermine an independent agency. Already, the Fed is accountable to Congress and the public and is subject to thorough auditing and oversight of its operations. It is scrutinized by the GAO. However, the GAO is not allowed to second-guess the FOMC. It would, according to Rivlin, politicize the system.

In short, the Federal Reserve's independence has become a model of central bank governance around the world and delegating monetary policy to an independent body was a sound idea. Rivlin ignores the challenges to independence presented in the previous section of this chapter. Her arguments are similar to those of Fed Chairs of the past and present. The best argument for Fed independence, however, is the present Chair, Janet Yellen, notable for her openness in the face of internal opposition at the Fed.

What Will End Negative Rates?

The central bankers are saying that ultra-loose monetary policy remains essential to prop up weak economies and hit their inflation targets. The Bank of Japan in the third week of September 2016 promised to keep 10-year government bonds yields around zero. Yes, those are 10-year government bonds. On September 21st the Federal Reserve backed off a rate rise yet again. In the wake of the Brexit vote, the Bank of England has cut its main policy rate to 0.25 percent, the lowest in its 300-year history. The ECB is clinging to negative rates.

A growing chorus of critics frets about the effects of a topsy-turvy place where savers are charged a fee, where the yields on a large fraction of rich world government debt come with a minus sign, and where central banks matter more than markets in deciding how real capital is allocated. Donald Trump, then the Republican presidential nominee, accused Janet

Yellen of keeping rates low for political reasons. But it is too simple to blame the central banks; they are also reacting to it. The decades-long decline in real long-term rates is driven by such real world elements as ageing populations and the integration of savings-rich China into the global economy. Nor are they being reckless, for in most of the supra-surplus world inflation is well below official targets. Only now has the BOJ explicitly pledged to overshoot its 2 percent inflation target. The Fed is really anxious to push up rates as soon as it can. A sluggish economy is not cooperating.

Yet distortions caused by the low-rate world are growing even as the gains are diminishing. The pension-plan deficits of companies and local governments have ballooned because it costs more to honor future pension promises when interest rates fall. Commercial banks, which normally make money from the difference between short-term and long-term rates have nowhere to go when zero is facing zero. It impairs their ability to make loans even to the most creditworthy. Low rates have skewed financial markets, ensuring a big sell-off in bond markets if rates were suddenly to rise. The perils accumulate the longer this goes on.

As to the truth, it is time to end our reliance on central banks. The most urgent priority is to once again use fiscal policy. The main tool for fighting recessions must shift from central banks to Treasuries. This means going beyond infrastructure investment, which nonetheless is a good thing. Much of the supra-surplus world could do with new railways, toll roads, and airports, and it will never be cheaper to build them. To be effective, fiscal policy must mimic the best features of monetary policy. In short, calling in fiscal policy from the bench and putting it in the lineup will end negative rates. *That* is the subject of the next chapter.

Chapter 19

THE MINIMUM WAGE AND THE REHABILITATION OF FISCAL POLICY

In recent times there has been a debate between the stimulus view and austerity view of economic policy.[1] Nowhere is the debate clearer than when it comes to fiscal policy. John Maynard Keynes and his General Theory are the most famous proponents of the stimulus perspective. Keynes says that government must stimulate the whole economy by giving millions of public jobs to people in fields like teaching, nursing, engineering, and construction work. This can be done indirectly by government deficit spending or by tax reduction. Deficit spending has been the surer path. Beyond the initial stimulus, each of those hired will spend new income this leads to the hiring of many more. There is a Keynesian multiplier effect.

The austerity view holds that there is too much government intervention in the economy. Specifically, there is too much government employment. The government is said to use resources inefficiently. Reducing taxes and the size of the government will unleash incentives in the private economy. Reduced government spending will permit the private sector to run most of the economy, even in areas traditionally thought of as the

---

[1] See David Card and Alan B. Krueger, *Myth and Measurement: The New Economics of the Minimum Wage* (Princeton, NJ: Princeton University Press, 2016).

purview of the public sector (schools and prisons, for instance). While the austerians are radicals in their thinking, it is fair to say that there are political limitations on using government spending to stimulate the economy We were cognizant of this when it came to the Obama stimulus of 2009. The austerians lose sleep over the expansion of public debt.

The Minimum Wage Disputants

The vast literature on the minimum wage is remarkable because it is about such small numbers. The first attempt to establish a national minimum wage came in 1933, when a $0.25 per hour standard was set as part of the National Industrial Recovery Act during the heart of the Great Depression. However, in the 1935 court case Schechter Poultry Corp. v. United States, the U.S. Supreme Court declared the act unconstitutional, and the minimum wage was abolished. The chickens had come home to roust. That's too bad because President Franklin D. Roosevelt at the time said, "No business which depends for existence on paying less than living wages to its workers has any right to continue in this country."[2] The minimum wage was reestablished in the U.S. In 1938 under the Fair Labor Standards Act, once again at a paltry $0.25 per hour ($4.23 in 2015 dollars). This time, the Act was upheld by the Supreme Court.

Since it was last reset on July 24, 2009, the federal minimum wage in the U.S. has been $7.25 per hour. Some U.S. Territories are exempt and some types of labor are also exempt. Employers in service industries may pay tipped labor a minimum of $2.13 an hour, as long as the hourly wage plus tip income equals at least the minimum wage. Persons under the age of 20 may be paid $4.25 an hour unless a higher state minimum exists. As of January 1, 2015 there were 29 states more generous than the federal government with a higher minimum wage. From 2014 to 2015, nine states increased their minimum wage levels though automatic adjustments, while increases in 10 other states occurred through legislative or ballot changes. Answering a call from President Barack Obama, Connecticut raised its minimum wage from $8.70 to $10.10 by 2017.

---

[2] Quoted in Teresa Tritch, "F.D.R. Makes the Case for the Minimum Wage," *New York Times*, March 7, 2014.

Notably, a number of U.S. Cities, including San Francisco, Seattle, and Los Angeles approved the gradual raising of their minimum wages to $15 an hour. Some $15 an hour has become the gold standard for the minimum wage. So far, Arizona, Ohio, Oregon, Missouri, Vermont, and Washington have linked their minimum wages to the consumer price index. A similar practice is found in San Francisco and Santa Fe.

Need we say, the austerians around the globe oppose the setting of a minimum wage; they would rather let the market decide. The central argument against the minimum is that it would raise unemployment. The same persons do not favor full employment. David Card and Alan B. Krueger have demolished the unemployment claim. They say that the weight of the evidence over the past two decades has supported their original view. It is supported by some 23 minimum wage studies published between 2000 and 2013.[3] There are side effects from a higher minimum wage. They concluded that increases in minimum wages lead to reductions in wage inequality and to increases in earnings and incomes for lower-income workers. Similar findings extend to the UK where the introduction of a national minimum wage had a strong effect on the "lower tail" of British wages, pushing up the wages of workers in as high as the 35th percentile of the overall wage distribution. Moreover, minimum wages tend to reduce poverty levels.

Card and Krueger's first case study focuses on the "natural experiment" generated by the April 1992 increase in the New Jersey minimum wage, from $4.25 to $5.05 per hour. They surveyed 410 fast-food restaurants in New Jersey and eastern Pennsylvania before and after, to determine how employment responded to the hike in the minimum wage. Regardless of the comparison used, the estimated employment effects of the minimum wage are virtually identical. Contrary to the stark predictions of conventional wisdom, they find that the rise in the New Jersey minimum wage seems to have increased employment at restaurants that were forced to raise pay to comply with the law. A second case study was conducted as a survey of fast-food restaurants in Texas. The federal minimum wage was raised from $3.80 to $4.25 an hour in April 1991. The results were similar to the those in the New Jersey-Pennsylvania study. Fast-food

---

[3] Card and Krueger, *op. cit.*, p. xiv.

restaurants in Texas that were forced to increase pay to meet the new federal minimum-wage standard had faster employment growth than did those that already were paying $4.25 an hour or more, and that therefore were unaffected by the law.[4] The 1988 increase in California's minimum wage also had a significant effect on wages in the state. The 27 percent increase in the minimum wage increased the average wages of teenagers by 10 percent, increased the average wages of employees in the retail-trade industry by 5 percent, and increased the average wages of restaurant workers by 8 percent. Moreover, the minimum wage had a positive effect on teenage employment.[5] Again, the conventional wisdom is disputed.

What with all the benefits from a higher minimum wage — a multiplier effect on wages in and outside the industry directly affected, increases in employment, and lower poverty rates — an increase in the national minimum wage to $15 an hour by 2017 seems like a win–win–win possibility. This would move many families into living-wage conditions. Not surprisingly, higher minimum wages are popular. A 1987 Gallup poll found that 66 percent of Republicans and 84 percent of Democrats favored an increase in the minimum wage. More recently, an October 1993 NBC–Wall Street Journal poll found 64 percent of adults in favor of another increase in the minimum wage. The minimum wage continues to attract the attention of policymakers in 2017 and beyond.

Conventional Fiscal Policy

Conventional fiscal policy should concern us because it has become rusty from disuse. In recent decades, the only game in town has been monetary policy, at home and abroad. Fiscal policy begins with net government spending, spending more than tax revenues, which usually requires running a budget deficit. The budget deficit is covered by the issuance of government bills and bonds. The spending includes that for goods and services, but also for transfer payments from governments to individuals or businesses. Purchases of goods and services increase aggregate demand. Also, if $1 billion is spent in transfer payments in the way of

---

[4] *Ibid.*, pp. 25–61.
[5] *Ibid.*, pp. 78–112.

unemployment compensation, this newly created income is soon spent, adding indirectly to aggregate demand.

There are actually two ways in which spending can be financed — one through taxation and the other through bond issuance. When government spending exceeds current tax revenue, a budget deficit is incurred. This is followed by clinched jaws and tight fists by conservatives. Anyway, the budget deficit can be financed by the issuance of government bonds, mostly long-term bonds. In turn, interest on the bonds add to the deficits. Hence, lower interest rates are beneficial in the conduct of fiscal policy. This is known as monetary accommodation. Though it is rare, government loans could be made at zero percent. There is a small amount of government revenue from government enterprises such as the Tennessee Valley Authority. If revenue exceeds spending, there is a fiscal surplus that not only surprises but cheers fiscal conservatives. The national debt, or accumulated deficits, are reduced by government surpluses.

The use of tax cuts to stimulate the economy is only slightly more complex. Since some income is saved, every dollar of a tax cut does not lead to spending of an equal amount. The extra spending amount depends on the marginal propensity to consume (MPC), that is the share of extra income that is spent. The MPC varies across the income distribution, falling as income rises. The U.S. has a mildly progressive income tax structure in which tax rates rise with income. The reasoning is that higher income at the margin goes to satisfy less urgent needs and wants. The pain for taxation at the upper income levels is less than at lower income levels. This progressiveness provides some automatic stabilization for the economy. As incomes fall, so do tax revenues, more so for the rich than for the poor. And vice-versa. When the economy is expanding, tax revenues rise more than in proportion to the rise in incomes. This automatically dampens the expansion of the economy, possibly precluding inflation. Politically, tax cuts are easy to implement; tax increases seldom happen. This makes tax policy lopsided for the business cycle.

We should reserve three cheers for the rich in one respect. Most government bonds are held by the very rich or by institutions; it is about 50:50. Thus, the rich are the lenders to the government and help to finance budget deficits. At the same time this has created a bondholding class with substantial power over public policy, far more than in proportion it its small population.[6]

The government can do what the public is forbidden to do; it can print money. Thus, when the government runs deficits, it writes checks at the Treasury for the amount of the bonds purchased. The fiscal power of the government is virtually unlimited. It is constrained only by the willingness of the public, corporations, banks, and the Federal Reserve to hold government bonds. (Debt did become so high in Greece and Spain in the past few years, that such willingness gave way.) In this way, the budget habits of the government can vary from that of the household. Austerians try to draw an analogy between the private household and the U.S. Treasury, but the world does not work that way. Still, from about 1800 to 1945, the dominant classical view in the Anglo-Saxon world that maintained fiscal policy was not needed for a market-based economy prevailed. No fiscal policy tools were required.

The Keynesians dominated economic policy in the Anglo-Saxon world during the 1950s and 1960s, decades of robust economic growth. The Keynesian use of fiscal tools was taught in almost every classroom and influenced most governments in the U.S. and Europe as well as much of Asia. When there was unemployment, governments should stimulate the economy by increasing government spending and reducing taxes became the mantra. During economic booms with inflation, government should shift into reverse and reduce spending and raise taxes to lower aggregate demand. American and European governments were all influenced by the Keynesian fiscal proposals.

The consequence of Maynard Keynes combined with other forces has been very low levels of British unemployment during the post-World War II years up to Thatcherism. In the U.S. this new ethic led to the Employment Act of 1946, which committed the Federal government to follow policies that would provide employment opportunities for those able, willing, and seeking work. Keynesian economic policies were vigorously pursued by the Truman administration, then a modified Keynesian

---

[6] For much more on the bondholding class, and how it influences public policy, see E. Ray Canterbery, *Wall Street Capitalism: The Theory of the Bondholding Class* (Singapore, New Jersey, London: World Scientific, 2000).

program was perhaps most successfully followed by the Kennedy and Johnson administrations prior to the escalation of the Vietnam War in 1968.[7]

There was an attempt to revive Keynesian economics during the Great Recession. When President Barack Obama too office in January 2009, the economy was in a shambles. More than 70,000 were losing their jobs every month, millions of houses were sliding towards foreclosure, and the largest industrial corporations were threatened with bankruptcy, as were the largest banks. There was a gap between actual aggregate demand and potential output of $1.2 trillion. Obama proposed that the economy should be stimulated by government projects, increased transfer payments, and tax cuts. In February of 2009, Congress passed the American Recovery and Reinvestment Act, the largest stimulus bill ever. The Congressional Budget Office found that between the time that the law was passed and the end of 2011, the total spending increases and revenue reductions resulting from the bill had been $739 billion. This fell short of the $1.2 trillion needed to fill the demand gap. Conservative Democrats and Republications prevented the bill from being any larger. As it was, all Republican senators except three voted "no" on the stimulus act. The spending bill should have been 60 percent more than the legislated amount.

In any case, of the $739 billion, only $224 billion in government purchases directly filled part of the $1.2 trillion spending gap. The tax cuts and transfer payment increments cushioned the falls in consumption, but did not have as great a multiplier or stimulus effect. Still, the Recovery Act was a traditional Keynesian attempt to counter a dramatic fall in aggregate demand and rise in unemployment. It was in the right direction but of insufficient magnitude, especially on the spending side.

These Keynesian policies went global. Nations around the world adopted comparable though mostly less ambitious fiscal stimulus policies. The European Economic Recovery Plan, adopted in the fall of 2008,

---

[7]For Keynes and Truman, see E. Ray Canterbery, *Harry S. Truman: The Economics of a Populist President* (Singapore, New Jersey, London: World Scientific, 2014). For the details of Keynesian policy as applied theory during the Kennedy years, see E. Ray Canterbery, *Economics on a New Frontier* (Belmont, CA: Wadsworth Publishing Co. 1968).

provided some 20 billion euros to a variety of projects; nations such as Germany and France followed with their own smaller stimulus plans. Japan initially planned a massive stimulus package, but the government ultimately instituted a much more modest mix of tax cuts and new spending measures. China's more ambitious plan totaled US$586 billion, the bulk of which went to public works, rail lines, roads, irrigation, and airports. Smaller economies such as South Korea and Australia also initiated Keynesian policies. It was a global Keynesian revival in the supra-surplus economies.

These orthodox Keynesian policies did much to slow the global decline. The deficits led to growing debt relative to GDPs. This "problem" was postponed until recovery set in, also a Keynesian strategy. The U.S. issued more Treasury bills and bonds, most of which were bought by the Federal Reserve and added massively to the Fed's assets. The policies did not work perfectly. For example, the tax cuts and tax rebates led to increased savings in 2008 and 2009. Consumers spent only 25 cents or 30 cents on every dollar they received from the government; the balance was used to repair balance sheets.

Unconventional Fiscal Policies

Other policies were ground in the mill of conventionality, but the Great Recession was not an ordinary event. Among unconventional policies is the use of guarantees of other people's money. This is a kind of fiscal policy because the guarantees often end up costing taxpayer's money. A typical guarantee is that the government will protect money that people have deposited in a bank from a run. During the Great Depression the U.S. adopted deposit insurance through the Federal Deposit Insurance Corporation (FDIC). The FDIC normally does not depend on taxpayer dollars; it assesses fees on the commercial banks. Also, the Federal Savings and Loan Insurance corporation (FSLIC), was founded in 1934 to protect deposits and savings and loans institutions.

These bank deposit guarantees became an issue in 2008 during the great financial crisis. The FDIC had been insuring deposits up to $100,000. (Similar insurance existed in other countries, though the ceiling varied by country.) In the U.S. alone, some 40 percent of deposits remained uninsured, a problem underscored by the bank runs on Countrywide, IndyMac, and Washington Mutual. The threat of still more runs triggered a round of new government guarantees. In September 2008, Ireland had to increase its deposit insurance to 100,000 euros, then fully guarantee all the deposits of its six largest banks. In the U.S., the FDIC raised the ceiling for insured bank deposits to $250,000. A few days later Germany guaranteed all of its private bank accounts; the next day Sweden extended insurance to all deposits to the sum of 500,000 krona (about US$75,000). Then, a week later Italy announced that none of its banks would be allowed to fail and that no depositor would suffer any loss. The next month Switzerland increased its ceiling on deposit insurance. The European Union guaranteed its banks' bonded debt in October 2008. The same month the FDIC guaranteed the principal and interest payments on debt issued by banks and bank holding companies up to a total of $1.5 trillion. Other countries followed with similar deposit and debt guarantees.

Ultimately it is the taxpayer that makes these guarantees good. This is highlighted by the FDIC fund dipping into negative territory in the third quarter of 2009. The taxpayer would need to shoulder part of the burden in the form of an FDIC bailout, much as it did in the wake of the savings and loan crisis.

Another kind of unconventional fiscal policy is the bailout. The big bailouts of the Great Recession in the U.S. began with Fannie Mae and Freddie Mac in September 2008. When the two mortgage giants came under government conservatorship, the George W. Bush Treasury pledged $400 billion to underwrite the takeover. This made explicit the Federal government's guarantee of their debt. The Treasury is on the line to cover some $5 trillion worth of obligations insured by the two institutions, along with another $1.5 trillion worth of debt that they issued. If housing prices continue to fall and many more mortgages go into foreclosure the Treasury could end up sustaining considerable losses. Prior to the Fannie and Freddie bailout, the Housing and Economic Recovery Act of July 2008 pledged some $320 billion to help struggling homeowners refinance into mortgages that were insured by the Federal Housing Administration.

This was part of a cluster of bailouts and guarantees funded by the Troubled Asset Relief Program (TARP). As noted earlier, the legislation initially allocated $700 billion to purchase toxic assets. The money was used to prop up banks and the automakers General Motors and Chrysler and their financial arms, GMAC and Chrysler Financial. This auto bailout amounted to $80 billion. This was just the beginning as a sizable share of the TARP funds — some $340 billion — was given to nearly 700 financial institutions, including giants like Citigroup, Bank of America, JPMorgan Chase, Goldman Sachs and AIG, as well as a host of smaller banks. Most of funds comprised capital injections from which the government purchased preferred shares in the institutions. Besides a steady dividend payment, these shares provided a partial ownership stake in the companies. This marked a radical departure for fiscal policy. American taxpayers became owners of large swaths of the financial system, not to mention of the automotive industry.

There was still more. The government formed a kind of insurance partnership with two giant ailing banks. The Treasury guaranteed several hundred billion dollars' worth of impaired assets held by the Bank of America and Citigroup. The pool of troubled assets totaled $118 billion in Bank of America's case, with a "deductible" of $10 billion. Bank of America would not even have to change its name under its new "ownership." This kind of partnership was adopted widely in the U.K., as well.

All of these radical measures combined managed to stabilize the global financial system. In turn, they helped to prevent (along with a super-easy monetary policy) the Great Recession from becoming another Great Depression at a time when aggregate demand was in free fall.

Keynes originally intended to save capitalism from its worst offenses and weaknesses. He never intended for the government to attain ownership of corporations, a modest form of socialism. Moreover, he never envisaged the use of government funds to bailout entire industries such as the financial system and the auto industry. All these policies were courageous and unconventional. TARP itself was an excursion into unexplored waters.

The most unconventional fiscal policy would be the use of helicopter money. In this, the central banks would be deploying monetary as fiscal policy. Some economists have argued that central bank independence has hampered the ability of monetary policy to combat inflation that's too low, the current era's problem. Using second-best policies have distorted financial markets and face diminishing returns, such as negative interest rates and large-sale bond purchases, shunning potentially more effective tools such as helicopter money. Helicopter money would involve an increase in public spending or tax cuts financed by the central banks. This takes central banks beyond their traditional realm of influencing the price and volume of credit to deciding how public funds are to be spent — the traditional domain of elected politicians. Since the Congress has rejected fiscal policy, there is a vacuum to be filled by monetary-fiscal policy.

Bank of Japan Governor Haruhiko Kuroda has warned that helicopter money would be an unacceptable intermingling of fiscal and monetary policy. In July 2016, the BOJ disappointed those hoping it might continue its experiment with helicopter money. After all, the Japanese economy is in a shambles. In Europe, Bundesbank President Jens Weidmann has cited similar concerns over the independence of the European Central Bank (ECB) as a reason not to deploy helicopter money. ECB President Mario Draghi says that the topic hasn't been discussed at policy meetings. There the helicopters have been grounded. Charles Goodhart, a former member of the Bank of England's (BOE's) monetary policy committee, has said the effects on inflationary expectations could be quite dramatic. He has said that helicopters have already been flying in huge formations in Japan. Asked about helicopter money in June 2016, Fed Chairwoman Janet Yellen said that, in unusual times when the concern is very weak growth or possibly deflation fiscal and monetary authorities should "not be working at cross-purposes."

Presently, fiscal and monetary policies are working at cross-purposes in the U.S., Japan, and Europe. Central banks have vastly expanded their balance sheets while governments have tightened their belts. Figure 19.1 shows how central bank assets have soared while budget deficits as shares of GDP have shrunk. The central banks are primed to use helicopter money; they can start liquidating their vast bond holdings. All that is required is a mechanism for doing so.

Former Fed Chairman Ben Bernanke has proposed a mechanism, a helicopter port, as it were, for giving flight to money. The Fed could credit a special Treasury account with funds if it assessed such a stimulus was needed to achieve its employment and inflation goals. The U.S. government would then determine how to spend the funds, or could leave them unspent. In the past other central banks around the world have followed

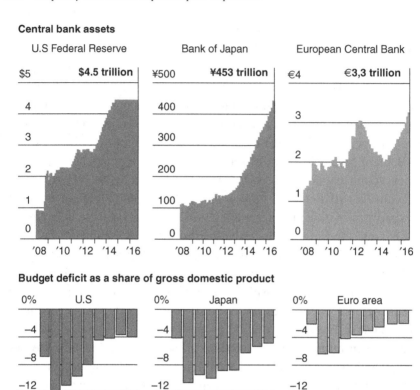

Figure 19.1 Cross-Purposes: Monetary V. Fiscal Policy. Central Banks have Vastly Expanded Their Balance Sheets while Governments Tightened their Belts.
Sources: St. Louis Federal Reserve (central bank assets); International Monetary Fund (deficits) The Wall Street Journal.

the Fed's lead. In practice, there could be little difference between current helicopter money and quantitative easing (QE), which cover a large swath of current government deficits.

Still another central banks action that borders on fiscal policy is the purchase of corporate bonds and equities of corporations. Also, this alters the normal relation of central banks and corporations under supra-surplus capitalism. Rather, it is an instance of central-bank capitalism. The BOE, the U.K.'s central bank, made its first foray into the corporate bond market on September 27, 2016. It bought the debt of companies in sectors including energy, transport and finance. The results published in 2017 by the BOE show that the corporate bond purchasing scheme leveled off in December 2016. But prices for sterling-denominated corporate bonds barely budged, according to investors. Anyway, this was only the first step, with the toes of the bank testing the waters. The central bank plans to buy 10 billion pounds ($13 billion) in corporate bonds in a bid to lower borrowing costs for companies and spur spending and investing, a role normally left to fiscal policy. The initiative has helped to boost bond issuance, a key goal. In an extraordinary announcement, the BOE said it would buy bonds that make a significant contribution to the U.K. economy, including Apple Inc., and German auto maker Daimler AG. In short, the bank's long arm reaches into the global economy.

The BOE is not alone. The ECB has been gobbling up corporate and government bonds for months and plans to buy assets valued at 80 billion euros, or about $90 billion, a month until March 2017. Between June 8 and September 23, 2016, it bought 27.9 billion euros of corporate debt. The question remains whether these programs will spur companies to invest in new products and services, given that Europe's underlying economic woes still are largely unresolved. As it stands, corporations have been using low interest rates to refinance debt rather than issue bonds to further growth. Real stimulus may await more traditional fiscal policies.

Chapter 20

TAXATION ON WEALTH

A Global Tax on Financial Capital

Thomas Piketty makes one policy proposal in his monumental work.[1] He recommends a global and progressive wealth tax for limiting wealth inequality. This is a utopian ideal that is a hard sell. It is difficult to imagine nations agreeing to it. Anyway, he sees such a tax as the only way to avoid a second Gilded Age. Since financial capital can move where taxes are lower, only a global tax would be effective, irrespective of the odds. Pikety wants the tax imposed annually on the value of assets each person owns. He suggests a tax of 1 percent on net assets worth between €1 million ($1.35 million) and €5 million ($5.75 million) and a tax of 2 percent on net assets worth more than €5 million. He raises the possibility of a 0.5 percent tax on wealth between €200,000 and €1 million, as well as a 5–10 percent tax on net assets exceeding €1 billion. The main tax on net worth exceeding €1 million would apply to about 2.5 percent of the EU population and would bring in revenue equal to 2 percent of European GDP. The low rates would provide little disincentive to accumulate wealth. The purpose of these taxes, according to Piketty, is to "regulate capitalism" so that income inequality does not get out of control. He wants to reduce r where now $r > g$. Of course, as we have noted earlier, g is getting smaller.

---

[1] Thomas Piketty, *Capital in the Twenty-first Century*, *op. cit.*, Chapter 5.

The Atkinson Proposals for Britain

Atkinson focuses on the question of wider access to net worth and owner-ship.[2] On the one hand, he calls for the establishment of a national savings program allowing each depositor to receive a guaranteed return on her capital (below a certain threshold of individual capital). On the other hand, alongside this national guaranteed and insured savings program Atkinson proposes establishing an "inheritance for all" program. This would take the form of a capital endowment to each young citizen as he or she reached adulthood, at the age of eighteen. All such endowments would be financed by estate taxes and a more progressive tax stucture on income. With current revenue from the British estate tax, it would be possible to finance a capital endowment of slightly more than £5,000 for each young adult. He advocates a far greater progressivity for larger estates, with the upper rate set at 65 percent, along with a similar income tax. These reforms would make it possible to finance a capital endowment on the order of £10,000 per young adult.

A Transactions Tax on Speculative Wealth

The fattest target for a tax on speculation is the oversized financial sector which has grown disproportionately to the industrial sector. A small finan-cial tax on financial assets could be levied. A minor tax would raise con-siderable revenue because of the presently vast size of financial assets outstanding. Beyond this, there is a need for a financial transactions tax on speculators.

Long-term capital gains — taking place over several years — within an industrial firm have long been considered the flywheel of capitalism. Rare is the economist who suggests that long-term capital gains are unde-sirable. I am with the majority on the blessings of strong *long-term* capital gains. Quick capital gains on secondary financial instruments are of a different character; generally, the purpose of such sudden sales is to make money out of money, something accomplished in a time too brief and too

---

[2] Anthony B. Atkinson, *Inequality: What Can be Done?* (Cambridge: Harvard University Press, 2015).

indirect to produce goods and services or real investment. If we prefer lasting to fleeting capitalism, we would discourage speculative gains. Such speculation led to the banking and money panic of 2008–2009.

A long time ago Nobelist James Tobin recommended a small transactions tax on foreign exchange and stocks to dampen speculation in such markets. I endorse the Tobin tax but suggest it be substantially greater than half a percent. A transactions tax also recommends itself for other kinds of domestic financial transfers. The purpose would not be to punish manufacturers for earning profits or stockholders for unearned dividends. The 30-year bond, for example, was intended to provide funds for long-term, real investment. Mortgages, for financing housing, is another example that comes easily to mind. Even equities were originally considered "long-term capital investments" both because perpetual corporations used them to provide finance for new factories and because households held them for such a long time.

A properly designed financial transactions tax would discourage speculation in securities. I recommend a transactions tax, not as a levy on productivity, which it isn't, but as a penalty for pure speculation. It is intended to punish people for the misuse of money and wealth. Such a tax, sufficient to sting but not so great as to eliminate all gains, would be directed at the leisure class of wealthholders, who have increased financial market volatility and made speculation more lucrative, moving from bonds into stocks and back again, and sometimes into derivatives.

Any person or institution buying and selling General Motors or any other stock in less than a year has either been imprudent in its purchasing decision or is speculating. A transactions tax, graduated from a high percentage near term and vaporizing at the end of a 2-year holding period would discourage short-term speculation in the stock markets. The design of the tax itself should be subject to long-term study.

Still, as a starting point for discussion, I would recommend a transactions tax of 12 percent on the value of the spot purchase (or sale in the case of a short position) for all stocks held for less than 30 days. Thereafter the transactions tax would be reduced by a half percentage point for each month that the shares are continually held. The tax would be applied to financial derivatives based upon stocks.

The purpose of a transactions tax penalty is not to discourage the buying and selling of securities. If speculators can gain more than 12 percent (after other fees) during the holding period they still make a profit, though a smaller one. Moreover, the government will have additional revenue going toward deficit reduction (and reduced interest) or toward particular programs.

Because most mature in less than a year U.S. Treasury bills are not a speculative threat. However, U.S. Treasury bonds and corporate bonds are intended to be long-term investments. Federal, state, and municipal bonds have a variety of maturities. The same 12 percent transactions tax could be levied on bonds maturing in 1 year and held for less than 30 days with a downward-sliding penalty equaling a full percentage point less every 30 days thereafter. If the bonds are held to maturity, no transactions tax would apply. For bonds maturing in 2 years, the 12 percent transactions tax would be phased out by a half percentage point every 30 days. The same kind of structure would apply to the transactions tax on bonds maturing in 3 or 4 years. Further, a tax good enough for standard financial instruments should be applied, perhaps with even greater enthusiasm, to financial derivatives based upon bonds.

After 4 years, we are looking at truly significant holding periods, and we do not wish to discourage individuals and institutions from buying such long-term bonds. The 12 percent transactions tax would be phased out at zero after holding a bond for 5 years, whatever the final maturity date. Thus, a bond maturing in 10 years or 30 years would be subject to no transactions tax if sold at the end of 5 years. A transactions tax structured to discourage the buying of long-term bonds would have a surprising benefit. By encouraging the purchase of long-term bonds that part of the bond market would be deepened and would enjoy greater liquidity, making it less subject to sudden collapse.[3]

---

[3] My transactions tax on infrastructure, graduated over the asset holder's holding period, was introduced in E. Ray Canterbery, *The Global Great Recession* (Singapore/New Jersey/London: World Scientific, 2011), pp. 305-308. It had its antecedents, which are discussed. In the same volume the idea of interest-free Treasury loans for infrastructure was introduced (see pp. 308-314). As ever, this too had its precursors, which are identified. The idea got as far as a proposed legislative bill, coming out of Freeport, Illinois.

Still, some will say that a transactions tax on financial debt instruments and equities will take some excitement out of the markets. They justifiably indict such as tax. However, the gaming tables and slot machines will still be open for business in Las Vegas, Reno, New Orleans, Atlantic City, and even Biloxi. Leisure-class speculators lusting after fast gains or losses can enjoy them in the same manner as the working class. Of course, to the extent that a transactions tax subdued financial speculation, real returns in industry would begin to supersede the paper profits from paper.

Chapter 21

THE CAMPAIGN OF 2016
AND THE TRUMP TRANSITION

If it had not been for the Truman close encounter with Thomas Dewey, the Donald Trump victory would have been the greatest upset in American history. Donald Trump, real estate tycoon and business deal maker, won the election of 2016 in the USA. Given his apparent arrogance and gun-slinging insults, how did he pull it off? A fractured, discontented electorate handed him the presidency. Key battleground states — Pennsylvania, Michigan and Wisconsin — had traditionally voted for the Democratic candidate. In fact, this has been the case in every presidential election for a generation. Ohio also has been under the Democrat's tent. Most of the pre-election polls reflected this "reality." However, Trump outperformed expectations in all states, moving most into the Republican column after President Barack Obama had twice swept the region. We would be remiss to leave out Florida and North Carolina also as key.

Deep racial, gender, economic and cultural divides nationally and across the Midwest and Great Lakes region were reflected in exit polls and unofficial returns. These helped drive Trump's success. Trump's popularity among white, mostly less educated, white voters helped his cause. Hillary Clinton's popularity among white and black women voters was not enough to offset Trump's advantage with men. All this was essential to Trump's capturing the Rust Belt and holding off Hillary elsewhere. Voters were describing themselves as "fed up," ready for something different, even if unpredictable. It is unclear what "fed up" meant. After all, the Obama administration was not *that* unpopular.

What accounted for the victorious vote for Trump? More of the electorate *did not* vote than *did* vote. Apparently too many Democrats and too many independents stayed away from the polls and that contributed to Hillary's defeat. As it turns out, many of those unhappy with the results went into the streets to protest the outcome of the election. In the days following the election riots broke out in some major cities, including Washington D.C.

The President's Business Acumen

At the heart of Trump's candidacy was his claim to be a brilliant businessman and therefore qualified to be a brilliant president. Yet his economics is the same old "trickle down" plan that has been rightly disparaged by anyone with any sense. Trump himself inherited $14 million from which he built his empire, hardly lifting himself by his own bootstraps American style. Then, he refused to release his own tax returns, despite paying no taxes for years. As to his business acumen, he has managed to file bankruptcy six times, while stiffing many he owed money. His foreign policy amounts to building a wall/fence between Mexico and the United States, stiffing the Mexicans to pay for it. This is not the way to deal with the problems brought by globalization. Hopefully, these aspects of President Trump's "business acumen" will not be exercised during his full term in office.

Much of the present book is about the problems related to inequality. Trump made clear during the campaign that he was not interested in reducing inequality. If anything, his overall, expressed plan would increase it. He would reduce taxes of the rich, and eliminate the estate tax, most of which is paid by one-percenters. His economics campaign goal was to widen the gap between the rich and the poor. Perhaps this was just campaign rhetoric. When asked if he regretted anything he said in the campaign, however, his reply was simply, "I won."

Trump's "Take the Oil" Plan

In the campaign, Trump suggested that we go into Iraq and "take the oil," which, he claims, is rightly ours. This is the worst idea since Hitler decided to invade Poland. We would have to occupy the entire oil-producing region of Iraq. Since oil is Iraq's sole export, they would fight to the last man to keep it. Saudi Arabia and other oil-producing nations would presume that "they would be next" in this reckless land grab. Our ally, Jordon, would be forced to take the side of Iraq, as would other Middle Eastern nations. The military expense of a war there would be astronomical, but it may explain why Trump has called for a great expansion in military expenditures. The growth in the military-industrial complex would be at the expense of social programs, which are currently underfunded.

"Taking the oil" means an endless occupation army in a Persian Gulf surrounded by enemies, without allies, and isolated hopelessly from the Islamic world. Such an occupation would polarize Americans more than ever and would reinvigorate the global *jihad*, as it would disgrace our fundamental values as a nation. With this, the Republican Party would own the greatest foreign policy disaster in American history.

The oil in question is distributed across Iraq, with the largest quantity in the south in and around Basra province. In the campaign, Trump said that he would leave a certain group behind to hold the oil wealth for America. Such a group would have to be the United States military, not ambassadors of good will. Since Basra has over 2.5 million people, almost all Shiite Arabs, their resistance alone would be challenging. But they would not be alone. The Shiite dominated government in Baghdad would support its citizens, adding to the struggle. It would turn attention away from fighting for Mosul and focus on recovering Basra.

Basra is in an uncomfortable place, being immediately next to Iran, which controls Iraq's only outlet to the sea. Tehran would certainly back the Shiite resistance in Basra, as it did when the British made the mistake of occupying the narrow bottleneck of Iraq's access to the sea. Trump *could* expand the oil takeover further south into Kuwait. The U.S. liberated Kuwait from Saddam Hussein a quarter-century ago and by Trump's warped logic, we would take their oil (and their country) as overdue spoils of war. That if nothing else, would unite the Arab and Muslim word against America. While the U.S. has a sizable military presence in Kuwait, it would require many more forces to occupy the country. The other targets could be Saudi Arabia's Eastern Provence and Qatar. Such a large takeover would give Washington control of the global energy system (except for solar energy), which may be what Trump has in mind.

For those hankering for World War III, such an occupation would be a godsend. As President, Trump backed away from this radical idea. Instead, his first foreign foray was into the Middle East, starting in Saudi Arabia and continuing to Israel. He was warmly received by the Saudis, doubtless influenced by his offer of some $500 billion in mutual military and other aid.

Hillary's New Deal

To be fair, we need to give Trump's opponent, Hillary Clinton, her due, despite her loss. In the campaign, Hillary restated the Democrats' old-time convictions about economic inequality and opportunity, convictions that have badly needed refurbishing and restating in the wake of the Great Recession. These were the convictions that Sen. Bernie Sanders' stunning primary challenge forced to the very center of the economic debate. On the convention stage, Sanders railed against "the 40-year decline of our middle class" and "the grotesque level of income and wealth inequality that we currently experience." Sen. Elizabeth Warren joined the battle, explaining how the system is rigged for CEOs and predators like Trump. And, Hillary, proclaimed that "Democrats are the part of working people." Further, "Our economy isn't working the way it should because our democracy isn't working the way it should." She touted a government program funded by targeted tax hikes on the rich, and the "biggest investment in new, good-paying jobs since World War II," to rebuild America's infrastructure.

Assembling various strains of reformist politics, Roosevelt's New Deal expounded a greatly enlarged conception of federal power to address the emergency of the Great Depression, to attack economic inequality and the power of those FDR called "economic royalists," and to expand public works for public benefits. Successive Democratic presidents adopted New Deal principles to the changing situation of a more affluent America after World War II, and put their own stamp on FDRs' legacy, from Harry S. Truman's Fair Deal to John F. Kennedy's New Frontier to Lyndon B. Johnson's Great Society.[1] There was a continuity in all this. Harry Truman

---

[1] For much more on Truman, see E. Ray Canterbery, *Harry S. Truman: The Economics of a Populist* President (Singapore, London, New Jersey: World Scientific, 2014). For more

started the prolonged battle for universal health care which LBJ advanced to the point of enacting Medicare and Medicaid in 1965. Democratic programs included elements such as raising the minimum wage (but not by much) and expanding aid to education.

Bill Clinton continued the tradition with his "Putting People first," his domestic program in the new Deal tradition. He devoted enormous energy toward a comprehensive health care reform, envisaged more than 40 years earlier by Truman. The defeat of Bill Clinton's health care reform paved the way for the election in 1994 of a more ideologically driven conservative Republican House majority, led by the new House speaker, Newt Gingrich. Thereafter, Clinton would have to bob and weave — as only he could — to advance his reforms.

Hillary was following in Bill's footsteps. With some adjustments in the federal tax code aimed chiefly at the top 1 percent and 0.1 percent of earners, $250 billion would be raised for the funding of roads, highways, and airports. An additional $25 billion would fund a project that was central to Bill Clinton's 1992 agenda and, which, as recently as 2011, House Republicans ridiculed as "dead on arrival" — an infrastructure bank that would leverage capital for more improvements. And that was just the start. Hillary's infrastructure improvement would also include making affordable broadband Internet available to every American household, while providing free Wi-Fi in public buildings and public transportation. They would include modernizing dams and levees, saving water resources and generating clean energy They would, in short, address problems worsened by neglect and by the supply-side priorities of the Reagan era. And as a plus, they would create as many as 3.25 million new jobs over 5 years from the direct spending alone. It would give a moribund economy a needed Keynesian yank.

Clinton's program for battling economic inequality was in the broad New Deal tradition. The proposals included middle-class tax credits to be covered by raising taxes on the very wealthiest Americans and by closing tax loopholes; raising the federal minimum wage by 66 percent to $12 an hour, while supporting a $15 minimum in individual cities and states; protecting labor union's collective-bargaining rights; and reducing

---

on JFK, see E. Ray Canterbery, *Economics on a New Frontier* (Belmont, CA.: Wadsworth, 1968).

child-care costs. At the same time, she called for the installation of a half a billion solar panels by the end of her first term with the goal of providing clean renewable energy to every household in the country by 2027.

Hillary's Specific Tax Proposals

Hillary Clinton proposed specific tax policies that would raise taxes on individual and business income. Her plan would have raised tax revenue by $498 billion over the next decade. Most of the revenue raised by Hillary's plan would come from a cap on itemized deductions, the Buffett Rule (a 30 percent *minimum tax* on those taxpayers earning a million dollars or more), and a 4 percent surtax on taxpayers with incomes over $5 million.[2] She would alter long-term capital gains rate schedule that would reduce revenue on both a static and dynamic basis due to the increased incentive to delay capital gains realizations. Based on the business-financed Tax Foundation's Taxes and Growth Model, the plan would reduce GNP by 1 percent over the long-term due to slightly higher marginal tax rates on capital and labor. This would be based on the conventional wisdom of economics. On a static basis, the tax plan would lead to 0.7 percent lower after-tax income for the top 10 percent of taxpayers and 1.7 percent lower income for the top 1 percent. On a dynamic basis, when accounting for reduced GDP, after-tax incomes of all taxpayers would fall by at least 0.9 percent. At the projected slowdown in growth and other elements, the plan would end up collecting "only" $191 billion over the long run. These results were based on a model with parameters determined in the past, not the present, and are highly suspect. Generally, we cannot accept this model as being reliable.

She proposed expanded government programs, particularly for infrastructure. To pay for these, she recommended raising and enacting new taxes on the rich. Her plan was to increase marginal tax rates for taxpayers with incomes over $5 million, enact a 30 percent minimum tax on those earning more than a million yearly (the Buffett Rule), alter the

---

[2] The original Obama "Buffett Rule" in 2011 would have placed the 30 percent minimum on about 0.3 percent of taxpayers, those then making a million dollars or more in income. Need we say, the proposal never got past a Republican-Senate.

Table 21.1 Tax Brackets Under Hillary Clinton's Tax Plan

Ordinary income	Capital (gains and dividends	Single filers	Married filers	Head of household
10%	0%	$0 to $9,275	$0 to $18,550	$0 to 813,250
15%	0%	$9,275 to $37,650	$18,550 to $75,300	$13,250 to $50,400
25%	15%	$37.650 to $91,150	$75,300 to $151,900	$50,400 to $130,150
28%	15%	$91,150 to $190,150	$151,900 to $231,450	$130,150 to $210,800
33%	15%	$190,150 to $413,350	$231,450 to $413,350	$210,800 to $413,310
35%	15%	$413,350 to $415,050	$413,350 to $466,950	$413,350 to $441,000
39.6%	20%	$415,050 to $5 million	$466,950 to $5 million	$441,000 to $5 million
43.6%	24%	$5 million and above	$5 million and above	$5 million and above

long-term capital gains tax rate schedule, and limit itemized deductions to a tax value of 28 percent.[3] At most, the taxes on the rich would affect only three-tenths of 1 percent of tax payers, the very wealthiest people in the USA. Her plan would also restore the estate tax to its 2009 parameters and would limit or eliminate other deductions for individuals and corporations.

Details of the tax changes are presented in Table 21.1, which shows the new capital gains tax schedule under Hillary's tax plan.

The graduated tax schedule has the same effect as my earlier proposal, except the changes from one holding period to the next are not as

[3]This was part of a plan by the Obama administration in 2011, which was rejected by a Republican majority. At most, the minimum tax affects only 0.3 percent of taxpayers, the tip of the top.

Table 21.2   Top Marginal Long-term Capital Gains Tax Rate Schedule under Hillary Clinton's Tax Plan

Years held	Marginal rate	Net investment income tax	Surtax on incomes over million	Combined rate on capital gains
Less than One	39.6%	3.8%	4%	47.4%
One to Two	39.6%	3.8%	4%	47.4%
Two to Three	36%	3.8%	4%	43.8%
Three to Four	32%	3.8%	4%	39.8%
Four to Five	28%	3.8%	4%	35.8%
Five to Six	24%	3.8%	4%	31.8%
More than Six	20%	3.8%	4%	27.8%

dramatic. Her table also shows the combined effects of her capital gains tax schedule.

In addition to these individual tax changes, she would have made some business tax changes. She would have eliminated the deductibility of reinsurance premium paid by corporations in foreign subsidiaries and provided an exclusion from income for reinsurance recovered for any arrangement where the deduction was disallowed. She would have established a business tax credit for profit-sharing and apprenticeships.

Among other changes, she would have restored the federal estate tax to 2009 levels. This would increase the estate tax rate to 45 percent and reduce the exemption to $3.5 million. She would also enact a tax on high-frequency trading, at an unspecified rate.[4]

Per estimates by the conservative Tax Foundation, not only would the tax plan reduce GDP by 1 percent, it would lead to 0.8 percent lower wages, a 2.8 percent smaller capital stock, and 311,000 fewer full-time

---

[4]Canterbery earlier detailed a graduated speculative tax on securities, wherein, for example, a 1 percent per month possible tax is applied to a 1-year bond if sold short of maturity. If the bond is held to maturity, the tax is zero. For the details, see Chapter 20 of this book. Clinton's tax on high-frequency trading may have brought her overall schedule closer to mine.

equivalent jobs. The smaller economy results from somewhat higher marginal tax rates on capital and labor income. This analysis is based on conventional wisdom about the effects of marginal tax rates on real capital investment and marginal tax rates affecting worker incentives. Again, the conventional wisdom is always or almost always suspect.

What would be the effect on revenue? The plan would increase federal revenue on a static basis by $498 billion over the next 10 years. Most of the revenue gain would be due to increased individual income tax revenue, which is projected to raise approximately $381 billion over the next decade. The changes to the estate tax would raise an additional $106 billion over the next decade. The remaining $11 billion would be raised through increased taxes on corporations. The largest sources of revenue are the new taxes targeted at high-income taxpayers. On a static basis, Hillary Clinton's plan would only reduce the after-tax incomes of top-income taxpayers. Those in the top 10 percent would see a reduction in *income* of 0.7 percent. The top 1 percent of all taxpayers would see a 1.7 percent reduction in after-tax income. On a dynamic basis, the plan would reduce after-tax incomes by an average of 1.3 percent. All deciles would see a reduction in after-tax income of at least 0.9 percent over the long-term. Taxpayers that fall in the bottom nine deciles would see after-tax incomes decline by between 0.9 and 1 percent. The top 10 percent of taxpayers would see a reduction in after-tax income of 0.7 percent. The top 1 percent of all taxpayers would see the largest decline in after-tax income — 2.7 percent. In short, the plan would dramatically alter the income distribution and by extension, the wealth distribution.

To conclude, Hillary Clinton would have enacted tax policies that would raise revenue over the next decade (the long run) and fund new or expanded programs. Based on the Tax Foundation's flawed report, most of her policies would end up losing revenue both on a static and a dynamic basis "due to the incentives it creates to hold on to assets longer." There would be slightly higher marginal tax rates on capital and labor income, "which would result in the reduction in the size of the U.S. economy in the long run." This, in turn, would decrease the revenue that the new tax policies would ultimately collect. The plan, as judged by the Tax Foundation, would lead to lower after-tax incomes for taxpayers at all income levels, but especially for taxpayers at the top of the pyramid. This is the redistribution that Hillary was seeking.

Changes from the January 2016 Analysis

In October, 2016 the business-oriented Tax Foundation did another simulation of the effects of Hillary Clinton's tax program. Her campaign had introduced some new policies that "significantly" altered the prior estimates. This was in response to several changes in the plan, the most important being in then Secretary Clinton's Child Tax Credit expansion. This expansion would have added $1,000 credit for children under 5 and would phase in at 45 percent. The current credit would have continued to phase in at 15 percent.

Another important change to the plan is then Secretary Clinton's expansion of her estate tax proposal. Previously, her plan only proposed raising the estate tax by reducing the exclusion from the present $5.45 million (10.9 million for couples) to $3.5 million ($7 million for couples), but also would tax larger estates progressively up to the top rate of 65 percent. In an apparent pairing with the estate tax was a modification to the step-up basis in capital gains.

In her second plan, she also would have introduced some business tax reforms. Her new plan includes an expansion of Section 179, an expansion of cash accounting, an increase in start-up cost deductions, and a new small business standard deduction. The campaign also introduced reforms to the Net Investment Income Tax and self-employment taxes that would make taxes on certain business owners lower and would limit the tax value of like-kind exchanges. Like-kind exchanges are pretty much as it sounds; these are exchanges which are alike in several dimensions.

In addition to incorporating all these changes in their estimates, the Tax Foundation claimed to have improved the estimates of the effects "of several existing policies." However, because of the "lack of clarity" in some of the proposals, their effects were not considered in the estimates.

The Economic Effects of the Second Hillary Plan

Once again, the Tax Foundation deployed its suspect Taxes and Growth Model. In it, the second Hillary plan would reduce the GDP by 2.6 percent in the long run. Capital investment would fall by 7.0 percent; the wage rate would fall 2.1 percent and full-time equivalent jobs would drop by 697,000. The closer we came to the election, the worse the estimates of Hillary's plan by the conservative Tax Foundation.

Hillary's 10–20–30 Plan to End Poverty

In 2009 Rep. Jim Clyburn suggested a 10–20–30 plan to grapple with persistent poverty. In it, any federal program subject to this plan would be required to direct at least 10 percent of total investment to counties where at least 20 percent of the population has lived under the federal poverty line for at least 30 years. The Recovery Act applied the 10–20–30 plan to three rural development investment programs totaling a modest $1.7 billion. In 2013, Rep. Clyburn introduced legislation to significantly expand the application of his plan. In a *New York Times* op-ed piece, Democratic presidential nominee Hillary Clinton presented her poverty plan. She wrote, "Tim Kaine and I will model our anti-poverty strategy on Congressman Jim Clyburn's 10–20–30 plan" to "ensure that our investments are reaching the communities suffering the most from decades of neglect." While Hillary Clinton has said that 10–20–30 "is a program that would target a lot of places in America, not only inner-city poverty but rural poverty, Indian country poverty, coal country poverty." But in practice, Clyburn's approach yields a collection of communities that are overwhelmingly rural. Upwards of 80 percent fall outside of metropolitan areas.

Brookings Institution constructed two maps — one based on the survey for the 10–20–30 plan and another on persistently poor small areas based on decennial census and census small area income and poverty estimates. These maps are reproduced in Figures 21.1 and 21.2. As Figure 21.2 shows, the originally selected communities miss a large swath of poverty-stricken areas, particularly in metropolitan regions. Clyburn's plan was unusual because it had the backing of both sides of the aisle. This bi-partisan coalition is as important as it is rare, but it makes sense to include more constituents in the anti-poverty program. This requires adopting Figure 21.2 as the appropriate map of poverty.

Trump: Building Walls Rather than Hands Across the Border

Donald Trump's signature policy remains building a wall between the U.S. and Mexico, for which our southern friends and neighbors will pay. However, he now admits that adding fences in-between walls would be

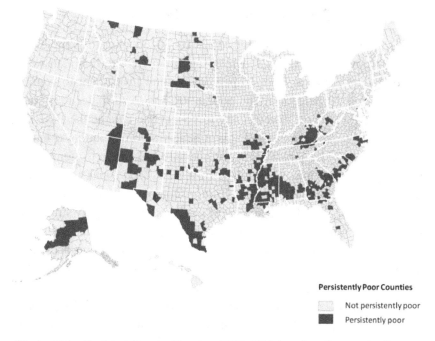

Persistently Poor Counties

Not persistently poor

Persistently poor

Figure 21.1 Persistent Poverty, Based on 2007–2011 American Community Survey
Source: Brookings Institution analysis of decennial census and American Community Survey data.

beneficial. This despite that fact that net migration flow across that long boarder has been southbound for years now. More people are crossing into Mexico than into the U.S. While we would win no international friendships with this plan, worse is Trump's insistence that the U.S. Treasury designate China a currency manipulator — meaning that Beijing is intervening in foreign-exchange markets to keep the yuan undervalued. This despite that the yuan would depreciate if the Chinese let it float — making China an even more formidable competitor. The same China has ratified the Paris agreement to limit carbon emissions. Yet President Trump insists that climate change is over-hyped by the media, apparently perpetuated by thousands of conspiring scientists in dozens of countries. In the same breath, he wants to lift all restrictions on all sources of American energy production. As to the truth, globalization cannot be reversed by unilaterally closing borders with walls and fences.

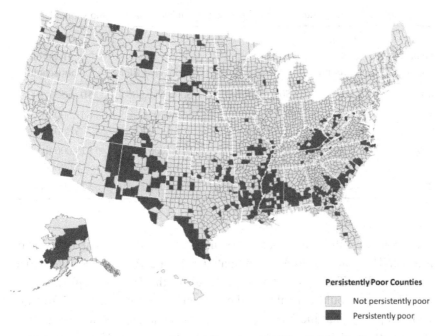

Figure 21.2 Persistent Poverty, Based on 2014 Small Area Estimates
Source: Brookings Institution analysis of decennial census and Census Small Area Income and Poverty Estimates data.

Donald Trump's Tax Plan

Mr. Trump's tax plan would substantially lower individual income taxes and the corporate income tax and eliminate some complex features of the current tax code. He would cut taxes by $11.98 trillion over the next decade on a static basis. The plan would end up reducing tax revenues by $10.14 trillion over the next decade when accounting for economic growth from increases in the supply of labor and capital. There would also be increased outlays due to higher interest on the debt, creating a 10-year deficit somewhat larger than the above estimates. With significantly reduced marginal tax rates and the cost of capita would lead to an 11 percent higher GDP over the long run, provided the tax cut could be appropriately financed. The plan would also lead to a 29 percent larger capital stock, 6.5 percent higher wages, and 5.3 million more full-time equivalent jobs. The slashing of

Table 21.3 Individual Income Tax Brackets under Donald Trump's Tax Plan

Ordinary income	Capital gains and dividends	Single filers	Married filers	Head of household
0%	0%	$0 to $25,000	$0 to $50,000	$0 to $37,500
10%	0%	$25,000 to $50,000	$50,000 to $100,000	$37,500 to $75,000
20%	15%	$50,000 to $150,000	$100,000 to $300,000	$75,000 to $225,000
25%	20%	$150,000 and up	$300,000 and up	$225,000 and up

taxes would result in higher after-tax incomes for taxpayers at all levels of income. The plan would also eliminate the Estate Tax and the Alternative Minimum Tax. Table 21.3 shows the details of the Trump tax plan.

The plan would consolidate the current seven tax brackets into four, with a top marginal income tax rate of 25 percent, and the lowest tax rate at the bottom of 0 percent. A top marginal tax rate of 20 percent would apply to long-term capital gains and qualified dividends.[5]

There would be substantial business tax changes. The corporate income tax rate would be lowered from 35 percent to only 15 percent. He would end the deferral of income from controlled foreign subsidiaries, but preserve the foreign tax credit. It would also enact a one-time deemed repatriation tax of 10 percent on all foreign profits currently deferred. There would be a provision for taxes pass-through businesses

---

[5] The idea of a simplified tax structure is not new. I and the Joint Committee on Taxation proposed a 10–25–30 set of tax brackets combined with a value-added tax (VAT) so popular in Europe. A negative income tax would apply to those earning a basket of necessities. A simulation study showed the benefits of such a plan. See E. Ray Canterbery, Eric W. Cook and Bernard A. Schmitt, "Gaining Progressivity and Revenue," *The Cato Journal* (Fall 1985), pp. 521–535. The article is reprinted in E. Ray Canterbery, Editor, *Beyond Conventional Economics* (Singapore, London, New Jersey: World Scientific, 2016), Chapter 46. Earlier, I had proposed a VAT as a form of incomes policy: see E. Ray Canterbery, "Tax Reform and Incomes Policy: a VATIP Proposal, *Journal of Post Keynesian Economics*, 5(3), 1983, pp. 430–439. The article is reprinted in Canterbery, *Beyond Conventional Economics, op. cit.*, Chapter 45.

at the rate of 15 percent commensurate with the traditional corporations. Further, he would cap the deductibility if interest expenses.

In the right-wing Tax Foundation Model, the increased incentives to work and invest from this tax plan would increase the size of the economy by 11 percent over the long run. The plan would lead to 5.4 percent higher wages and a 29 percent larger capital stock. The larger economy is mainly the result of the significant reduction in the service price of capital due to the rate reductions for corporations and pass-through businesses. In addition, the reduction of marginal tax rates on individual income would increase the incentive to work and result in 5.3 million full-time equivalent jobs.

There would be distributional effects from the tax plan. The greatest benefits are reserved for the highest income class, especially the one-percenters. Taxpayers in the bottom deciles (the 0–10 and 10–20 percent deciles), would see increases in after-tax adjusted gross income (AGI) of 1.4 and 0.5 percent, respectively. Middle-income taxpayers with incomes that fall within the 30th and 80th percentiles would see larger of increases in their after-tax AGI, of between 3.0 and 8.3 percent. Taxpayers with incomes that fall in the highest income class (the 90–100 percent decile) would see an increase in after-tax income of 14.5 percent. The top 1 per-cent of all taxpayers would see a whopping 21.5 percent increase in after-tax income. On a dynamic basis, the plan would increase after-tax incomes by 20 percent on average. Taxpayers in the bottom three deciles would see their after-tax AGIs increase between 10.6 and 11.5 percent. The top 1 percent of all taxpayers would see an increase in after-tax AGI of 27.0 percent. This is Donald Trump's tax bracket.

To conclude, the combination of tax simplification and lower tax rates would lower marginal tax rates on workers and significantly reduce the cost of capital. These changes in the incentive to work and invest would greatly increase the U.S. economy's size in the long run, leading to higher incomes for taxpayers at all income levels. The federal deficit would increase by over $10 trillion, both on a static and dynamic basis.

A similar plan was enacted by Ronald Reagan. It had the opposite of the intended effects, with the economy enduring a sharp decline, the most precipitous since the Great Depression of the 1930s. The federal deficits soared. Hopefully, President Trump's plan will not give tax simplification a bad name.

Tax Plans: Viva La Difference

Besides gender, nothing separated the two presidential candidates like their tax plans. In almost every meaningful respect, these plans are mirror images. The Trump plan would cut taxes by $6.2 trillion over a decade, delivering about half the benefits to the top 1 percent. Middle-income households, on average, would see tax cuts, too, but they are so small as to be almost invisible. Mrs. Clinton's plan would boost taxes by a net $1.4 trillion, concentrated on the wealthiest households. The top 1 percent would see after-tax income *fall* 7.4 percent and would face an average tax increase of $117,760 in 2017. Most people in lower income groups would get small tax cuts. To pay for the targeted tax cuts, she would raise taxes on the wages, business income, capital gains and estates of the richest Americans, new taxes to make them pay what she says is their "fair share" She would double the $1,000 child tax credit for children ages 4 and under, which would deliver benefits directly to low-income families.

In the Transition

Many are thankful that the presidential campaign of 2016 was over in November 2016. It was the ugliest, nastiest slugfest in modern political history. We were hopeful that President Trump would reject some of the more radical conservative ideas that he had expressed in the campaign. Economists noted that his tax proposals would, if legislated, worsen the income and wealth distributions and possibly lead to more rioting in major cities, such as New York, Chicago and Detroit. If ever there was a good time for industrial peace, it is now. And the wealth and income distributions were at their most unequal since 2007, when the Great Recession began.[6]

---

[6] I remain steadfast in having named the "Great Recession." See the comment in E. Ray Canterbery, *The Making of Economics*, Vol. III, 4th edition (New Jersey/London/Singapore/Hong Kong: World Scientific, 2010) pp. 216–217. I, along with then President Barrack Obama, saw the effects of the Great Recession extending well beyond June 2009, the "official" ending date per the NBER.

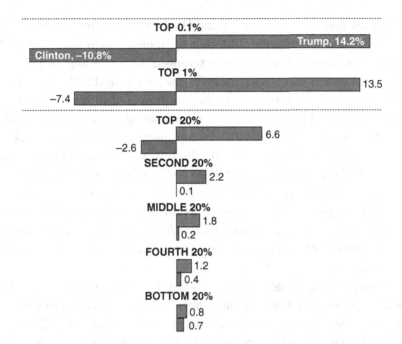

Figure 21.3 Percentage Change in after-tax Income by Candidate's Tax Plan and Income Level (2017)
Source: Tax Policy Center. The Wall Street Journal.

In what was supposed to be a transition, President-elect Trump virtually took the reins of the Presidency out of the hands of then President Barack Obama. He made pronouncements that undercut the powers of the then current President. He said he would repeal Obamacare at a time when Paul Ryan, the House majority leader was pleading for compromise. Ryan and other Republicans expressed a desire to keep what was working and do away with the parts that were failing, but not abandon it altogether.

As President-elect, Mr. Trump wanted "Boeing to make a lot of money," but "the $4 billion for a new Air Force One should be canceled." Boeing was in competition with Europe's Airbus. Was it to be "Air Force None?" Besides being a decision affecting future Presidents without their consent, it was a decision affecting trade relations with Europe, which were subject to renegotiation. Again, he was going over the head of a sitting President of the United States. Did he really want the contract to go to a European competitor? Moreover, Boeing would have to lay off dozens of workers if the plane was scrapped. Later, Trump said that he had spoken with Boeing representatives and they agreed to "cost savings" on the new airplane. Trump threatened to place a tariff on any goods or services produced by American companies abroad and imported to the U.S.[7] Meanwhile, President-elect Trump made a deal with Softback of Japan, which agreed to invest $50 billion in the U.S. and create some 50,000 jobs here. Speaking of future Presidents, Trump said that he "was going to serve eight years," with the second election a foregone conclusion. This arrogance, while it may have been expected, was not becoming of a President replacing Barack Obama. Again, while we were initially hopeful, we quickly found that this post-campaign rhetoric was simply that — rhetoric.

Donald Trump made a dramatic move to save 800 jobs at Carrier, based in Farmington, Connecticut; it attracted praise from his supporters. Somehow, they saw the President-elect as a man of his word. However, experts viewed the deal as a political stunt and a dangerous precedent that doesn't alter underlying conditions in the economy. Trump's negotiations with Carrier were troubling and did not reflect sound economic policy. It was the President-elect's direct intervention, using the power of an office which he had yet to occupy, that made this transaction newsworthy.

We somehow knew that Trump's deal-making would go on, even as President. As a real-estate tycoon he built tall buildings, renovated the Old Post Office near the White House (now the Trump International Hotel) and built private golf clubs around the world as well as casinos. Trump is faced with a Ricardian dilemma, since the land under the Old Post Office is owned by the government. While the states and local economic development groups dole out corporate retention subsidies daily, Trump was using the power of the President's office for such subsidies. For example, Carrier was given a modest state subsidy that it did not need to stay competitive. Economists generally find such subsidy-driven arrangements to be inefficient. The Brookings Institution suggested a few ways that the

---

[7] Paul Ryan, the speaker of the House, said he would not support the tariff plan, and that it may take 7 years to evolve. Later, he offered qualified support for new tariffs.

ribbon-cutter-in-chief could carry out future place-based interventions in a more sustainable, scaled manner.[8]

The meddling with Presidential politics by President-elect Trump did not end at the water's edge. China's influence in the global economy grows with its rapidly growing economy. If we exclude the nations comprising the European Union, China has the second largest GDP in the world according to the IMF, the World Bank, and the UN. In 1979 diplomatic relations were established between the USA and the Republic of China (PRC). Since, no American President or President-elect has had a face-to-face meeting with his Taiwan counterpart. When Taiwan's President Tsai Ing-wen gave a congratulatory call on his nomination, President-elect Trump spoke by phone on December 2, 2016 with her. Though *she* had called, it nonetheless heightened concerns about Trump's foreign policy deftness. Washington DC had accepted the PRC as the sole legal government of all of China in 1979, agreeing to conduct relations with Taiwan on strictly an unofficial basis. This phone call from Taiwan was viewed as a break with the past in Chinese relations. It put Taiwan on the front burner in the eyes of the Chinese. Taiwan's security depends on restraint across the Taiwan Strait on the part of Beijing. Trump said that during the discussion they noted the "close economic, political and security ties" between the U.S. and Taiwan. While one can empathize with President Tsai's desire to establish contact with and gain respect from an incoming U.S. President, in his discussion the President-elect was ignoring historic and strategic factors that all eight Presidents since Nixon have understood and acceded to. Notably, the Chinese vented their anger with Taiwan, not Mr. Trump. China plays its political-economic cards close to its chest.

Trump did consult Obama about his appointments, but there was little-to-no evidence that Obama had much influence. As defense secretary, Obama named James "Mad Dog" Mattis. He is a retired Marine General selected shortly after Trump's election. With a nickname like that, one cannot be reassured about the appointment. To take office, Congress will have to pass legislation to bypass a federal law stating that defense secretaries

---

[8] See "Redefining the Art of the Deal," Brookings Institution, *Policy Briefs*, December 5, 2016, pp. 2–3.

must *not* have been on active duty in the previous 7 years. The exception was made *once*, for legendary General George C. Marshall in 1950. One plus for Trump — Mattis is a close friend of Israel. A complacent Congress quickly gave a pass to the new defense secretary. We are reminded that civilian control of the military is a fundamental principle of democracy.

Trump initially urged Mitt Romney to be the new Secretary of State, but later settled for a retired general, Rex Tillerson as his choice. The number of current or ex-generals soon began to fill the Cabinet. Just as it began to look like a military academy, the President-elect turned toward those who were rich. Historians say that it is the richest Cabinet in U.S. history. In defense, Trump said in a Des Moines, Iowa rally, "because I want people that made a future, because now they are negotiating with you, okay?" How rich? CBS News estimated that seven of Trump's picks combined are worth $11 *billion*. Bernie Sanders, who lost to Hillary Clinton as the Democratic nominee, said, "I guess they have a few poor millionaires on it, but mostly its billionaires." Exxon Mobil CEO Rex Tillerson is among the "poor" with *only* $228 million in assets.[9] Neither President Obama nor President George W. Bush had a single billionaire in their first Cabinet. Wilbur Ross, the very rich Secretary of Commerce appointee, said "they were attuned to the plight of working Americans."

Kellyanne Conway was selected as White House Counselor, elevating her to the West Wing of the White House. She had led Trump's campaign. She was a divisive choice. Conway irritated some Trump aides with her outspoken opposition to Mitt Romney, the 2012 Republican nominee for President, for Secretary of State. This she confided to Trump privately. As to Hillary Clinton, the 2016 Democratic nominee for President, Trump initially declared, "Lock her up!" After the election, he said, "The Clintons' are nice people." Still later, he and Bill Clinton chose to engage in a heated conversation. Trump gave the impression that he was a sore winner.

Reince Priebus was named as Chief of Staff. He was to be senior counselor to the President and chief West Wing strategist. He is past chairman of the Republican National Committee (RNC) and a friend of

---

[9] The references to net worth of the candidates is from the Forbes 400, Special Issue, 2016 Edition.

Paul D. Ryan, the Majority Leader and often critic of Donald Trump. Priebus is said to have embraced a fringe ideology (of the right-wing, if not of the West Wing). Adam Jentleson, a spokesman for Senator Harry Reid, the Democratic leader, said, "It is easy to see why the K.K.K. views Trump as their champion when Trump appoints one of the foremost peddlers of white supremacy views and rhetoric as his top aide." As his partner, Stephen Bannon, one time Goldman Sachs banker, who is infamous for his scorched earth style of politics, was appointed as White House Counselor. Some of Bannon's supporters have traded in conspiracy theories and sometimes racist messages at *Breithart News*, the Bannon website for the past decade. The website, for example, called Bill Kristal a "renegade Jew," though Kristal should have been friendly with a conservative. Bannon soon was pushed into the background, but not out of ear-shot of the President.

Jared Kushner, Trump's son-in-law and close adviser during the campaign, was named as an influential counselor, though his exact duties went unspecified. This led some Democrats to criticize the appointment as an example of nepotism. Federal law prohibits the hiring of relatives in government agencies; it is unclear whether this applies to the White House. Anyway, Trump does not need any further legal drama. Mr. Kushner has no government experience, but was an informal Trump adviser during the campaign. While Kushner is well-heeled, he is poor compared with Vincent Viola as Secretary of the Army ($1.8 billion in net worth) or the controversial Betsy DeVos as Secretary of Education ($5.1 billion).

We could go on and on regarding the Trump appointments, but we need not. The main point has been established: given his plan for taxes and his appointments, President Trump does not seem to favor income and wealth equality or economic justice. A movement toward greater income and wealth distributions equalities has been a major theme of this book.

Bernie Sanders and the Modern Monetary Theory (MMT)

Bernie Sanders never really went away, even though he came in third in a three-way contest for the Presidency. What is remarkable, if more than a few votes in a few select districts had gone his way, he would have won.

After all, it is said that more did not vote than did. Moreover, an economic movement is associated with the name of Bernie's chief economic advisor, Stephanie Kelton, now an economist at the University of Missouri, Kansas City. She became an advisor to Bernie when recommended by several prominent left-wing economists, including Dean Baker and Jamie Galbraith. "She's 48 years old, whip-smart, impeccably coiffed, and brims with enthusiasm - important for someone who spends half her time telling Wall Street types to rethink their basic approach to economics."[10]

A little background will help. In early 2013, Congress was in a crisis mode, what with House Republicans opposed to raising the debt ceiling without cuts to spending, and Democrats, weary also of debt, not signing on the Republicans' austerity program.

A curious solution came out of the cybersphere: why not mint at the Treasury a $1 trillion coin, deposit it in the Treasury's account at the Federal Reserve, and get on with business. It eventually got a name as a hashtag: #mintcoin. Politics was the problem, not money. The #mintcoin is in the same family as the bitcoin.

The idea of a trillion dollar coin would have been quickly dismissed, except for the adherents of the doctrine of Modern Monetary Theory (MMT). The trillion dollar coin drove home the idea of money as a social contract. Namely, there are no limits to government spending. Once we change the way people think about money, everyone can be provided for. Kelton spoke about the coin on MSNBC. The appeal was made to Republicans and Democrats alike. Moreover, the MMT has its roots in Adam Smith and John Maynard Keynes along with Hyman Minsky and Abba Lerner. Old ideas have been put in the same wine bottle, and assembled into modern macroeconomics.

The idea of a big-expenditure economic stimulus to rebuild the nation's superstructure was common ground for Trump and Sanders voters who liked the idea of jobs perhaps more than they disliked deficit spending. As it turns out, if that is what voters want, then MMT is that rare economic doctrine that not only validates their hunches, but contends that

---

[10]Atossa Araxia Abrahamian, "Debt is not the End: The Rock-Star Appeal of Modern Monetary Theory for the Sanders Generation," *The Nation* (May 22/29, 2017), p. 14.

the unholy combination is the key to a healthy, stable, and prosperous economy for everyone.

Modern Monetary Theory emerged as a school of thought in the 1990s, when Kelton and her colleagues in mainly heterodox economics departments like the University of Missouri, Kansas City, and Bard's Levy Institute, published something called "Post-Keynesian Thought." The leaders included Hyman Minsky at Levy, Warren Mosler, a wealthy financier, and L. Randall Wray at Kansas City and author of a book on Minsky. Mosler argued that taxes create the demand for federal spending and that deficits don't cause countries to default on their debt. Stephanie Kelton initially disagreed with Mosler, but was convinced by Randall Wray to do her own work, in which she arrived at the same place as Mosler. In turn, Mosler found kindred spirits in the Post-Keynesians. As I and others have noted, there is scant reason for any society to tolerate unemployment. In Europe, where a generation of young people remain under- or unemployed, more expenditures, better social welfare, and a guaranteed job are especially attractive options. According to Jamie Galbraith, "The contribution of MMT is not the discovery of new facts. It's a teaching core of things which are factually uncontroversial." He concludes that what's threatening the establishment "is that the narrative is very compelling."[11]

---

[11] Ibid., p. 15.

APPENDIX 1

Appendix 1.A   Rank Order of Countries by GDP (Nominal).

List by the International Monetary Fund (2016)			List by the World Bank (2016)			List by the United Nations (2015)		
Rank	Country	GDP (US$MM)	Rank	Country	GDP (US$MM)	Rank	Country	GDP (US$MM)
	World	752,78,049		World	755,43,543		World	741,96,404
1	United States	186,24,450	1	United States	185,69,100	1	United States	180,36,648
—	European Union [1]	164,08,364	—	European Union [1]	163,97,980	—	European Union [1]	168,32,631
2	China [2]	112,32,108	2	China [5]	111,99,145	2	China [5]	111,58,457
3	Japan	49,36,543	3	Japan	49,39,384	3	Japan	43,83,076
4	Germany	34,79,232	4	Germany	34,66,757	4	Germany	33,63,600
5	United Kingdom	26,29,188	5	United Kingdom	26,18,886	5	United Kingdom	28,58,003
6	France	24,66,472	6	France	24,65,454	6	France	24,18,946
7	India	22,63,792	7	India	22,63,522	7	India	21,16,239
8	Italy	18,50,735	8	Italy	18,49,970	8	Italy	18,21,580
9	Brazil	17,98,622	9	Brazil	17,96,187	9	Brazil	17,72,591
10	Canada	15,29,760	10	Canada	15,29,760	10	Canada	15,52,808
11	South Korea	14,11,042	11	South Korea	14,11,246	11	South Korea	13,77,873
12	Russia [3]	12,83,162	12	Russia [3]	12,83,162	12	Russia [3]	13,26,016
13	Australia	12,61,645	13	Spain	12,32,088	13	Australia	12,30,859
14	Spain	12,32,597	14	Australia	12,04,616	14	Spain	11,92,955

Rank	Country	Value	Rank	Country	Value	Rank	Country	Value
15	Mexico	10,46,925	15	Mexico	10,45,998	15	Mexico	11,40,724
16	Indonesia	9,32,448	16	Indonesia	9,32,259	16	Indonesia	8,61,934
17	Turkey	8,63,390	17	Turkey	8,57,749	17	Netherlands	7,50,318
18	Netherlands	7,77,548	18	Netherlands	7,70,845	18	Turkey	7,17,887
19	Switzerland	6,69,038	19	Switzerland	6,59,827	19	Switzerland	6,70,789
20	Saudi Arabia	6,46,438	20	Saudi Arabia	6,46,438	20	Saudi Arabia	6,53,219
21	Argentina	5,45,124	21	Argentina	5,45,866	21	Sweden	5,71,090
22	Taiwan	5,28,550	22	Sweden	5,11,000	22	Nigeria	5,68,499
23	Sweden	5,11,397	23	Poland	4,69,509	23	Poland	5,44,959
24	Poland	4,67,591	24	Belgium	4,66,366	24	Argentina	5,43,490
25	Belgium	4,66,960	25	Iran	4,25,326	25	Belgium	5,31,547
26	Thailand	4,06,949	26	Thailand	4,06,840	26	Venezuela	5,09,968
27	Nigeria	4,05,952	27	Nigeria	4,05,083	27	Norway	5,00,519
28	Austria	3,86,752	28	Austria	3,86,428	28	Austria	4,36,888
29	Venezuela	3,76,755	29	Venezuela	3,71,337	29	Iran	4,25,326
30	Norway	3,71,353	30	Norway	3,70,557	30	Thailand	4,04,824
31	United Arab Emirates	3,70,449	31	United Arab Emirates	3,48,743	31	United Arab Emirates	3,99,451
32	Egypt	3,32,349	32	Egypt	3,36,297	32	Colombia	3,77,740
33	Hong Kong	3,20,668	33	Hong Kong	3,20,912	33	South Africa	3,49,819
34	Israel	3,18,386	34	Israel	3,18,744	34	Denmark	3,46,119

(Continued)

Appendix 1.A   *(Continued)*

List by the International Monetary Fund (2016)			List by the World Bank (2016)			List by the United Nations (2015)		
Rank	Country	GDP (US$MM)	Rank	Country	GDP (US$MM)	Rank	Country	GDP (US$MM)
	World	752,78,049		World	755,43,543		World	741,96,404
35	Denmark	3,06,730	35	Denmark	3,06,143	35	Malaysia	3,26,933
36	Philippines	3,04,696	36	Philippines	3,04,905	36	Singapore	3,07,872
37	Singapore	2,96,967	37	Singapore	2,96,966	37	Israel	3,05,673
38	Malaysia	2,96,359	38	Malaysia	2,96,359	38	Philippines	2,90,896
39	South Africa	2,94,132	39	South Africa	2,94,841	39	Egypt	2,82,242
40	Ireland	2,93,605	40	Ireland	2,94,054	40	Hong Kong	2,74,027
41	Colombia	2,82,357	41	Pakistan	2,83,660	41	Finland	2,72,217
42	Pakistan	2,78,913	42	Colombia	2,82,463	42	Chile	2,58,062
43	Chile	2,47,025	43	Chile	2,47,028	43	Pakistan	2,51,255
44	Finland	2,36,883	44	Finland	2,36,785	44	Ireland	2,50,814
45	Venezuela	2,36,443	45	Bangladesh	2,21,415	45	Greece	2,35,574
46	Bangladesh	2,27,901	46	Portugal	2,04,565	46	Portugal	2,30,117
47	Portugal	2,04,761	47	Vietnam	2,02,616	47	Iraq	2,25,422
48	Vietnam	2,01,326	48	Greece	1,94,559	48	Kazakhstan	2,16,036
49	Peru	1,95,140	49	Czech Republic	1,92,925	49	Algeria	2,13,518

#			#			#		
50	Greece	1,94,248	50	Peru	1,92,094	50	Qatar	2,11,817
51	Czech Republic	1,92,991	51	Romania	1,86,691	51	Czech Republic	2,05,270
52	Romania	1,87,039	52	New Zealand	1,85,017	52	Peru	2,01,809
53	New Zealand	1,81,991	53	Iraq	1,71,489	53	Romania	1,99,045
54	Iraq	1,67,026	54	Algeria	1,56,080	54	New Zealand	1,98,652
55	Algeria	1,60,784	55	Qatar	1,52,469	55	Vietnam	1,86,205
56	Qatar	1,56,734	56	Kazakhstan	1,33,657	56	Bangladesh	1,73,062
57	Kazakhstan	1,33,757	57	Hungary	1,24,343	57	Kuwait	1,63,637
58	Hungary	1,25,675	58	Kuwait	1,12,812	58	Angola	1,46,676
59	Kuwait	1,09,859	59	Puerto Rico	1,03,135	59	Hungary	1,38,347
60	Morocco	1,03,615	60	Morocco [6]	1,01,445	60	Ukraine	1,31,806
61	Puerto Rico	1,01,304	61	Ecuador	97,802	61	Morocco	1,10,009
62	Ecuador	98,010	62	Sudan	95,584	62	Puerto Rico	1,03,676
63	Angola	95,821	63	Ukraine	93,270	63	Ecuador	1,00,917
64	Sudan	94,421	64	Angola	89,633	64	Slovakia	1,00,249
65	Ukraine	93,263	65	Slovakia	89,552	65	Cuba	87,206
66	Slovakia	89,525	66	Sri Lanka	81,322	66	Sudan	81,894
67	Sri Lanka	82,615	67	Ethiopia	72,374	67	Oman	81,797
68	Syria [4]	77,460	68	Dominican Republic	71,584	68	Belarus	76,139
69	Ethiopia	72,523	69	Kenya	70,529	69	Azerbaijan	75,193

(*Continued*)

Appendix 1.A   *(Continued)*

	List by the International Monetary Fund (2016)			List by the World Bank (2016)			List by the United Nations (2015)	
Rank	Country	GDP (US$MM)	Rank	Country	GDP (US$MM)	Rank	Country	GDP (US$MM)
	World	752,78,049		World	755,43,543		World	741,96,404
70	Dominican Republic	72,194	70	Guatemala	68,763	70	Sri Lanka	74,941
71	Kenya	68,919	71	Myanmar	67,430	71	Myanmar	66,478
72	Guatemala	68,175	72	Uzbekistan	67,220	72	Luxembourg	64,874
73	Uzbekistan	66,502	73	Oman	66,293	73	Dominican Republic	63,969
74	Myanmar	66,324	74	Luxembourg	59,948	74	Uzbekistan	63,030
75	Oman	63,171	75	Costa Rica	57,436	75	Kenya	60,936
76	Luxembourg	59,468	76	Panama	55,188	76	Guatemala	58,827
77	Costa Rica	58,109	77	Uruguay	52,420	77	Uruguay	57,471
78	Panama	55,122	78	Bulgaria	52,395	78	Croatia	57,137
79	Uruguay	54,567	79	Croatia	50,425	79	Bulgaria	56,718
80	Bulgaria	52,418	80	Lebanon	47,537	80	Macau	55,502
81	Lebanon	51,991	81	Belarus	47,433	81	Ethiopia	53,638
82	Croatia	50,441	82	Tanzania [7]	47,431	82	Lebanon	49,631
83	Belarus	48,847	83	Macau	44,803	83	Costa Rica	49,553
84	Tanzania	47,184	84	Slovenia	43,991	84	Slovenia	49,491

Rank	Country	Value	Rank	Country	Value	Rank	Country	Value
85	Macau	44,110	85	Lithuania	42,739	85	Panama	49,166
86	Slovenia	44,009	86	Ghana	42,690	86	Lithuania	48,392
87	Ghana	43,264	87	Tunisia	42,063	87	Tanzania	48,030
88	Lithuania	42,749	88	Jordan	38,655	88	Turkmenistan	47,932
89	Tunisia	41,869	89	Azerbaijan	37,848	89	Tunisia	47,423
90	Democratic Republic of the Congo	41,615	90	Serbia	37,745	90	Serbia	43,866
91	Jordan	38,743	91	Turkmenistan	36,180	91	Libya	41,319
92	Serbia	37,745	92	Côte d'Ivoire	36,165	92	Ghana	37,177
93	Azerbaijan	37,556	93	Democratic Republic of the Congo	34,999	93	Yemen	37,131
94	Turkmenistan	36,180	94	Bolivia	33,806	94	Democratic Republic of the Congo	35,909
95	Côte d'Ivoire	35,489	95	Bahrain	31,859	95	Jordan	35,827
96	Bolivia	34,831	96	Libya	29,153	96	Côte d'Ivoire	34,254
97	Libya	33,157	97	Latvia	27,677	97	Bahrain	33,850
98	Bahrain	31,907	98	Paraguay	27,441	98	Bolivia	32,996
99	Cameroon	29,334	99	Yemen	27,318	99	Cameroon	32,051
100	Latvia	27,684	100	El Salvador	26,797	100	Latvia	31,286
101	Paraguay	27,441	101	Uganda	25,528	101	Paraguay	30,985
102	Yemen	27,318	102	Cameroon	24,204	102	Trinidad and Tobago	28,069

(Continued)

Appendix 1.A   *(Continued)*

List by the International Monetary Fund (2016)			List by the World Bank (2016)			List by the United Nations (2015)		
Rank	**Country**	**GDP (US$MM)**	**Rank**	**Country**	**GDP (US$MM)**	**Rank**	**Country**	**GDP (US$MM)**
	World	**752,78,049**		**World**	**755,43,543**		**World**	**741,96,404**
103	El Salvador	26,709	103	Estonia	23,137	103	Uganda	27,465
104	Uganda	26,195	104	Honduras	21,517	104	Zambia	26,963
105	Estonia	23,130	105	Nepal	21,144	105	Estonia	26,485
106	Honduras	21,364	106	Trinidad and Tobago	20,989	106	El Salvador	25,164
107	Zambia	21,310	107	Iceland	20,047	107	Cyprus	23,077
108	Nepal	21,154	108	Cambodia	20,017	108	Afghanistan	21,122
109	Trinidad and Tobago	20,966	109	Cyprus [8]	19,802	109	Honduras	19,497
110	Iceland	20,047	110	Zambia	19,551	110	Nepal	19,489
111	Papua New Guinea	20,003	111	Afghanistan	19,469	111	Bosnia and Herzegovina	18,491
112	Cyprus	19,810	112	Papua New Guinea	16,929	112	Gabon	17,412
113	Cambodia	19,398	113	Bosnia and Herzegovina	16,560	113	North Korea	17,396
114	Afghanistan	18,886	114	Zimbabwe	16,289	114	Brunei	17,104
115	Bosnia and Herzegovina	16,605	115	Laos	15,903	115	Mozambique	17,081

Rank	Country	Value	Rank	Country	Value	Rank	Country	Value
116	Botswana	15,018	116	Botswana	15,275	116	Iceland	17,036
117	Senegal	14,785	117	Senegal	14,765	117	Cambodia	16,778
118	Gabon	14,273	118	Georgia [9]	14,333	118	Equatorial Guinea	16,731
119	Georgia	14,222	119	Gabon	14,214	119	Papua New Guinea	16,576
120	Zimbabwe	14,174	120	Mali	14,045	120	Georgia	16,530
121	Mali	13,960	121	Jamaica	14,027	121	Botswana	15,813
122	Jamaica	13,950	122	South Sudan	13,282	122	Senegal	15,658
123	Laos	13,790	123	Nicaragua	13,231	123	Zimbabwe	14,719
124	Nicaragua	13,049	124	Mauritius	12,164	124	Congo Republic of the	14,077
125	Albania	12,126	125	Burkina Faso	12,115	125	Jamaica	13,927
126	Mauritius	11,950	126	Albania	11,927	126	Namibia	13,429
127	Burkina Faso	11,182	127	Brunei	11,400	127	Albania	13,413
128	Equatorial Guinea	11,636	128	Mongolia	11,160	128	Chad	12,791
129	Mozambique	11,283	129	Mozambique	11,015	129	Arab Palestinian areas	12,766
130	Brunei	11,182	130	Malta	10,949	130	Burkina Faso	12,756
131	Mongolia	11,031	131	Macedonia	10,900	131	Mauritius	12,616
132	Malta	10,953	132	Armenia	10,547	132	Mongolia	12,067
133	Macedonia	10,912	133	Namibia	10,267	133	Mali	11,979
134	Namibia	10,646	134	Equatorial Guinea	10,179	134	Nicaragua	11,806

(Continued)

Appendix 1.A   *(Continued)*

List by the International Monetary Fund (2016)			List by the World Bank (2016)			List by the United Nations (2015)		
Rank	Country	GDP (US$MM)	Rank	Country	GDP (US$MM)	Rank	Country	GDP (US$MM)
	World	752,78,049		World	755,43,543		World	741,96,404
135	Armenia	10,499	135	Madagascar	9,991	135	Laos	11,749
136	Chad	10,103	136	Chad	9,601	136	Macedonia	11,319
137	Madagascar	9,740	137	The Bahamas	9,047	137	South Sudan	11,007
138	Bahamas	8,939	138	Benin	8,583	138	Armenia	10,889
139	Benin	8,577	139	Rwanda	8,376	139	Madagascar	10,674
140	Rwanda	8,406	140	Haiti	8,023	140	Malta	10,536
141	Haiti	8,257	141	Republic of the Congo	7,834	141	New Caledonia	10,234
142	Republic of Congo	7,955	142	Niger	7,509	142	Benin	9,575
143	Niger	7,479	143	Kosovo	7,047	143	Tajikistan	9,242
144	Kosovo	7,047	144	Tajikistan	6,952	144	Haiti	8,599
145	Tajikistan	6,922	145	Moldova [10]	6,750	145	The Bahamas	8,510
146	Moldova	6,750	146	Kyrgyzstan	6,551	146	Niger	8,169
147	Kyrgyzstan	6,551	147	Guinea	6,299	147	Moldova	7,944
148	Guinea	6,512	148	Somalia	6,217	148	Rwanda	7,903
149	Malawi	5,492	149	Bermuda	5,574	149	Kyrgyzstan	7,404

Rank	Country	Value	Rank	Country	Value	Country	Value
150	Eritrea	5,352	150	Liechtenstein	5,488	Kosovo	7,387
151	Mauritania	4,714	151	Malawi	5,442	Monaco	7,060
152	Fiji	4,640	152	Mauritania	4,635	Guinea	6,579
153	Barbados	4,588	153	Fiji	4,632	Liechtenstein	5,855
154	Togo	4,434	154	Barbados	4,588	Malawi	5,720
155	Montenegro	4,126	155	Togo	4,400	French Polynesia	5,623
156	Sierra Leone	3,981	156	Montenegro	4,173	Bermuda	5,601
157	Swaziland	3,770	157	Swaziland	3,727	Suriname	5,210
158	Suriname	3,570	158	Sierra Leone	3,669	Mauritania	5,092
159	Guyana	3,437	159	Suriname	3,621	Timor-Leste	4,970
160	Maldives	3,379	160	Maldives	3,591	Sierra Leone	4,893
161	Burundi	3,133	161	Guyana	3,446	Montenegro	4,588
162	South Sudan	2,914	162	Andorra	3,249	Togo	4,576
163	Timor-Leste	2,498	163	Burundi	3,007	Fiji	4,532
164	Lesotho	2,267	164	Faroe Islands	2,613	Swaziland	4,482
165	Bhutan	2,115	165	Greenland	2,441	Barbados	4,353
166	Liberia	2,111	166	Bhutan	2,237	Eritrea	3,858
167	Djibouti	1,894	167	Lesotho	2,200	Cayman Islands	3,480
168	Central African Republic	1,780	168	Liberia	2,101	Andorra	3,278
169	Belize	1,743	169	Belize	1,765	Curaçao	3,159

(Continued)

Appendix 1.A *(Continued)*

List by the International Monetary Fund (2016)			List by the World Bank (2016)			List by the United Nations (2015)		
Rank	Country	GDP (US$MM)	Rank	Country	GDP (US$MM)	Rank	Country	GDP (US$MM)
	World	752,78,049		World	755,43,543		World	741,96,404
170	Cabo Verde	1,636	170	Central African Republic	1,756	170	Guyana	3,086
171	San Marino	1,592	171	Cape Verde	1,617	171	Maldives	3,032
172	Seychelles	1,405	172	Djibouti	1,589	172	Burundi	2,869
173	Antigua and Barbuda	1,398	173	Antigua and Barbuda	1,449	173	Aruba	2,664
174	St. Lucia	1,385	174	Seychelles	1,427	174	Greenland	2,441
175	Solomon Islands	1,184	175	Timor-Leste	1,417	175	Liberia	2,122
176	Guinea-Bissau	1,155	176	Saint Lucia	1,379	176	Lesotho	2,081
177	Grenada	1,027	177	Solomon Islands	1,202	177	Bhutan	1,965
178	The Gambia	965	178	Guinea-Bissau	1,126	178	Cape Verde	1,855
179	St. Kitts and Nevis	903	179	Grenada	1,016	179	San Marino	1,845
180	Samoa	786	180	The Gambia	965	180	Central African Republic	1,838
181	St. Vincent and the Grenadines	775	181	Saint Kitts and Nevis	917	181	Belize	1,699

Rank	Country	Value
182	Vanuatu	773
183	Comoros	620
184	Dominica	520
185	Tonga	403
186	São Tomé and Príncipe	350
187	Federated States of Micronesia	322
188	Palau	293
189	Marshall Islands	183
190	Kiribati	167
191	Tuvalu	34

Rank	Country	Value
182	Samoa	786
183	Vanuatu	774
184	Saint Vincent and the Grenadines	771
185	Comoros	617
186	Dominica	525
187	Tonga	395
188	São Tomé and Príncipe	351
189	Federated States of Micronesia	322
190	Palau	293
191	Marshall Islands	183
192	Kiribati	166
193	Nauru	102
194	Tuvalu	34

Rank	Country	Value
182	Djibouti	1,589
183	Seychelles	1,511
184	Saint Lucia	1,406
185	Somalia	1,375
186	Zanzibar	1,289
187	Antigua and Barbuda	1,248
188	Guinea-Bissau	1,209
189	Solomon Islands	1,103
190	Sint Maarten	1,059
191	British Virgin Islands	902
192	Grenada	884
193	Saint Kitts and Nevis	852
194	The Gambia	851
195	Samoa	824
196	Vanuatu	812

(*Continued*)

Appendix 1.A *(Continued)*

List by the International Monetary Fund (2016)			List by the World Bank (2016)			List by the United Nations (2015)		
Rank	Country	GDP (US$MM)	Rank	Country	GDP (US$MM)	Rank	Country	GDP (US$MM)
	World	752,78,049		World	755,43,543		World	741,96,404
						197	Turks and Caicos Islands	797
						198	Saint Vincent and the Grenadines	729
						199	Comoros	648
						200	Dominica	533
						201	Tonga	435
						202	São Tomé and Príncipe	337
						203	Federated States of Micronesia	308
						204	Cook Islands	311
						205	Anguilla	311
						206	Palau	234
						207	Marshall Islands	209
						208	Nauru	182

209	Kiribati	180
210	Montserrat	63
211	Tuvalu	38

Source: Wikipedia, the free encyclopedia.

Notes:

1. The European Union (EU) is an economic and political union of 28 member states that are located primarily in Europe.
2. Figures exclude Taiwan, and special administrative regions of Hong Kong and Macau.
3. Figures exclude Republic of Crimea and Sevastopol.
4. Data for Syria's 2014 GDP is from the September 2011 WEO Database, the latest available from the IMF.
5. Figures exclude special administrative regions of Hong Kong and Macau.
6. Includes Former Spanish Sahara.
7. Covers mainland Tanzania only.
8. Data are for the area controlled by the Government of the Republic of Cyprus.
9. Excludes Abkhazia and South Ossetia.
10. Excludes data for Transnistria.

Appendix 1.B The Legatum Prosperity Index (Global Rankings, 2016)

Overall Rank	Country*	Economic Quality [1]	Business Environment [2]	Governance [3]	Education [4]	Health [5]	Safety & Security [6]	Personal Freedom [7]	Social Capital [8]	Natural Environment [9]
1	New Zealand	1	2	2	15	12	19	3	1	13
2	Norway	7	10	3	5	13	6	11	6	5
3	Finland	12	8	1	3	21	18	8	11	2
4	Switzerland	4	9	6	1	3	8	18	16	8
5	Canada	13	3	9	14	16	22	2	3	19
6	Australia	15	7	13	4	8	20	12	2	14
7	Netherlands	2	14	4	2	5	12	7	13	36
8	Sweden	3	13	5	13	6	10	14	18	9
9	Denmark	6	11	7	12	23	5	13	7	18
10	United Kingdom	10	5	11	6	20	13	15	12	10
11	Germany	5	12	10	16	10	7	21	9	6
12	Luxembourg	9	29	8	27	1	2	1	23	3
13	Ireland	25	15	14	7	24	16	5	10	25
14	Iceland	18	17	12	28	22	4	4	5	17
15	Austria	11	20	15	11	25	9	23	15	12
16	Belgium	16	19	16	9	11	30	9	24	26
17	United States	14	1	22	8	32	52	26	4	35

18	France	17	18	23	18	14	28	22	49	4
19	Singapore	8	6	18	10	2	1	97	31	11
20	Slovenia	30	60	38	23	35	14	20	22	1
21	Spain	38	42	35	22	17	15	16	29	15
22	Japan	19	21	17	20	4	3	49	101	48
23	Hong Kong	20	4	27	21	7	11	45	53	98
24	Malta	33	73	21	42	18	17	17	8	90
25	Portugal	35	40	28	61	41	25	10	42	27
26	Estonia	27	26	20	29	55	43	32	71	7
27	Czech Republic	26	30	34	24	27	27	28	78	32
28	Uruguay	40	39	19	73	38	55	6	27	67
29	Costa Rica	62	38	31	51	33	67	19	39	40
30	Mauritius	42	32	26	63	43	36	29	40	62
31	Chile	57	43	25	36	51	49	34	63	20
32	Italy	43	68	49	26	34	24	27	51	60
33	Cyprus	39	33	29	57	42	26	35	32	77
34	Poland	37	45	36	33	47	21	39	85	46
35	South Korea	29	36	41	17	19	29	73	105	91
36	Slovakia	46	49	48	30	46	23	43	86	34
37	Latvia	34	34	39	32	82	42	57	94	16

(Continued)

Appendix 1.B (Continued)

Overall Rank	Country*	Economic Quality [1]	Business Environment [2]	Governance [3]	Education [4]	Health [5]	Safety & Security [6]	Personal Freedom [7]	Social Capital [8]	Natural Environment [9]
38	Malaysia	23	16	40	31	37	58	112	33	49
39	Panama	47	22	56	69	72	75	31	26	42
40	Israel	32	25	24	19	9	94	91	46	133
41	United Arab Emirates	21	23	53	66	28	32	109	25	43
42	Lithuania	45	55	37	43	80	45	41	125	33
43	Croatia	61	89	44	37	56	31	38	113	30
44	Greece	77	61	42	62	36	33	63	100	24
45	Trinidad and Tobago	56	47	45	65	74	88	47	20	39
46	Qatar	24	24	60	93	15	41	98	36	69
47	Hungary	52	56	46	38	50	38	46	114	93
48	South Africa	111	37	33	70	126	115	24	37	45
49	Argentina	78	96	86	55	44	66	25	57	63
50	Romania	65	41	64	47	85	46	48	97	61
51	Suriname	89	137	58	74	54	56	30	61	23
52	Brazil	44	90	74	81	81	89	36	52	28
53	Macedonia	93	44	62	40	66	37	69	119	85

54	Botswana	99	70	30	78	84	110	51	41	51
55	Jamaica	75	27	63	84	63	117	62	34	59
56	Sri Lanka	41	76	66	58	39	83	110	19	57
57	Bulgaria	73	71	78	39	91	48	66	111	41
58	Montenegro	96	52	59	52	69	35	54	117	125
59	Ecuador	72	103	83	75	60	84	61	75	22
60	Philippines	69	62	57	68	98	141	58	21	44
61	Indonesia	55	75	50	72	95	50	128	14	73
62	Thailand	22	64	99	59	30	86	121	28	79
63	Dominican Republic	86	99	85	96	73	114	40	44	21
64	Peru	58	48	76	89	90	106	68	69	38
65	Mexico	81	31	77	64	64	133	55	126	53
66	Serbia	101	102	70	46	86	40	59	127	105
67	Bahrain	31	46	91	67	29	51	127	56	119
68	Namibia	112	65	32	111	108	122	33	50	74
69	Nicaragua	88	93	88	104	78	108	37	55	31
70	Oman	51	54	90	77	26	34	104	66	137
71	Kuwait	59	94	97	95	31	39	108	35	99
72	Colombia	76	28	89	79	65	142	44	64	52
73	Paraguay	68	91	116	99	57	59	56	76	64

(Continued)

360 Inequality and Global Supra-surplus Capitalism

Appendix 1.B (Continued)

Overall Rank	Country*	Economic Quality [1]	Business Environment [2]	Governance [3]	Education [4]	Health [5]	Safety & Security [6]	Personal Freedom [7]	Social Capital [8]	Natural Environment [9]
74	Albania	107	67	71	76	49	68	60	106	121
75	Vietnam	36	80	104	50	62	53	124	58	80
76	Mongolia	64	82	81	48	93	105	83	30	108
77	Kyrgyzstan	71	87	113	60	61	81	86	47	68
78	Turkey	49	74	65	80	52	126	94	104	55
79	Bolivia	80	123	73	82	105	77	42	72	81
80	Guyana	97	115	61	100	94	79	75	43	65
81	Belize	106	128	80	94	70	91	53	91	29
82	Kazakhstan	48	53	105	35	75	65	122	109	97
83	El Salvador	79	57	67	91	58	125	64	88	114
84	Georgia	94	66	54	54	96	78	79	139	124
85	Saudi Arabia	70	50	95	83	45	74	133	45	71
86	Guatemala	83	51	103	110	104	116	85	38	37
87	Ghana	109	81	43	109	115	85	71	89	88
88	Rwanda	95	35	52	123	77	98	84	99	110
89	Jordan	90	112	79	86	48	54	119	68	103
90	China	28	63	123	34	40	64	138	140	134
91	Cambodia	54	79	124	88	102	102	72	95	100

92	Honduras	110	72	101	87	79	128	76	83	86
93	Tunisia	92	95	55	105	71	61	115	136	84
94	Nepal	53	107	87	116	112	82	50	67	129
95	Russia	63	69	108	25	101	119	141	116	56
96	Moldova	84	77	98	49	103	73	87	123	142
97	Kenya	108	59	68	103	119	137	100	17	96
98	Belarus	50	92	135	41	89	57	134	121	102
99	Armenia	115	83	107	56	100	70	99	141	104
100	Tajikistan	103	108	126	53	67	47	130	81	127
101	Morocco	66	84	118	118	87	44	118	144	66
102	Laos	60	105	122	107	97	92	103	60	120
103	Azerbaijan	102	78	127	44	76	71	116	133	141
104	India	67	86	47	102	113	135	102	84	140
105	Lebanon	82	100	131	101	83	80	120	129	82
106	Senegal	121	106	51	134	114	104	52	77	117
107	Ukraine	85	97	128	45	111	134	93	135	112
108	Zambia	134	58	72	115	120	99	96	92	92
109	Tanzania	100	109	82	114	124	100	111	70	83
110	Malawi	123	125	75	121	116	113	82	110	54
111	Algeria	116	131	120	90	53	60	136	138	75
112	Burkina Faso	117	113	102	137	123	62	70	79	78

(Continued)

Appendix 1.B *(Continued)*

Overall Rank	Country*	Economic Quality [1]	Business Environment [2]	Governance [3]	Education [4]	Health [5]	Safety & Security [6]	Personal Freedom [7]	Social Capital [8]	Natural Environment [9]
113	Djibouti	120	144	114	85	117	72	90	124	70
114	Bangladesh	87	116	109	119	99	76	105	122	138
115	Lesotho	146	119	69	120	118	107	81	90	132
116	Uganda	74	98	111	122	140	132	106	48	115
117	Egypt	105	101	117	92	88	93	146	134	131
118	Iran	114	114	136	71	92	120	145	74	111
119	Zimbabwe	104	136	130	97	107	109	113	103	123
120	Gabon	128	118	132	112	132	97	92	102	109
121	Venezuela	127	145	146	98	68	129	95	130	50
122	Mozambique	129	122	96	135	144	103	67	87	101
123	Ivory Coast	119	104	106	136	143	118	78	118	72
124	Madagascar	133	133	112	131	137	63	80	115	116
125	Sierra Leone	118	124	94	139	139	95	89	65	130
126	Togo	122	129	125	129	141	96	74	146	94
127	Cameroon	113	111	133	113	130	139	125	80	76
128	Benin	124	120	84	143	145	90	65	147	87
129	Swaziland	135	88	140	106	106	101	135	73	135
130	Congo	143	126	148	124	134	124	77	128	47

131	Comoros	130	135	119	130	129	69	131	93	107
132	Ethiopia	91	132	115	128	128	123	126	120	122
133	Liberia	132	110	92	140	146	121	107	96	95
134	Mali	131	121	110	145	122	130	88	98	126
135	Nigeria	139	85	121	117	142	145	123	59	106
136	Libya	137	147	144	108	59	138	144	54	136
137	Niger	136	134	93	147	135	87	117	108	128
138	Guinea	126	130	129	146	147	111	114	112	58
139	Pakistan	98	117	100	125	121	143	132	137	149
140	Burundi	138	138	141	127	110	136	101	149	113
141	Angola	140	148	138	132	127	127	129	142	139
142	Mauritania	148	139	137	138	109	112	143	82	146
143	Iraq	142	146	134	126	131	147	139	62	148
144	Chad	144	140	145	149	149	131	137	132	118
145	Democratic Republic of Congo	147	141	143	133	136	148	140	131	144
146	Sudan	141	142	142	144	133	144	148	107	143
147	Central African Republic	145	143	139	148	148	149	142	143	89

(Continued)

Appendix 1.B *(Continued)*

Overall Rank	Country*	Economic Quality [1]	Business Environment [2]	Governance [3]	Education [4]	Health [5]	Safety & Security [6]	Personal Freedom [7]	Social Capital [8]	Natural Environment [9]
148	Afghanistan	125	127	147	141	138	146	149	145	147
149	Yemen	149	149	149	142	125	140	147	148	145

*The term 'country' is used to refer to the 149 societies included in the Index. These include 148 nations and one Special Administrative Region of China, Hong Kong.

Source: The Legatum Prosperity Index, Legatum Institute Foundation.

Notes:

1. The Economic Quality sub-index ranks countries on the openness of their economy, macroeconomic indicators, foundations for growth, economic opportunity, and financial sector efficiency.

2. The Business Environment sub-index measures a country's entrepreneurial environment, its business infrastructure, barriers to innovation, and labour market flexibility.

3. The Governance subindex measures a country's performance in three areas: effective governance, democracy and political participation, and rule of law.

4. The Education sub-index ranks countries on access to education, quality of education, and human capital.

5. The Health sub-index measures a country's performance in three areas: basic physical and mental health, health infrastructure, and preventative care.

6. The Safety & Security sub-index ranks countries based on national security and personal safety.

7. The Personal Freedom sub-index measures national progress towards basic legal rights, individual freedoms, and social tolerance.

8. The Social Capital sub-index measures the strength of personal relationships, social network support, social norms, and civic participation in a country.

9. The Natural Environment sub-index measures a country's performance in three areas: the quality of the natural environment, environmental pressures, and preservation efforts.

APPENDIX 2

Table A2.1   Advanced Economies by Subgroup

Major Currency Areas

United States

Euro Area

Japan

Euro Area

Austria	Greece	Netherlands
Belgium	Ireland	Portugal
Cyprus	Italy	Slovak Republic
Estonia	Latvia	Slovenia
Finland	Lithuania	Spain
France	Luxembourg	
Germany	Malta	

Major Advanced Economies

Canada	Italy	United States
France	Japan	
Germany	United Kingdom	

(Continued)

Table A2.1   (*Continued*)

Other Advanced Economies

Australia	Korea	Singapore
Czech Republic	Macao SAR²	Sweden
Denmark	New Zealand	Switzerland
Hong Kong SAR¹	Norway	Taiwan Province of China
Iceland	Puerto Rico	
Israel	San Marino	

¹On July 1, 1997, Hong Kong was returned to the People's Republic of China and became a Special Administrative Region of China.
²On December 20, 1999, Macao was returned to the People's Republic of China and became a Special Administrative Region of China.
Source: International Monetary Fund, "World Economic Outlook: Too Slow For Too Long", April 2016.

Table A2.2   European Union

Austria	Germany	Poland
Belgium	Greece	Portugal
Bulgaria	Hungary	Romania
Croatia	Ireland	Slovak Republic
Cyprus	Italy	Slovenia
Czech Republic	Latvia	Spain
Denmark	Lithuania	Sweden
Estonia	Luxembourg	United Kingdom
Finland	Malta	
France	Netherlands	

Source: International Monetary Fund, "World Economic Outlook: Too Slow For Too Long", April 2016.

Table A2.3 Emerging Market and Developing Economies by Region and Main Source of Export Earnings

	Fuel	Nonfuel Primary Products
Commonwealth of Independent States		
	Azerbaijan	Uzbekistan
	Kazakhstan	
	Russia	
	Turkmenistan[1]	
Emerging and Developing Asia		
	Brunei Darussalam	Marshall Islands
	Timor-Leste	Mongolia
		Papua New Guinea
		Solomon Islands
		Tuvalu
Latin America and the Caribbean		
	Bolivia	Argentina
	Colombia	Chile
	Ecuador	Guyana
	Trinidad and Tobago	Paraguay
	Venezuela	Suriname
		Uruguay
Middle East, North Africa, Afghanistan, and Pakistan		
	Algeria	Afghanistan
	Bahrain	Mauritania
	Iran	Sudan
	Iraq	
	Kuwait	
	Libya	
	Oman	
	Qatar	
	Saudi Arabia	
	United Arab Emirates	
	Yemen	

[1] Turkmenistan, which is not a member of the Commonwealth of Independent States, is included in this group for reasons of geography and similarity in economic structure.

(Continued)

Table A2.3 *(Continued)*

	Fuel	Nonfuel Primary Products
Sub-Saharan Africa		
	Angola	Burkina Faso
	Chad	Burundi
	Republic of Congo	Central African Republic
	Equatorial Guinea	Democratic Republic of the Congo
	Gabon	Côte d'Ivoire
	Nigeria	Eritrea
	South Sudan	Guinea-Bissau
		Liberia
		Malawi
		Mali
		Niger
		Sierra Leone
		South Africa
		Zambia

Source: International Monetary Fund, "World Economic Outlook: Too Slow For Too Long", April 2016.

Printed in the United States
By Bookmasters